Economics as

Also by Wilfred Beckerman

The British Economy in 1975 (with associates)

International Comparison of Real Incomes

An Introduction to National Income Analysis

In Defence of Economic Growth (USA edition under title *Two Cheers for the Affluent Society*)

Measures of Leisure, Equality and Welfare

Poverty and the Impact of Income Maintenance Programmes

Growth, the Environment and the Distribution of Incomes

Poverty and Social Security in Britain since 1961 (with Stephen Clark)

Small is Stupid

A Poverty of Reason: Sustainable Development and Economic Growth

Justice, Posterity, and the Environment (with Joanna Pasek)

Wilfred Beckerman

Economics as Applied Ethics

Fact and Value in Economic Policy

Second Edition

Wilfred Beckerman
University College London
London, United Kingdom

ISBN 978-3-319-50318-9   ISBN 978-3-319-50319-6 (eBook)
DOI 10.1007/978-3-319-50319-6

Library of Congress Control Number: 2017933430

Cover illustration: Michael Burrell / Alamy Stock Photo

This Palgrave Macmillan imprint is published by Springer Nature
The registered company is Springer International Publishing AG
The registered company address is: Gewerbestrasse 11, 6330 Cham, Switzerland

PREFACE

This is a substantially revised version of the first edition. Some of the chapters have been largely rewritten, notably the chapters on 'happiness', the valuation of life and the problem of equality. In addition, Chapter 1 of the first edition has been scrapped and substantial changes have been made to all the opening chapters in order to bring out more clearly the main theme of this book. This is an attempt to provide a simple method for analysing any problem in economic policy. The method is basically a distinction between what parts of the problem are questions of fact and what parts are questions of value judgement.

Consequently, after an initial explanation of the basic concepts involved, the rest of the book comprises a discussion of the way that this distinction crops up in the analysis of applied economic problems. This begins with a general explanation of the role of facts and value judgements in the general theory of welfare economics, and is followed by the application of this distinction to some major contemporary economic problems, such as equality or obligations to other countries or future generations.

Thus I make no attempt to provide a general survey of ethics in economics, on which there are already several excellent texts available. Instead I focus on trying to provide a practical key to the analysis of economic policy issues. I believe that this key – namely the separation of questions of fact from questions of value – is one that can also be used profitably to unlock the complexities of non-economic problems as well. But that is another matter. All that I try to do is to bring out into the open the value judgements hidden away in the general theory of welfare economics and in the analysis of many economic policy problems of our time.

ACKNOWLEDGEMENTS

The title of this book has been taken – with his permission – from the opening remarks made by John Broome at a public meeting in Oxford in November 2009 that was focused on the great contributions made by Amartya Sen to our understanding of the relationship between ethics and economics. As I indicate in Chapter 1 of this book, in the course of writing it I drew very heavily on their work as well as that of the late Ian Little. This does not mean that they would agree with all of what I say.

I am indebted to my old friend and ex-colleague, Paul Streeten, who first opened my eyes to the importance of the link between ethics and economics.

I am also indebted to the many people with whom I have discussed some of the contents of the book, and to the following people who have kindly read – and commented on – individual chapters of the first edition of this book. These are the late Tony Atkinson, Ken Binmore, John Broome, Roger Crisp, Nicholas Fahy, James Forder, Sudhir Hazareesingh, the late Ian Little, Tom Nagel, Joanna Pasek, Adam Swift and Clark Wolf, as well as to my Balliol colleagues and ex-colleagues, including the late Bob Hargrave, Kinch Hoekstra, John Latsis and Jessica Moss, for guidance on many philosophical topics, and to my UCL colleague, Uwe Peters, for important amendments at a late stage in the drafting of this book.

I am also greatly indebted to my wife, Joanna Pasek, with whom I have discussed the topics covered in this book over many years and who has been a source of patient encouragement and enlightenment throughout. I am also grateful to the discussion over the years with her students in the Economics Department at University College London.

Finally, my greatest debt is to my old friend Nick Morris. In addition to help with the overall structure of the book as well as with the statistical material in Chapter 15, Nick Morris took over the co-ordination of the team of proof-readers in my family (Debbie Beckerman, Keith Jones, Beatrice Beckerman, and Agnieszka Pasek), and then master-minded the whole process of producing a printable version. Without his help this book might never have seen the light of day.

In the Acknowledgements to his recent book, *The Idea of Justice*, Amartya Sen lists about 360 people who have contributed in one way or another to the development of the views expressed in his book. By comparison, my little list of only about twenty or so people is rather brief. I am sure that help from 360 people would have made my book better – though probably not as good as his, of course. But the problem is that I do not even know 360 people! However, such little merit – if any - that my book may have has to be shared out among only about twenty people, not 360! Of course, I, alone, take all the blame for its defects.

CONTENTS

LIST OF FIGURES

CHAPTER 1

Introduction

This book is not about ethics in economics, which can cover a vast range of topics, such as business ethics or the morally questionable behaviour of many of the actors in the world of business, or some important ethical aspects of economic theory. There are several excellent books that deal with such issues.

This book is very different. It is designed to do two things. First, it is designed to provide a simple method for breaking down the analysis of economic policy issues into what are matters of fact and what are matters of values. Second, for this purpose it highlights the main value judgements – mostly of an ethical nature – that tend to be ignored in the analysis of what policies contribute to society's economic welfare. Of course, the fact/value distinction is not as sharp as might be supposed. Even the 'facts' are not totally objective. Many of the people involved in collecting and presenting the 'facts' have their own agendas or biases. Furthermore, there is no value-free method of measuring most economic variables, such as the degree of income inequality or the level of unemployment or national income.

But for present purposes the fact/value distinction is useful and important. It should help people who hold conflicting views on economic policy issues – and any other issues for that matter – to identify how far their differences reflect different assumptions about the relevant facts and how far they reflect differences in values. Thus it should enable reasonable people to arrive at a peaceful agreement about what – if anything – they still differ about.

© The Author(s) 2017
W. Beckerman, *Economics as Applied Ethics*,
DOI 10.1007/978-3-319-50319-6_1

1

Economics is an applied science, like medicine or engineering. Few people would want to study medicine if there were no intention of improving people's health. In the same way the study of economics would be far less attractive if it were not to be used to tackle the economic ailments of society. As Pigou, the father of welfare economics, put it, 'If it were not for the hope that a scientific study of men's social actions may lead, not necessarily directly or immediately, but at some time and in some way, to practical results in social improvement, not a few students of these actions would regard the time devoted to their study as time misspent'.

In order to understand how our bodies work, medicine has to call on many other disciplines, such as anatomy, physiology, biochemistry, pharmacology, psychology and so on. Similarly in order to find out how economies work, economics has to take account of many special disciplines, such as statistics, history, politics, sociology and psychology. But in order to judge how it *ought* to work it also has to take account of ethics. Indeed, it would be difficult to think of any important current economic policy question that did not raise questions about society's ethical values. These range from issues such as the concern with increasing economic inequality in society to relatively technical questions such as how much ought to be spent on improving transport facilities.

The first two chapters will explain the key to the method I believe is essential in the analysis of most problems of social policy. This method consists of making a clear distinction between questions of fact and questions of value. In spite of contributions to economics made by pioneers such as Bergson, Samuelson, Little and Graaff, the role of value judgements in economics is not always adequately recognised. Perhaps this is why economics has been described as 'the dismal science'. Following the first two chapters in which the basic concepts used are explained there are a few chapters that discuss the role of value judgements in the general theory of welfare economics. This will include some discussion of what is meant by the 'welfare' of individuals and of society as a whole. These will be followed by chapters in which some of the applications of the method to certain specific contemporary problems are examined in more detail, such as how we define the boundaries of the society in whose welfare we are interested, and what concept of 'equality' we should be concerned with.

I assume that most readers of this book have some knowledge of elementary economic theory, or are prepared to acquire some in the course of reading it, if only by accident. For the analogy between medicine and economics goes further. Outside primitive societies one would not take much notice of a medical practitioner who did not have a basic medical training. Similarly, one ought not to attach too much importance to the economic pronouncements of pundits who have no basic economic knowledge, especially if they are politicians or businessmen who have their own axes to grind. Let me give one example.

Not long after I arrived as a Fellow of Balliol College, Oxford, in 1964, I was invited to attend some special College dinner at which most of the other guests were successful businessmen. (Any reader of this book can guess why.) At various points during the evening I was introduced to several of them as the new economist on the block. Every one of them quickly proceeded to explain to me what was wrong with the British economy at that time. What was interesting was that many of their diagnoses were totally contradictory. For example, one said that the trouble with the British economy was that it was too difficult to make a profit. And another said that the trouble with the British economy was that it was too easy to make a profit. Not one of them mentioned the real reason, namely that Britain was stuck with a fixed and uncompetitive exchange rate.

Today most 'men of affairs' may be a little less confident about the way to solve the grave economic problems facing most developed countries. But this book is not directly addressed to those problems, although it is hoped that the method of analysis set out in this book will contribute to sensible discussion of them.

PART I

Basic Principles

CHAPTER 2

Preview

1 Value Judgements in Welfare Economics

Throughout this book emphasis is placed on the importance in economic policy analysis of the distinction between 'positive propositions', which rely on facts, and 'value judgements', which do not. Between them they provide the basis for 'normative propositions', which are propositions about what one *ought* to do, or what society *ought* to do. For example, the *normative* proposition that society *ought* to impose heavy taxes on tobacco could be defended on the basis of (i) a *positive* proposition that smoking is bad for people's health and (ii) another *positive* proposition that better health makes people happier and, finally, (iii) the *value judgement* that being happy is *intrinsically* valuable, so that it needs no further justification (though it can still be disputed).

In this book I try to show how essential are these distinctions in welfare economics, which is about how a society's economy ought to work. The next chapter of the book explains how these concepts are used. Later chapters show how ubiquitous are value judgements in the analysis of economic policy problems. This might come as a surprise to most people, including even some economists. For it is probably widely believed that economics is all about facts and statistics.

Alas, if that were only the case! But it isn't. So here I shall summarise some of the most important of the value judgements that I shall highlight in the book.

© The Author(s) 2017
W. Beckerman, *Economics as Applied Ethics*,
DOI 10.1007/978-3-319-50319-6_2

2   THE WELFARE OF THE INDIVIDUAL

So let us start at the beginning, which is the 'welfare' of the individual. Probably most people intending to read this book will already be familiar with a central concept in economics, namely the concept of 'utility'. (Every student of the subject has heard about the 'law of diminishing marginal utility'.) Individuals are assumed to derive utility from various goods, services and activities. And the structure of theoretical welfare economics begins with an analysis of how a 'rational' consumer maximises his utility given his tastes, his income and the prices of the goods and services available on the market. It is generally assumed that he knows what he is doing and that the choices he makes really do contribute to his 'welfare'.

But we have always known that this is not the case. We have always known that people often lack the necessary information to enable them to choose between various options according to how far they will actually add to their welfare. And we have all known a few people who we believe are incapable of always choosing as wisely as they should if their ultimate objective is to maximise their welfare. Consequently, in the last two decades or so a vast amount of evidence has been obtained, thanks to the work of behavioural psychologists and economists, that has confirmed in some detail the many reasons for the gap between people's revealed preferences on the market and what is in the real interests of their welfare.

So right at the start of the analysis of any policy problems, we have to decide whether to accept (i) the normative proposition that society *ought* to accept consumer sovereignty as expressed in their market choices and the resulting pattern of prices, even knowing that this will often not promote their real welfare, or (ii) the normative proposition that we *ought* to take a paternalistic position and interfere with their market choices. This would depend on how much weight we attach to the value judgement that personal freedom to choose is intrinsically good as against the value judgement that raising people's welfare is intrinsically good. This conflict of values is ubiquitous in policy. For example, ought society to impose heavy taxes on goods like tobacco, alcohol or fattening food? Or ought one oblige people to wear seatbelts in cars? And should there be safety regulations in places of work?

On top of all that we are faced with the fact that 'welfare' is not an objective concept anyway. We may all differ about what constitutes the real welfare of an individual.

3 FROM THE INDIVIDUAL TO SOCIETY

However this is just the start of our problems. For what public policy is about is what promotes the welfare of society as a whole. It is true that most works on ethics – going back as far as Aristotle's *Nicomachean Ethics* (about 330 BC) – focus mainly on how *individuals* ought to behave in order to be 'moral' people and promote their welfare. But Aristotle also thought that 'For while the good of an individual is a desirable thing, what is good for a people or for cities is a nobler and more godlike thing'.[1] Hence, the subject of this book is welfare of societies, although, of course, this has to be related directly or indirectly to the welfare of individuals.

And we usually cheerfully assume that the welfare of society as a whole is just some sort of aggregate of the welfare of the individuals in that society. But this is a bit vague. And on examination it turns out that to go from the welfare of the individual to the welfare of society as a whole raises the need to make a lot more value judgements.

The reason for this is that society does not have a 'mind' in the same way that an individual does – at least most of them. Yet we would like to think that there is some method by which the preferences of all the people in society could be combined and that respected certain compelling criteria of rational choice. For example, if an individual prefers X to Y and Y to Z, we would expect him to prefer X to Z. Respect for this 'transitivity' of preferences is assumed to be an axiom of rational choice.

And one could postulate other axioms of 'rational choice' for a collection of individuals, such as that if the welfare of any one (or more) of them increases and none of them suffers a decline in welfare, then we can say that the welfare of the whole collection has risen.

But it has been famously shown by Ken Arrow that it is impossible to construct a rule for aggregating the preferences of a number of individuals in such a way that it will respect all the axioms that one would normally demand of rational collective choice. The significance of this problem has been disputed. For it has been argued that one should not expect the concept of rationality that we demand for individual choices to apply to a whole society. This may well be so. But, nevertheless, it leaves one very uneasy about the legitimacy of drawing conclusions concerning the 'welfare' of a collection of individuals on the basis of any information about their individual welfares. Various constitutional methods have been adopted for this purpose, but the choice between them is ultimately a matter of value judgement, not simple logic.

4   EQUALITY AND THE DISTRIBUTION PROBLEM

Anyway, few people would like to live in a society that simply maximised its aggregate welfare irrespective of the way that this welfare is distributed. Most people attach importance to the equality of its distribution. However, people differ greatly in the sort of equality that they think is desirable. The usual suspects are equality of opportunity, or of income, or of welfare, or of capabilities, or something else. Which one do you prefer?

And each of these concepts is subject to different interpretations. For example, should equality of opportunity mean only that jobs or other positions in society should only be given to the people who are best qualified for it by virtue of their talents and education? Or should society go further and seek greater equality in the opportunities open to people to attain such qualifications? And if one goes down this road where does one stop? People are born in different circumstances, in different countries, with different natural abilities and so on. Some people are just less careful than are others in the choice of their parents.

And when we have arrived at some value judgement as to what concept of equality we believe to be intrinsically 'good', we still have to decide whether its 'goodness' depends on whether it is distributed equally over whole lifetimes, or during any one particular time period, such as a year? For example, suppose people have exactly the same total incomes over their whole life, but their incomes start from a low level when they are young, reach a peak in, say, late middle age, and then decline in old age. At any one point of time, therefore, incomes will be distributed unequally. Should this matter? Should we ignore the plight of some destitute old person simply because he had not saved enough when he was young? Are we not concerned with possible poverty of some old people?

In fact, are we really concerned with equality at all, rather than just poverty? If we lived in a society that was generally very well off and there was no poverty would we still worry if the wealth of its inhabitants was unequally distributed?

This brings us to another question: do we believe equality to be *intrinsically* valuable rather than being solely instrumentally valuable? For it can be argued that our concern with equality arises purely because of its *instrumental* value in promoting harmonious working and living conditions, promoting prosperity, or preventing the sort of political frictions that seemed to have emerged as a result of increasing inequality in developed countries over the last few decades.

If we make the value judgement that equality is *intrinsically* valuable, then that is the end of the debate, apart from the need to spell out more precisely what particular concept of equality is the one that we think is intrinsically valuable. But if we believe that equality of some kind or other is instrumentally valuable then we are back in the field of 'positive propositions', where we are obliged to provide some factual evidence.

5   VALUING LIFE: THE ULTIMATE VALUE JUDGEMENT

Enormous amounts of money are spent on projects that, one way or another, are connected to life and death. The most obvious case is expenditure on the health services. Decisions are constantly having to be made about the relative amount of money to be devoted to different forms of health care. But in other fields of public policy, such as those related to transport expenditures, or regulations concerning safety at work, the analysis of certain projects has to take account of their effect on safety and risk to life.

But the fact is that there are many things in life that do not have a price. And life is one of them. For there is nothing that can be regarded as equivalent to it. And prices are just one way in which equivalence between different goods and services is expressed. So when decisions have to be taken involving life or death it is futile to try to attach a price to life. The decisions will therefore have to rely partly on what will invariably be painful value judgements.

What can be given a price, however, is how much people value differences in the *risk* to life. People may be able to say how much they are prepared to pay for an increase in their safety or how much they are prepared to accept as compensation for a decrease in it. Some of the methods used to make such evaluations, as well as the reasons why life itself cannot be given a price, are discussed in Chapter 14.

6   NATIONAL INCOME AND GDP

There is one ingredient in most discussions of economic policy about which most people are fairly neutral – if not bored stiff. This is the concept of gross domestic product (GDP), which is closely related to a country's national income. But the way that this ought to be measured has been the subject of continuous debate for many decades. And the fairly universal current agreement that now prevails about the correct way to measure

GDP means that most people are unaware of the value judgements that are reflected in it.

However, they need not detain us here since they are not the kind of value judgements that most need to be borne in mind in normal everyday economic policy analysis. So it must suffice here to give just two examples. One of these has, perhaps, the longest ancestry. It is the example given about a century ago by the great economist A.C. Pigou, who pointed out that if he married his housekeeper national income would be reduced. This is because the value of the work done in one's household by one's wife is not included in national income, whereas the wages of a housekeeper are included.

Another example is the inclusion in GDP estimates of expenditures on services like the maintenance of law and order. For it is often claimed that these are really just inputs needed for the operation of the economy and the viability of society. Hence, so the argument goes, their inclusion in the final net output of the economy is like including the value of the steel used in the construction of automobiles in the measure of national income or output as well as the value of the automobiles. Double counting! The cardinal sin of national accounts.

7   HAPPINESS

Anyway, why does public policy attach so much importance to GDP? Surely it is only *instrumentally* valuable? Isn't what we really want to measure is how happy people are? After all, aren't economists always talking about 'utility', and isn't this closely related to some concept of happiness?

Of course, measuring GDP and measuring 'happiness' are not necessarily mutually exclusive activities. Even if we accept that GDP is only instrumentally valuable, it would still be useful to know a lot about how it is doing – rising or falling; what determines it; and how it is used, since all these things will affect how it is making its contribution to happiness.

So in the last few years there has been an explosion of interest in what is known as 'happiness economics', and many estimates have been published that makes some people happier than others, and why it varies between countries, and how it has changed, if at all, over time in individual countries.

One thing has certainly changed over time, and that is the concept of happiness itself, which has changed considerably since the days of the ancient Greek philosophers. In those days the concept of *eudaimonia*, which approximates to the modern concept of happiness, referred mainly to what would be a morally desirable way for a person to live. This concept of happiness is clearly a value judgement.

What value judgements are embodied in contemporary measurements of happiness is not very clear. They seem to follow Jeremy Bentham in accepting that society should aim at maximising the happiness (or 'utility', which Bentham regarded as its equivalent) of society as a whole. Apart from despots few people would contest this. Nevertheless, it does differ from the Aristotelian concern with what was morally 'good' for the individual. And it leaves little room for qualification along the lines of Amartya Sen's famous critique of welfarism.

It also seems to differ from John Stuart Mill's explicit distinction between more or less morally commendable ways by which people are made happy. But the distinction is probably implicitly in the choice of variables selected in these studies as being those that contribute to making people happy. For example, they include variables such as income, health, educational attainment, personal relationships and so on, but do not include drink, drugs or sadistic activities.

But I hardly need elaborate on the vast scope for different value judgements as to what particular concept of happiness is the one at which the authorities ought to aim. I am sure that any reader of this book is quite capable of doing so without any further assistance from me. So I shall now move on to another completely different set of value judgements that are much involved in many important areas of economic policy. These are judgements about the boundaries of the society the welfare of which we are interested in.

8 The Boundary in Space and International Justice

How much ought we to spend on foreign aid? Should we allow imports of goods produced with the aid of child labour? Ought immigration policy to be based solely on economic calculation? All such questions involve issues of international justice and our moral obligations to citizens of other countries. In other words they raise the question of where, in space, we draw the boundary around the society the welfare of which we are seeking to promote.

As indicated earlier in connection with the problem of equality, the concept of justice is complicated enough when we limit its application to the way any individual society is organised. So it might be thought that it would be even more complicated when we turn to justice between different countries. But, paradoxically, this is not the case!

The reason for this is simply that, with a few exceptions, philosophers have not yet had time to make it so. The problem of international justice has not been with us all that long. Until relatively recently it was limited to questions such as proper respect for international treaties, or deals made by trading partners across national borders and so on. But during the course of the last century the degree of economic interaction between countries has rapidly expanded.

So philosophers have only had a few decades in which to come to grips with the issues of justice that this economic integration has thrown up. By comparison they have had thousands of years in which to explore the question of justice within any society. Nevertheless, they have responded to the challenge brilliantly. So while no clearly exhaustive and mutually exclusive classification of different theories of international justice is possible some major strands of thought can be identified. The flavour of these is as follows.

At one extreme there are theories which may be described as 'cosmopolitan'. The distinctive feature of these theories is that everybody, irrespective of their place of birth, has to be granted the same rights and privileges, has an equal claim on the riches of the world, and has an equal right to respect for his or her integrity and freedom.

This corresponds to the various declarations of human rights that have been proclaimed at various times and in various countries ranging from the French Revolution at the end of the eighteenth century down to the United Nations Declaration of Human Rights. Needless to say, as Hamlet would have put it, all these declarations have been more honoured in the breach than in the observance. This is chiefly because they are not usually accompanied by a corresponding declaration of 'obligations' which everybody and every country is bound to respect and implement, or by the institution of any international authority that can ensure this respect.

At the other extreme are 'communitarian' theories. A central feature of these is that the structure of rights and obligations within any society will legitimately represent the particular histories of the individual communities in which they have developed. In other words, there can be no compelling general theory of what principles of justice should apply to everybody in the world. This means that the particular rights and obligations associated with any theory of justice should not be expected to be the same in all communities.

Another crucial class of theories of justice that has been applied internationally is the contractarian class of theory, of which John Rawls has been the most influential in modern times. The essence of his theory is that the principles of justice are those that would be drawn up by rational participants in some imaginary 'original position' in which they did not know what position they would eventually come to occupy in the real world. Hence they would take an impartial view of the sort of society in which they would like to be born and the corresponding rights and obligations that ought to be specified in the principles of justice in that society.

But, whereas Rawls limited his analysis to the principles of justice that will prevail within any particular society, some philosophers have claimed that the participants in the original position will also take account of the possibility of being born in a very poor country. Hence, if they were – as Rawls assumed – both rational and risk averse, the principles of justice on which they would agree would include provision for assistance to poor countries.

Clearly, these and other theories of international justice present one with a choice of value judgement. And the same applies to the question of the boundary in time that we should draw around the society the welfare of which we aim to promote.

9   THE BOUNDARY IN TIME AND INTERGENERATIONAL
JUSTICE

The problem of justice between generations that may not even overlap has been around for even less time than the problem of international justice. In the last few decades it has been sparked by growing fears that the world was running out of the natural resources required for economic sustainability. But more recently it has been reinforced by the more serious fear that excessive burning of fossil fuels and its concomitant emission of carbon molecules into the atmosphere will induce intolerable global warming. This would greatly reduce future standards of living and even threaten the continuous existence of the human race.

The gravity of this threat is a very complex scientific matter on which I would not attempt to pass judgement. But the value judgement involved is fairly clear. It is a question of how far we value the interest of future generations by comparison with our own. Earlier philosophers had little need to pay any attention to this question. It is true that John Locke is frequently quoted as having done so, but, as I explain in Chapter 18, this is usually based on a misreading (or often, not even any sort of reading) of what Locke actually wrote. A little later in the eighteenth century David Hume does make allusion here and there to the fact that we would normally attach more value to the welfare of those near and dear to us than to people who are more distantly related to us, if at all.

But contemporary philosophers have had to get to grips with the problem of intergenerational justice. It even plays a crucial role in the selection of the appropriate discount rate to be used in public projects the costs and benefits of which will be spread over many years into the future. Rawls did address intergenerational justice in a rather cursory manner and suggested that it was probably an intractable problem. And his somewhat half-hearted contribution to a solution, which was a theory of 'just savings', was never very convincing.

So we are left where we started. How far should we value the welfare of future generations relative to that of people alive today? Full-bloodied utilitarians would like to give them equal weight. But, in practice, nobody would do so in the ordinary course of their lives or even feel morally obliged to do so.

An alternative approach would be to follow Adam Smith and David Hume and recognise that justice does not exhaust the whole of morality. We frequently treat other people with sympathy and concern without limiting this treatment to the claims of 'justice' or respect for their rights. From this point of view, the claims of the welfare of future generations are very much like the claims of poorer countries.

Like other sentiments, such as love, loyalty, duty or aesthetic appreciation, they are unquantifiable. Seeking an objective scientifically defined number for, say, the value of a life, or the discount rate to be used in the economic analysis of public projects that may affect distant generations, or the proportion of national income devoted to aid for distant people in other countries is to pursue a chimera.

Thus we have to face the fact that although value judgements are not woven into the fabric of the universe they are woven into the fabric of welfare economics. So the art of economic analysis is to separate them out from the positive propositions. In the following chapters I try to spell out how to do this.

NOTE

1. About 339 BC, *Nicomachean Ethics,* trans. Crisp, page vii.

CHAPTER 3

The Main Concepts

1 David Hume and the Health Fanatic

In order to be able to make full use of the simple key to the analysis of economic policy questions that I have promised to supply in Chapter 1, it is necessary to clarify a few basic concepts. Boring, perhaps, but essential, like some boring facts that one invariably has to learn in order to practise any applied science. The essence of the concepts that constitute the simple key to the analysis of policy problems, including economic policy problems, was set out about 250 years ago by the great philosopher, David Hume.

Hume pointed out that if you ask somebody

> ... *why he desires health* he may ... reply, that *it is necessary for the exercise of his calling.* If you ask, *why he is anxious on that head,* he will answer, *because he desires to get money.* If you demand *why? It is the instrument of pleasure,* says he. And beyond this it is an absurdity to ask for a reason. It is impossible there can be a progress *in infinitum;* and that one thing can always be a reason, why another is desired. Something must be desirable on its own account, and because of its immediate accord or agreement with human sentiment and affection. (Italics in the original)[1]

This book would be worthwhile if it did no more than drive home this message.

Hume's example illustrates in a very simple way the difference between two kinds of proposition. The first kind are 'positive propositions'. As explained in more detail later, these are propositions like 'Mount Everest is

© The Author(s) 2017
W. Beckerman, *Economics as Applied Ethics,*
DOI 10.1007/978-3-319-50319-6_3

the highest mountain in the world' or that 'other things being equal, a rise in the relative price of apples will generally reduce the demand for them'. The truth or otherwise of such propositions can be checked – at least in principle – by reference to some facts.

The second kind of proposition is a 'value judgement', like 'happiness is *intrinsically* good' or 'killing people is *intrinsically* bad'. In the next section I shall discuss these propositions in slightly more detail. Meanwhile, it is useful to see how these two types of proposition work in David Hume's example. In Hume's story the man in question is claiming that health has '*instrumental*' value for him. His claim involves two positive propositions; namely that good health is necessary for his calling and that his calling is necessary for earning money. These positive propositions are open to reasonable challenge. For example, it could be argued – however implausibly – that he would make more money if he stopped wasting his time in the gym or swimming up and down the pool, and spent it directly trying to make money instead. But Hume's point is the one that is central to the whole thrust of this book, namely that even if we accept the sequence of positive propositions in question, in the end we have to make a value judgement, such as that happiness – or pleasure in Hume's example – has intrinsic value.

2   Value Judgements and Intrinsic Values

So what exactly is meant by the term 'value judgement'? Unfortunately, there does not seem to be any universal agreement among philosophers about what the term really means. So I shall not presume here to give an authoritative definition of the concept. Not being a philosopher I need not fear breaking any union rules if I state that I shall simply use the term 'value judgement' to indicate judgements that do not depend on factual observation or evidence in the way that, say, positive propositions depend. They cannot be shown to be either unequivocally true or false. They represent *intrinsic* values.

This definition of the concept of a 'value judgement' may appear to depart from the normal meaning of the words 'value' and 'judgement' taken separately. In ordinary life one may pass judgements about the value of all sorts of things without, in any way, implying that they have intrinsic value as distinct from instrumental value. For example, when one judges that a certain vase is valuable, one may be referring merely to its market value and not implying that it is intrinsically valuable. But when the two words 'value' and 'judgement' are combined in the term 'value judgement' they take on a special meaning in which something or other is claimed to have *intrinsic* value.

It is true that there has been much discussion in philosophy over the years about whether all value judgements have to be justified, in the end, by some reference to facts. But although this meta-ethical topic has provided a good living for many philosophers over the ages, I shall bypass it and simply use the term 'value judgements' as defined earlier to refer to values that are held to be *intrinsically* valuable – that is, valuable for their own sake and not because they contribute to some other value.

The point is that many philosophers would agree that intrinsic values, including ethical principles, are not part of the fabric of the universe like the speed of light that can, *in principle*, be confirmed or refuted by appeal to some facts, or that can be deduced from some axioms by a process of logical reasoning. David Hume went as far as to argue, in his *Treatise on Human Nature,* that 'reason' has no place in the justification of values, or what he called the 'passions'. According to Hume reason only comes into play in the evaluation of what we now call 'positive propositions'. He argues that 'Reason is the discovery of truth or falsehood. Truth or falsehood consists of an agreement or disagreement either to the *real* relations of ideas, or to *real* existence and matter of fact . . . Moral distinctions, therefore, are not the offspring of reason. Reason is wholly inactive, and can never be the source of so active a principle as conscience, or a sense of morals'.[2] In a similar vein John Stuart Mill summed up the situation when he stated that 'Questions of ultimate ends are not amenable to direct proof'.[3]

Of course, if the question in Hume's example were put to somebody else she might not have followed the same sequence of reasons as did the man in that example. Instead, she might have gone directly to the assertion that health had intrinsic value. And that view is not open to reasoned challenge, even though some people might regard it as being a bit bizarre. It would be a value judgement, so that is the end of the story. But the point that Hume was making was that even if we accept the chain of positive propositions attributed to the man in his example, in the end he still has to justify his policy by reference to some intrinsic value, which, in his case, is his pleasure.

And it is possible that another person to whom Hume's question is put might have replied that he regarded health as having both intrinsic value – a value judgement – and the *instrumental* value of leading to happiness via the money-making route set out. In the former case it is the end of the story. In the latter case the positive propositions involved may be subject to challenge, but even if they are accepted, it is still necessary to justify the pursuit of health by some value judgement, such as that happiness is intrinsically valuable. There cannot be any generally accepted list of top-level intrinsic values. For example, at the level of the individual, they might comprise Aristotle's list of basic values, including virtue, honour, pleasure and understanding.[4] Still at the level of what are intrinsic values for an individual, some contemporary philosophers have listed 'certain states of consciousness; personal relationships; intellectual, artistic, and moral excellence; knowledge; and human life itself'.[5]

But some valuable features of society as a whole are about relations between the constituent individuals, and are not simply aggregates or averages of individual values. This would be the case, for example, with justice or social harmony. These are characteristics of society as a whole, not of individuals. Indeed, on the first page of his famous book, *A Theory of Justice*, John Rawls wrote that 'Justice is the first virtue of social institutions, as truth is of systems of thought'.[6]

Aesthetic judgements are also a form of value judgement since they are not amenable to empirical verification. For example, no appeal to facts can help decide whether some pieces of music are 'better' than others. Some people may claim that this is not true and that, for example, some music is 'better' than other music on account of certain 'facts', such as its harmonic subtlety, popularity or richness of emotional response. But while some of the facts may be indisputable the choice of criteria is a value judgement. Suppose a piece of music is judged better on one of these criteria but worse on another. What factual evidence could prove which criterion is more important? And how is it that some music that had been poorly regarded in the past is now very popular, or vice versa? Had some new factual evidence come to light, or did tastes or values simply change?

How does the previous distinction between positive propositions and value judgements operate in welfare economics? To answer this question we need to say a little more about 'positive propositions' and to introduce also the concept of a 'normative proposition'.

3 NORMATIVE PROPOSITIONS AND POSITIVE PROPOSITIONS

A 'normative proposition' is an 'ought' proposition – that is, an assertion about what *ought* to be done, like 'you *ought* to be kind to animals' or 'you *ought* to respect your teachers' or 'we *ought* to raise taxes on fattening food'. Such propositions differ sharply from 'is' propositions – that is, 'positive propositions' – such as those explained in Chapter 3, namely that Mount Everest is the highest mountain in the world, or that, other things remaining equal, the demand for apples is inversely related to their price. The distinction between normative and positive propositions corresponds to the famous distinction drawn by David Hume between 'ought' propositions and 'is' propositions. Hume was highly critical of a widespread tendency to jump too readily from the latter to the former.[7] Unfortunately, his criticisms were not enough to banish this tendency and it is still widespread. In fact, the main object of this book could be seen as an attempt to fight against its widespread persistence in the analysis of economic policy.

As indicated earlier, since *positive propositions* are factual statements about the way the world *is*, including statements about how it is believed to work, it must be possible – at least in principle – to check their truth by reference to some facts. They may be simple descriptive propositions, such as that the population of the USA is greater than that of Canada. Or they may describe certain causal relationships that are believed to hold between certain economic variables, such as the relationship between inequality and economic growth.

Of course, value judgements will influence the choice of 'facts', or the particular economic relationships, that are examined. This is why there can never be a value-free *positive economics*. For the choice of problems to be studied – such as the causes of inflation, or the effect of growth on the environment, or the degree of inequality in society and so on – depend on value judgements. Value judgements will also enter into the definition of the variables included in any analysis. For example, in an analysis of, say, the degree of economic inequality in society, there are different ways of measuring inequality. These include inequality of incomes between individuals, families, households, post-tax income or pre-tax income, lifetime income or annual income and so on. But when one has selected a particular definition in the light – partly or fully – of one's value judgement as to which definition is more 'important', the subsequent relationship between whatever concepts of inequality one has selected and, say, the rate of economic growth, is a matter of positive propositions. But given the particular definitions and methods adopted the statistical relationship between the selected variables *as defined* is a matter of fact and is the basis of a positive proposition. For example, this could take the form of the proposition that greater equality – as defined – does not conflict with economic growth – as defined. In other words, the truth or otherwise positive propositions can be verified, in principle, by reference to the 'facts' *as they have been defined*. So, positive propositions are value-free, although positive *economics* cannot be value-free, since the choice of problems to be studied and the way that the variables are defined depend partly on subjective value judgements.

Of course, the empirical verification of positive propositions in economics is not a simple matter. Economists cannot carry out controlled experiments as in the natural sciences or cut up corpses in order to improve their understanding of how they function. Their substitutes for these are comparisons across space – for example, between countries or regions or individuals – or comparisons over time. But in all cases the interpretation of the comparisons is invariably complicated by differences in other important variables.

Indeed, many important positive propositions in economics are still the subject of serious – and often heated – debate. These include propositions such as those about the effect of taxes on people's willingness to work, or the effect of the interest rate on the level of investment, or the effect of a budget deficit on an economy's rate of growth, etc. Propositions of this type have been the subject of an immense amount of very skilful and ingenious empirical testing, without, in many cases, arriving at indisputable results. What all such propositions have in common is that, *in principle*, given the definition of the variables involved, their truth or falsity can be established by appeal to some facts.

In practice, most informed debate about any particular economic policy or project revolves around differences in predictions about its likely effects. People – such as some politicians, or journalists, or commentators – who claim to know what these effects will be without having some model in mind of which positive propositions are relevant and what evidence for them exists are deluding themselves. But, even where there is agreement over the relevant positive propositions, the *desirability* of the policy or project in question will still depend on ultimate objectives. And these will depend on '*value judgements*'.

Before moving on, however, mention ought also to be made of one class of proposition that can be shown, in principle, to be true or false, without recourse to empirical verification. These are purely logical propositions such as those of mathematics, which, given some axioms, depend solely on the laws of logic. But such propositions are not relevant to the subject matter of this book. What is of interest here is the distinction between positive propositions and value judgements, since this is at the heart of the simple key to the analysis of economic policy issues which this book is designed to provide.

So, having set out the basic concepts needed for a fruitful analysis of any policy problems, how do they arise in the particular area with which we are concerned here, namely welfare economics? To answer this question it is useful to explain first what welfare economics is all about.

4 What Is Welfare Economics?

Welfare economics is that part of economic theory that is concerned with how far the economy is operating 'efficiently'. But the concept of 'efficiency' is meaningless except in relation to objectives. An axe may be an efficient instrument for chopping up wood, but not for trimming one's toe-nails. So what is the objective to which economic efficiency is directed? It is to make the maximum possible contribution – given available resources, techniques and people's preferences – to society's economic welfare. But 'society's economic welfare' is obviously a very subjective concept about which reasonable people may differ. For example, what do we mean by 'welfare' in general, or 'economic welfare' in particular, and what 'society' we are concerned with? And how can one assess the total welfare of a society without taking account of the way it is distributed among its members?

Furthermore, in most economic policy issues there is often no clear distinction between the objectives – that is, the 'ends' – to which one is aiming and the 'means' that may be employed to pursue those ends. For example, the ability to participate in the political life of one's community is both an 'end' in itself as well as a 'means' to influence its policies. At a more prosaic level if the authorities decided to reduce the country's dependence on imported fuel it is unlikely that they would do so by forcing aged pensioners to go down the coal mines, on the grounds that they have a low opportunity cost, since this particular 'means' to the adopted 'end' would probably conflict with most people's values, such as the rights of old people to freedom and a quiet life. The well-known definition of economics as 'the science which studies human behaviour as a relationship between ends and scarce means which have alternative uses' does not prescribe what the 'ends' ought to be.[8]

Thus whether an economy is operating in a manner best adapted to the promotion of society's economic welfare depends on 'value judgements', which are often – but not always – of an ethical nature, about both ultimate objectives and the means employed to pursue them.[9] As Amartya Sen has put it, an '.... ethics-related view of societal achievement cannot stop the evaluation short at some arbitrary point like satisfying 'efficiency'.[10] Nevertheless, given some value judgements that define our objectives, it is, of course, impossible to proceed to judgement as to how far these objectives are being achieved and, if not, what ought to be done about it, without some facts, which are in the domain of what is known as 'positive economics'

'Welfare economics' is sometimes distinguished from 'normative economics'. This distinction is significant only if 'welfare economics' is defined narrowly as being limited to the basic theory of what is known as the 'optimum' allocation of resources and the types of market failure – such as externalities, imperfect competition and so on – that prevent resources from being allocated optimally. Defined in this manner, welfare economics does not necessarily prescribe what ought to be done to improve the working of the market or to achieve other objectives that may even conflict with an 'optimum' allocation of resources.

'Normative economics', however, is usually interpreted more broadly. It encompasses considerations that lie outside the domain of pure economic theory, and which usually fall within the wider domain of ethics. It allows for the pursuit of values that may even conflict with a narrow concept of society's purely economic interests. In fact, the founding fathers of the subject – notably Pigou, Bergson, Samuelson, Little and Graaff – actually used the term 'welfare economics' in the broader sense. So out of respect for them I shall use it to correspond to the broader definition and to go beyond the basic theory of resource allocation and productive 'efficiency'. So I shall use the terms 'welfare economics' and 'normative economics' interchangeably.

For present purposes a more important – and generally adopted – distinction is one that I do follow in this book. It is the one described by one distinguished contributor to welfare economics, Tibor Scitovsky, in the following terms 'Modern economic theory draws a sharp distinction between *positive economics*, which explains the working of the economic system, and welfare economics, which prescribes policy'.[11]

Positive economics is that part of economics that purports to explain *how* markets work; what determines how much people want to buy or sell, and how their willingness to do either depends on their incomes, prices, expectations, tastes and a host of other influences. Thus it comprises propositions such as that, other things being equal, a fall in a country's exchange rate will lead to a rise in the demand for its exports.

By contrast, welfare economics is *prescriptive,* it provides the basis for normative propositions about what *ought* to be the case. It would include, for example, the proposition that incomes ought to be taxed, or that policies ought to be implemented to deal with environmental externalities. Normative propositions are thus at the cutting edge of welfare economics, and they rest on a combination of positive propositions and value judgements.

Certain features of society may possess *instrumental* value such as, for example, an educated population or an impartial legal system. They may be instrumentally valuable on account of the contribution they are believed to make to some other value, like freedom or justice. They are often referred to as *'derived'* values. But the proposition that they are *instrumentally* valuable must be a positive proposition so that, in principle, its truth or falsity can be checked by appeal to some facts. Indeed there is considerable statistical evidence of a positive relationship between the average educational level of a society and the average self-reported happiness of its citizens. Of course, education may also possess intrinsic value. Most people probably share Aristotle's view that, for an individual, knowledge possesses both *intrinsic* and *instrumental* value.

In the end, in welfare economics, it is the normative propositions that are the object of the whole exercise. On the basis of positive propositions and value judgements one can arrive at normative propositions. And, conversely, normative propositions have to be justified in terms of value judgements and, where relevant, positive propositions. Value judgements do not have to be ethical judgements. For example, you may believe that health is intrinsically good but would not claim that somebody who did not try to stay healthy was evil. Nor would one maintain that somebody who does not believe that education is intrinsically valuable is in some way immoral.

Thus all normative propositions are prescriptive, or 'ought', propositions. They all have to be justified, *in the end*, by some form of *'value judgement'*, such as that being richer or having beautiful flowers is *intrinsically* good, or that killing people is *intrinsically* bad. As such they are not open to empirical verification. This does not mean that there is no room for discussion as to the consistency of some particular values with others, as in the aforementioned example of the value judgement that 'killing people is bad'. Similarly, somebody who is against abortion on the grounds that human life is 'sacred' might want to ask himself whether this is consistent with his views on the morality of capital punishment, or some other social value, and if there is a conflict of values how he would trade them off. In such cases one comes up against the possible conflict between intrinsic values, which are discussed in more detail in Chapter 10 in connection with the ethical doctrine known as 'Utilitarianism'.

5   THE CONSTRUCTION OF WELFARE/NORMATIVE ECONOMICS

In welfare economics value judgements are subjective judgements about what values society should adopt for the purposes of defining its economic objectives and the means that should be used to promote them. They are not *necessarily* ethical judgements in the usual sense of the term 'ethical'. But in economic policy debate the value judgements usually do involve ethics, if only implicitly. For, in principle, economic policy choices should be based on (i) models of how economies, or parts of it, are believed to operate; and (ii) the relevant objectives that society ought to pursue and the acceptability of possible means to pursue the objectives. The first part of this system comprises the 'positive economics', which relies on what one believes to be 'facts'; and the second part relies on some value judgements, which may be noble or obvious, but which are not subjects for empirical verification.

The recipe for normative propositions in economics could be set out as shown in Fig. 3.1. First, make some *'behavioural'* (psychological) assumptions about how economic 'agents' – consumers and producers – react to the economic environment with which they are faced. This would include their assets, relative prices, demand for their services and so on. These behavioural assumptions could include, for example, the assumption that rational agents attempt to select, from the options open to them, the ones they prefer. Then mix these behavioural assumptions with some assumptions about technology – such as the law of diminishing marginal product. With this mixture one can

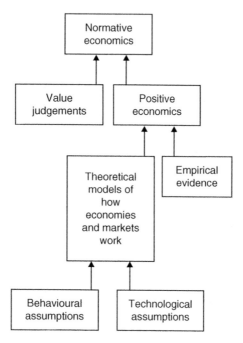

Fig. 3.1 Structure of economic policy choice

construct a nice *theoretical* model of the way that markets would function. If one can then stir in some factual evidence to demonstrate how far the theoretical assumptions of the model are valid one arrives at some *positive economics*.

Most empirical work in positive economics is devoted precisely to the verification of these assumptions. And even some highly plausible behavioural assumptions have been challenged. For example, many studies by behavioural psychologists have shown that consumers' behaviour is not as 'rational' as is generally assumed in the models (Chapter 5). Indeed, it has been claimed that the rational choice model that is at the heart of positive micro-economic theory is not a 'positive' theory to start with and is really a 'normative' theory of how people *ought* to behave.[12] On the other hand, many statistical studies do confirm that, in the end, some of the basic predictions of the theory hold good. Demand curves do tend to slope down from left to right – on the whole – and where they do not there is usually a convincing theoretical explanation.

But, as we have seen, even when the economist has established a plausible, workable model of how the economy – or that part of it in which one is interested – is believed to work, it is still impossible to make normative policy prescriptions without, at some stage, introducing some value judgements.

For David Hume there was only one basic value for an individual that was desirable for its own sake, namely 'pleasure' or 'happiness'. In later years, in the hands of Jeremy Bentham and others this was identified with 'utility'. Furthermore the 'utility' of society was simply the sum total of the utility of the individuals comprised in that society. This school of thought – namely that there was one top-level value, utility – became known as 'Utilitarianism', a school of thought that still commands very widespread assent. It is discussed in more detail in Chapters 9 and 10.

It is also widely contested. Many philosophers believe that there are several independent intrinsic values and that they are incommensurate. In fact most of us subscribe to several values which often appear to conflict. For example, one might be faced with an occasional conflict between truth and loyalty to some other individual or institution. And, at the level of society as a whole, it may be believed that the intrinsic value, justice, conflicts with other intrinsic values, such as freedom or the role of prosperity in raising happiness by one means or another.

But whether one is a Utilitarian, or a pluralist who believes that there are several top-level values, it is still true that, faced with any normative proposition, one cannot go on for ever asking for the reason behind the reason for it without reaching the point where reason has no more role to play and one has reached an *intrinsic* value judgement, like 'pleasure' in Hume's example at the beginning of this chapter.

As indicated earlier, most research and public debates about economic policies tend to ignore – quite reasonably – the value judgements involved and concentrate on disagreements about the consequences of different policies. This book is intended to remind readers that the value judgements are there, and are an essential part of welfare economics and that their neglect can often lead to an easy acceptance of certain policies that depend on some possibly contentious value judgements. Without some idea of what *ends* we want to attain there is little point in knowing what economic *means* will attain them most 'efficiently'. It would be like studying anatomy or physiology without expecting it to be of any practical use. A value-free welfare economics would be rather frustrating.

NOTES

1. Hume, 1739, 1998 edn., ed. Beauchamp: Appendix 1, para. 19.
2. Hume, 1739, www.davidhume.org:3.1.11.10. Hume's defence of his theory of morality in general and of justice in particular was also presented, more briefly, just over ten years later, in *An Enquiry concerning the Principles of Morals*.
3. Mill, 1861:I,5.
4. *Ethics, 1097b2–21*. Aristotle did not, however, regard these as what he called 'final values', of which, in his opinion, there was only one, namely 'happiness' (interpreted in a rather special manner). The reason he gives for this is that although we might pursue them for their own sake, one might also pursue them for the sake of our happiness, whereas the converse does not apply.
5. Scanlon, 1998:87.
6. Clarendon Press, Oxford, 1972.
7. Hume, 1739, *ibid*:3.1.1.27.
8. This definition originated in the important and influential book by Lionel Robbins, 1932. It abstracted from the question of how far an economy's 'scarce means' are fully employed, since it was focused on the problem of allocation under conditions of scarcity.
9. See an interesting discussion of this point in Jonathan B. Wight, *op.cit.* 59 *et seq.*
10. Sen, 1987:4.
11. Scitovsky, 1941:77.
12. See Hands, 2009:13.

CHAPTER 4

Fact and Value in Personal Choice

1   The Pain of Personal Choice

While value judgements determine our objectives, the means at our disposal to pursue different objectives are usually limited. This is why economics has been described as 'the logic of choice'. Values conflict at both the personal and the public level. At the personal level people are constantly making choices in their daily lives. Life is one long trade-off. Even simple things like choosing which vegetables go best with whatever else we are eating involves an unconscious trade-off of values. There are lots of things we would like to do but there are constraints on how many can be done. Finance will be one constraint. Even Bill Gates would probably like to donate more money to charitable activities but is constrained by the finance at his disposal, as well as his time.

Indeed, time is a constraint to which almost everybody is subject. One is constantly having to decide whether to read a book, go to the cinema, get on with one's work, listen to music, chat to one's friends and so on. Faced with such choices one will often make some sort of comparison between the advantages and disadvantages of the various options, but the comparison is likely to be very rough and ready and often subconscious, instinctive and impulsive. And some of the choices may have important longer-term consequences, and in a world of uncertainty they will represent judgements about probabilities.

For example, consider the case of a student who is trying to decide which job to take up after graduating. He will probably take several factors

© The Author(s) 2017
W. Beckerman, *Economics as Applied Ethics*,
DOI 10.1007/978-3-319-50319-6_4

into account. These would include, for example, the salary offered in different lines of employment, promotion prospects, the location of the work, its intrinsic interest, the prestige of the career it might lead to or how far it will provide opportunities to meet interesting or attractive people. These considerations will be partly 'factual'. But they will also be partly matters of taste or values – for example, what the student regards as 'interesting' work or people, and how much importance he attaches to the various considerations.[1]

And suppose his parents say he *ought* to become a dentist because the pay is high and there are good career prospects. But he may reply that material prosperity is not all that important in his scale of values, and the work looks unpleasant. He is inclined to pursue an academic career instead. The pay is low but the work is very interesting, and many people engage in it for love of the work, their contribution to the dissemination of knowledge, and the stimulus they get from their students and colleagues. In this example, then, the student and his parents are reaching different normative propositions as to what he *ought* to do. They may differ both as to the facts and the values. Some of the considerations taken into account by the student and his parents are fairly factual.

For example they may all agree on the pay prospects, but may disagree about the interest of the work. Propositions about whether the salary is high or not are *positive propositions*, the truth of which can be established by reference to some facts, at least in principle. But differences in the relative weight that they attach to, say, prosperity as compared to the intrinsic interest of the work or the appeal of the pursuit of knowledge are differences in values about which no empirical information can provide an answer.

2   THE BASIC THEORY OF CONSUMERS' CHOICE

Economic theory has helped us understand the psychological processes that help us make our choices. One of the greatest advances in economic theory was the concept of 'diminishing marginal utility', one which probably anybody with the slightest familiarity with economic theory has heard of. Indeed, the concept of 'utility' plays a central role in economics. It also plays a central role in the welfare economics concept of the 'Pareto optimum'. Hence Chapter 9 is devoted to a discussion of the closely related ethical theory of 'Utilitarianism'. The concept of 'utility' has often been rather loosely identified with 'welfare' or 'happiness' (as in classical Utilitarianism). In this chapter I shall concentrate on the concept of 'utility', and in the next chapter I shall discuss the concept of 'Pareto optimum'.

Words like 'utility' or 'welfare' or 'better-offness' usually denote states of mind, though they sometimes have other interpretations. But for most purposes we cannot actually observe states of mind. We can only observe what choices people make, which we generally assume to 'reveal' their preferences. But do their choices accurately reflect their 'true' preferences? And do their preferences accurately reflect their welfare? In the jargon, 'Are their preference orderings identical to their welfare orderings?' We all know people (including ourselves) whose choices we believe to have been unwise, such as taking this job rather than some other, or dating this young lady or that young man rather than another, or taking a holiday in this place rather than that place, and so on. So we have to admit that to go from observed choices to 'better offness' is a big jump, involving both positive assumptions about people's psychologies as well as value judgements about what constitutes being 'better off'.

3   THE 'UTILITY FUNCTION' IN ECONOMICS

In Chapter 3 we saw that models of the way economies operate – that is, positive economics – are built up on foundations that comprise (i) 'behavioural' assumptions – that is, assumptions about the way that economic agents react to their economic environments in pursuit of their presumed objectives, and (ii) technological assumptions about productive activities (defining 'productive' very widely). The models also take as given some initial endowments of capital (including natural and 'human' capital) and labour.

A crucial element in the behavioural assumptions is the concept of the utility-maximising consumer and the accompanying concept of the 'utility function'. In modern economics this merely represents a ranking of preferences that an individual may attach to different collections of goods and services. No precise psychological explanation of preferences is proposed and it is just assumed that if somebody chooses X rather than Y this merely 'reveals' his preference for X over Y without implying any particular psychological state of mind that explained the preference – that is, *why* he preferred X to Y. For purposes of positive economics such psychological explanations of consumers' choices are unnecessary.

Consider an agent (e.g. a consumer) who is faced with a number of options that depend on his 'environment' (i.e. his circumstances). Suppose that if he compares two of these options, say X and Y, he can either prefer X to Y or Y to X or be indifferent between them. Repeat this for all possible pairs of options. Assume now that his preferences are *transitive* – that is, that if he prefers X to Y and Y to Z he will prefer X to Z. In that case, he can rank all the options in the order X > Y > Z, that corresponds to his preferences, or – to use the more formal term – he can attach an 'ordering' to the different options available to him. If another option, A, is introduced, and he can rank, say X > A, and A > Y, we can introduce this into the preference orderings, so that we have X > A > Y > Z. Such an ordering is then called his 'utility function'.

It tells us nothing about *why* he prefers X to Y and so on. His utility function is defined as a representation of this ordering, and nothing more. In economics, utility just means the value of the function that represents a person's preferences.[2] In other words, the utility function 'is a function that assigns a number called a "utility" to each of the options in such a way that one option gets a higher number than another if and only if it is preferred. It represents the order of preferences by means of utilities'.[3]

The contemporary interpretation of utility is clearly set out by Binmore as follows:

> The modern theory . . . *disowns* its Benthamite origins and cannot be properly understood if these trappings of its childhood are not entirely discarded. . . . A rational individual is only said to behave as though he were satisfying preferences or maximising a utility function and nothing is claimed at all about the internal mental processes that may have led him to do so. A utility function, in the modern sense, is nothing more than a mathematically tractable means of expressing the fact that an individual's choice behaviour is consistent.[4]

4   PREFERENCES AND THEORIES OF 'THE GOOD'

It might seem that ostentatious rejection of the classical utilitarian interpretation of 'utility' as virtually synonymous with words such as 'happiness' or 'welfare' is a case of 'The lady doth protest too much' [Hamlet]. For in spite of the gradual replacement of the old utilitarian identification of utility with welfare by the modern concept of a utility function it is generally assumed in welfare economics that people's preferences do, in fact, correspond to their own welfares. As Broome puts it, 'Welfare economists move, almost without noticing it, between saying a person prefers one thing to another and saying she is better off with the first than with the second'.[5]

The reason for this is that preferences play a dual role in welfare economics. In one role they are assumed to determine people's choices. It is assumed that if people prefer A to B it must be because they expect A to add more to their welfare. Given these assumptions, preferences then play a second role, namely to provide the basis for passing judgements about the welfare of society as a whole. As Sen puts it, 'This dual link between choice and preference on the one hand and preference and welfare on the other is crucial to the normative aspects of general equilibrium theory. All the important results in this field depend on this relationship between behaviour and welfare through the intermediary of preferences'.[6]

This feature of welfare economics embodies a particular theory of the 'good' (for an individual, not society), namely the *preference-satisfaction theory of good*. There are, however, other theories of the 'good' or of what constitutes 'welfare' or 'well-being'. The theory generally adopted by economists for practical purposes is the *'mental state'* theory, such as the utilitarian theory according to which well-being is a function of people's mental state, such as how happy they *feel*. The father of welfare economics, Pigou, clearly adopted a mental state account when he wrote that 'the elements of welfare are states of consciousness and, perhaps, of their relations'.[7] Another theory of the good is the *'objective list'* theory, according to which welfare has to be measured in terms of various specific items on a list, such as average expectation of life, levels of literacy, access to clean drinking water, and so on.[8] This is, in effect, embodied in various measures of national welfare, such as the United Nations *Human Development Index*.

According to Broome '...the preference-satisfaction theory is obviously false and no one really believes it!'[9] Even economists, who rely heavily on it, do not really believe it. It is another instance – like attitudes to interpersonal comparisons of utility – of the professional schizophrenia to which economists are prone. Indeed, in welfare economics the identification of welfare with the satisfaction of preferences is so automatic and ubiquitous that economists tend to forget how controversial it is. And controversial it certainly is.

5   The Economic Concept of Rational Choice

But can we go further and see whether people express their preferences in a manner that would enable us to predict how their choice would respond to changes in their circumstance – such as in incomes or prices. To do this we would need to identify some *rational* system behind their choices. And the system we adopt is as follows.

We assume that consumers have some goals and that they attempt to pursue these goals in a 'rational' manner. In economics rational behaviour is *instrumentally* rational. 'The concept of rational behaviour arises from the empirical fact that human behaviour is to a large extent goal-directed behaviour. Basically, rational behaviour is simply behaviour consistently pursuing some well-defined goals, and pursuing them according to some well-defined set of preferences or priorities'.[10] What these goals and preference orderings happen to be will vary from one individual to another and economists need not make any specific assumptions about whether, for example, the goal is maximisation of happiness or some other objective.

The fundamental axioms of rational choice are:

(a) *Consistency.* This means that you cannot prefer A to B at one moment and then prefer B to A later, unless there is a relevant change in the environment within which you are choosing. In other words a person's preference relations between collections of goods and services X, Y, Z and so on, are not haphazard and random. The assumption of stable utility functions does not, of course, exclude changes in preferences as a result of changes in a person's circumstances. For example, a person may have fallen ill, which will change the position of health expenditures in his ranking. Or his partner may have run off with the local baker. In this case there will be two types of effect. First, he may become miserable even without any change in his preference pattern at all. It just changes the amount of 'happiness' corresponding to any of his 'indifference' curves. But, second, he is likely to change his expenditure rankings in many ways. He might even stop eating madeleines.

Furthermore, consistency is not a *sufficient* condition for rationality. A madman who believes he is Louis XVI is making assumptions about his environment that patently conflict with some of its indisputable features. So even if he pursued his objectives in a consistent manner one might still regard his behaviour as 'irrational'. On the other hand, one might say that, like people who bought certain bank shares before they went bankrupt, he is simply the victim of mistaken information. Consistency, like comparability, is, however, a *necessary* condition for rationality. Without this consistency assumption, 'well-ordered utility functions' would not be very 'well-ordered', so the whole structure of micro-economic theory would collapse.

(b) *Transitivity*. This means that if a consumer prefers A to B and B to C, he must prefer A to C. Again, without this assumption it would be difficult, if not, impossible to postulate well-behaved utility functions.

It is true that, as discussed in detail in the next chapter, the assumption that people's choices strictly follow the criteria of rational choice is unwarranted. But there is also enough evidence to show that it is a sufficiently good assumption to permit the construction of reasonable working models of how the market behaves that could be compared with value judgements about how markets *ought* to behave. But the implications of the fact that people's choices are not always entirely rational *on the above narrow conception of rationality* raise important conflicts of value judgements that are discussed in the next chapter.

NOTES

1. As Arrow points out, the distinction between 'tastes' and 'values' is a very flimsy one. ['Social Choice and Individual Values', 2nd edition, 1963:18].
2. Broome refers to this as being now the 'official definition' of utility in economics (Broome, 1999:21).
3. Broome, *ibid.*:186.
4. Binmore, 1974:50–51.
5. Binmore, *ibid.*:4.
6. Sen 1982:66–67.
7. Pigou, 1932 edn:10.
8. See Hausman and McPherson, *op.cit.* (2nd edn, 2006) ch. 8, for a comprehensive survey of the main theories.
9. Broome, 1999:4.
10. Harsanyi, 1977:42.

CHAPTER 5

How to Make 'Bad' Choices

1   Why People Make 'Bad' Choices

According to the late Milton Friedman and other members of the 'Chicago School' of economics we have to assume that people – except lunatics and children – rationally pursue their own interests. But a casual observation of the state of the world suggests that, in fact, most people *are* either lunatics or children, so this does not leave us with a large class of people whose choices are to be respected.

There is ample evidence from both common observation (including introspection) and careful professional psychological studies that many – and probably most, if not all – people frequently make choices that are not really in their best interests. (For present purposes I shall define these as 'bad' choices although it is arguable that in many cases such choices can be defended.) Behavioural psychologists have identified various classes of reasons for such 'self-defeating' behaviour. One is that people simply lack full self-knowledge of their own preferences. Another is that their strategies are based on an imperfect recollection, or interpretation, of past experiences in certain situations. Also, in particular, emotional stress plays a large part in such behaviour. Under emotional distress, people shift towards favouring high-risk, high-payoff options, even if these are objectively poor choices.

Another common cause of self-defeating action is a concern for social considerations. People may pay too much attention to what other people think. Or they may get very upset in response to a blow to their pride,

© The Author(s) 2017
W. Beckerman, *Economics as Applied Ethics*,
DOI 10.1007/978-3-319-50319-6_5

'...and the rush to prove something great about themselves overrides their normal and rational way of dealing with life'.[1] Also a variety of social considerations tend to lock people into consumption habits and constrain their freedom of choice, such as class, family, culture, ideology, national character and so on.[2]

Thanks to the work of many behavioural psychologists such as Daniel Kahneman and colleagues, various other explanations of such behaviour have been proposed. Kahneman distinguishes between two modes of thinking, namely System 1 and System 2.[3] The latter comprises a careful reflection and analysis of the available options. The former relies much more on guesswork, intuition and previous experience. It saves time and mental energy. People need some kind of energy to weigh up all the costs and benefits of any choice and many people do not have it, or have used it up, at some crucial point.[4] But it means that one is prone to make several mistakes which, as Kahneman and his colleagues have shown, in many common types of System 1 thinking, have certain features in common.

One of these is a common tendency to be optimistic about one's own capabilities. For example, surveys have shown that, in the USA, about 80% of motorists think that they are better drivers than the average. Another common type of mistake is what is known as the 'anchoring' effect. This effect can be seen in numerous transactions, such as in influencing how much one is prepared to bid when negotiating to buy a house or a car, where it is rare to put in a bid very far removed from some initial asking price.

The 'endowment' effect is a further example of what seem to be inconsistent choices. This is where people value more highly some object that they happen to own – quite apart from sentimental attachment and so on – than would be justified by some objective valuation based on how much they value other objects that they do not own but that have equal monetary value.

An example of what seem to be inconsistent choices among highly educated people is recent analysis of the choices made by a large sample (386) of employees of the highly respected Boston University. They were all asked their preferences as regards the way they would like their consumption levels to vary over their lives, given their existing income prospects. For example, those who did not care much about a likely severe fall in consumption levels in old age would save less than those who did. So their preferred profiles of consumption over their lives had implications for what their savings and insurance behaviour ought to be. But when their actual savings and insurance behaviour were examined it was shown that most of them were far from following the required strategy. There was, in fact, very little correlation between their preferred lifetime consumption profiles and those that would result from their actual savings and insurance behaviour. And the strategies were just as inconsistent for high-income professors who had significant financial knowledge as for low-income staff without such knowledge.[5]

However, it should not be thought that reliance on System 2 rather than System 1 for purposes of making choices always produces more welfare-enhancing outcomes. Indeed, some studies suggest that even if people are reflective and suffer from none of the mentioned impediments to Kahneman's System 2, they still sometimes make choices that aren't in their best interests. For example, some students who were given the time to follow System 2 and reflect on and assess all the attributes of university courses from which they could choose subsequently made less optimal course choices than the students who were not asked to reflect much on the choice. Similarly, other students who were allowed to reflect carefully on their choices were more influenced by irrelevant factors – for example, by the way in which the choice scenarios were framed rather than by the rationality of either option – than were the other test participants. So we have to face the fact that even when we have enough mental resources and motivation to engage in thorough reflection on our choices, we can still make choices that are not in our best interests.

This is particularly the case in choices involving the future. For it is generally accepted that people suffer from what Pigou called 'defective telescopic faculty' when it comes to taking account of future costs and benefits. This is particularly important since many choices require forecasting future costs and benefits. Sometimes these involve short-term pleasures but long-term pains. In such cases if people discount future costs too heavily they will fail to maximise their welfare over the relevant time period. Also, in most cases the present benefits are certain and the future costs are uncertain, which makes it even more tempting to discount them very heavily. There are many ways in which failure to take due account of longer-term consequences leads to decisions that reduce people's longer term welfare. Eating too many fattening foods, smoking, drugs, unprotected sex, excessive drinking, are all examples of this failure to make choices that maximise one's welfare over time.

One real-world implication of an apparent inconsistency in choice is the experience of some companies' policies concerning their employees' contribution to pension schemes. Instead of leaving it up to employees to make the positive decision to contribute to their pensions, many companies in the USA have switched to making the contributions automatic while giving the employees the right to opt out of the scheme. Thus the scheme was not paternalistic in the sense of imposing choices on the employees. Anyway, the result in these cases was a big increase in employees' participation in the schemes, and only a few opted out. In other words, when it was a question of opting in, few took up the option, which seems to indicate a preference for staying out. But when it was a case of opting out, few took up the option, which indicated a preference for staying in. Clearly there is some inconsistency here with respect to which option employees thought was in their best interests (Sunstein, 2005, ch. 8). It is true that the different income effects of the alternative transactions could explain very small disparities but the large disparities observed go well beyond that.

Of course, even if people are reflective and rational and suffer from none of the impediments to Sunstein's System 2 thinking mentioned earlier, welfare maximising choice may be very difficult simply because the options will often seem incommensurate. At the beginning of this chapter we considered the conflict between values arising in a student's choice of career. In that example there was a conflict between the values of the student and the values of his parents. But on either side there was no doubt some conflict of values. The student in question probably took account of the value that a more lucrative occupation would permit, such as more appealing cultural activities, including foreign travel, or going to the opera, not to mention the ability to eat high-class food washed down with Chateau Mouton Rothschild claret. If, in the end, he chose a less lucrative career on account of its inherent interest and so on, this could have been the outcome of a very difficult choice between conflicting values. And conflicts of values are ubiquitous at the level both of the individual and society as a whole.

The general problem of incommensurability of values, which is one of the main objections to classical Utilitarianism, is discussed in Chapter 10. Some of the resulting problems in economic policy are discussed in Chapter 6. But there is one particular conflict of values that arises directly from the previous discussion of the ways in which people's ignorance of the effects of some of their choices may do them harm. For this raises the question of how far one should force people to make choices that are believed to be in their best interests. In other words how far should society trade off the value of 'consumer sovereignty', or 'personal autonomy' against paternalism and its accompanying restriction on individual liberty.

2   INFORMATION AND 'RATIONAL IGNORANCE'

Even when people are not irrational in the manner described earlier they will still very often make choices that do not best promote their welfare on account of lack of information. Lack of information is obviously an all-pervasive feature of most decisions that people take, ranging from what career path they embark on to which toothpaste best protects their teeth. This is particularly the case when the choices involve – as is often the case – judgements about risk and probabilities. For example, it is well known that people are far more worried about the probability of being killed in a railway or aircraft accident than in a road accident, though the statistical evidence suggests that the latter probability is much greater.

However, information gaps do not necessarily indicate a failure to behave rationally. There is what is known as 'rational ignorance'. Consumers may sometimes lack information because they have ration-ally decided that the costs to them – in terms of time or money – of getting the extra information is not worth it in terms of the likely pay-off. Consider the following example that must be replicated in one form or another every day by thousands of tourists all over the world. Outside the Duomo in Florence there are kiosks that sell, among other things, postcards – photographs of the Duomo, or of Michelangelo's statue of David after he had slain Goliath, or of some famous Raphael or Botticelli painting and so on. About a 10-minute walk north of the Duomo, in the direction of the Piazza Annunziata, there are a couple of bookshops that sell exactly the same postcards as those outside the Duomo, but at a much lower price. How is this possible? Quite simply, coach-loads of tourists are deposited outside the Duomo for a short time; they take their photographs of the façade and the adjacent Giotto tower and perhaps the Ghiberti low-reliefs around the Baptistery out-side the Duomo, and then may spend a few minutes buying postcards from the closest kiosks. It would be uneconomical for them to waste time walking all around the area in order to check whether they could save a few cents by buying the same cards elsewhere. It is this allowance by most people for the costs of acquiring information that is known as 'rational ignorance'. By contrast, most people go to much more trouble to obtain information when making big investments, such as buying a car, or a house, where it is worth doing so.

And in some cases the relevant information is about the future, which is never known to us completely. Lack of information and inability to predict future tastes and preferences is amply demonstrated by the high divorce rates. Given high divorce rates and the assumption that, in most cases, divorce is a last-resort option, marriage is clearly a gamble. Indeed, I am surprised that it is still legal. Instead – unlike gambling for money – it is actively encouraged, unless one is married to more than one person at a time. At least when one gambles on a horse to win a race it is possible to study the horse's past form, including its record over similar distances and under similar circumstances. Such information is not usually available for marriage.

Also, while it may often be perfectly rational to make choices without obtaining all the relevant information, information is not a commodity like any other commodity. For one cannot know what is the optimum amount of investment one should make to obtain information until one already has the information. So in many cases lack of information probably does cut the link between preferences and welfare, as when people are not aware that they need the information or that it is available – for example, taking a highly paid job unaware that it was likely to be only a short-term job and that it will not prepare them for subsequent employment. Not knowing what one needs to know may be particularly important in certain situations, such as the trade in toxic waste (discussed in more detail in Chapter 8).

Furthermore, much information has the character of a public good – that is, that there is no extra marginal cost in allowing an extra person to have access to a piece of information once that information is available to other people. It is rather like a radio or TV broadcast, where once the programme is on the air, so that some people can enjoy it, there is no further cost in allowing other people to share in it. It is well known that in a free market the supply of information in public goods is unlikely to be optimal. Hence, in the case of many forms of information, there can be no presumption that people enjoy a socially optimal amount of it.

3   Consumer Sovereignty or Paternalism?

Given the general scepticism about the crude 'preference-satisfaction theory of good', how can individuals' preference satisfaction be a good starting point for judgements about social welfare? Most economists recognise that people's 'manifest' preferences (to use Harsanyi's term), namely the ones that determine market outcomes, including prices, are often bad guides to their welfare, for the various reasons enumerated earlier. Consequently, many economists and philosophers believe that one should often overrule 'revealed preferences' and force or push consumers into expenditure choices that the authorities believe would better promote their welfare. In other words, consumer sovereignty would often give way to paternalism.

There are, of course, innumerable actual examples of not relying entirely on people's preferences, including what are known as 'merit goods' (or their counterpart 'demerit goods'). The most important example is basic education. Education benefits partly the community at large, of course, and so has an element of externality in it that would justify a subsidy even if it were a purely private good. But some people might still not take advantage of the opportunity to educate their children more cheaply. They might prefer to be able to spend more on drink, or a better car, or a foreign holiday. Thus education is usually made compulsory.

There are many other examples of a paternalist attitude, as when, for example, regulations are introduced that prevent people doing harm to themselves on account of the sort of psychological forces outlined previously. For example, there are lots of instances where we all accept that public restriction on freedom of choice is justified, such as prescription medicines, Health and Safety Regulations, as well as some instances where it is more debatable – drugs, smoking in public places, fatty foods and so on.[6] And because people are known to underestimate the probability of their being involved in a road accident, many people would not wear seat belts unless they were compulsory (and did not do so for many years before they were made compulsory). So Parliament decided that people would have to be made to wear them.

In the defence of such measures it can be argued that one is not really challenging the validity of people's ends, but only helping them to achieve them. In other words, the objection to such interference with people's choices reflects a failure to distinguish between ends and means – that is, society should not try to interfere with people's ends, but should be allowed to correct their errors about the means to achieve them. For example, one can assume that most people have top-level values to go on living. But suppose we have good reason to believe that if they postpone giving up smoking, or dieting and so on, they will die earlier – that is, we believe that they are failing to promote their ends. Thus, for example, seat belts in cars, or helmets for motorcyclists, would support their objective of long life.

However, there is a long-established tradition in support of the view that people are better judges of their own interest than are some outside authorities. For example, in his famous book, *On Liberty*, first published in 1859, John Stuart Mill devoted a whole chapter to the question of the extent to which the authorities should overrule the preferences of ordinary people, in the course of which he wrote that

> ...the only purpose for which power can be rightfully exercised over any member of a civilized community, against his will, is to prevent harm to others. His own good, either physical or mental, is not a sufficient warrant. He cannot rightfully be compelled to do or forbear because it will be better for him to do so, because it will make him happier, because, in the option of others, to do so would be wise or even right.

And this view has been echoed by other philosophers throughout the ages, as, for example, Robert Nozick, who wrote in 1974 that 'Two noteworthy implications [of his, i.e. Nozick's, view] are that the state may not use its coercive apparatus for the purpose of getting some citizens to aid others, or in order to prohibit activities to people for their *own* good or protection'.[7]

Of course, Mill – and even Nozick – could not have been aware of all the modern evidence for believing that people are not best judges of their own interests. So it is arguable that they were quite wrong about the basic assumption that people are the best judges of their interests. On the other hand, as Robert Sugden has cogently argued, there is not much evidence that authorities are any better.[8] It is highly plausible that in some cases 'nanny knows best', but even in such cases does this really justify overriding consumers' preferences in most other cases at the cost of a probable mistaken belief of what is in their interests? It would be wrong to assume that the alternative to reliance on fallible consumers is intervention by some public authority that is all-seeing, fully informed, efficient, honest, rational and impartial. Nowhere is the 'agent-principal' distinction more important than in most public authorities, where the principals are the public and the agents are the officials who have their own agendas.

Furthermore, freedom to choose, even if it may mean making mistakes, may be an independent top-level value. People may attach 'end value' to freedom to choose even if they know they may not make the wisest choices. Hence, the objective of maximising people's welfare by preventing their free choice in certain situations may be subordinated to the objective of respect for their rights.

In any case, one may be reluctant to brush aside people's revealed preferences on the grounds that this would be the first step down a slippery slope via paternalism and authoritarianism to tyranny. For one has to be aware of the danger of excessive paternalism. Many tyrannies have been based on the view that people do not know what is best for them or that, even if they do, they ought to be motivated by a sense of duty to do what is best for the society in which they live. A cavalier rejection of democratic respect for people's preferences can lead to very undesirable outcomes, not to mention an unjustified infringement of people's liberties.

On the other hand, it can be argued that it is morally admirable to respect and promote the 'projects' (life aims) of other people because they have value. So a certain amount of paternalism is justified in order to help them pursue their objective, even though we may think that they are mistaken in their beliefs about how to promote their objectives. In other words a certain amount of paternalism could be defended on the grounds that it does not represent a challenge to people's values, but is merely a way of helping them promote those values.

Again there is no scientific way of trading off the objective of paternalistic welfare maximisation against the objective of respect for consumers' 'rights', including their right to make their own mistakes about the means they adopt to pursue their ends. Faced with a difficult choice between these conflicting values, one compromise policy is the 'nudge approach' that has been advocated notably by Thaler and Sunstein.[9] In the UK there is now an official 'nudge unit', known as 'The Behavioural Insights Team', which takes account of recent academic research into behaviour to devise 'nudge' policies that will be of value to people and the community by making it easier for people to take the decisions that will best promote their welfare. Most obvious are 'opt-out against opt-in' policies for, say, pension schemes. But other 'nudge' policies would include, for example, health warnings on cigarette packaging, or clear indication of possibly harmful ingredients in some foodstuffs and so on.

However, even the 'nudge' approach is based on the assumption that people would be better off making choice A rather than choice B. This is then assumed to justify framing people's choices in a way that will increase the chances of their making choice A, without falling into the paternalist trap of forcing them to do so. Neither of these assumptions is clearly compelling. For example, consider the aforementioned example of obliging employees to opt-out of a pension scheme rather than having to opt-in, so that the default is membership of the scheme. It is assumed that people who remain in the scheme but who might otherwise have failed to opt-in will be better off as a result. But it is possible that they would have been better off if they had not joined the pension scheme and had made their own arrangements for their old age, or even not at all for that matter.

Thus, again, there do not seem to be any clear-cut answers. In certain cases – such as the availability of possibly dangerous medicines – the case for paternalism may be very strong, but the case for restrictions on the consumption of fattening foods may be less so. The net social welfare gain from one policy or another may be difficult to access. And even if some reasonable rough balance sheet can be drawn up, there is still the problem of balancing the net gain or loss against the violation of personal liberty.

4   ALTRUISM AND COMMITMENT

One important reason why the axioms of rationality specified earlier do not guarantee that people's choices will promote their 'welfare' is that some people may deliberately and consciously choose not to maximise their own welfare. The welfare that most people expect to derive from their choices may depend partly on the effect they expect to have on the welfare of other people. Such modes of behaviour may satisfy the two axioms of rational choice without being motivated purely by self-interest. And modern theories of human behaviour in terms of game theory, particularly their behaviour in repeated games, which is the situation that people are faced with in society, explicitly allow for people's preferences to include considerations such as altruism. For, over the course of human history, some concern for the interests of others has helped establish viable societies which indirectly promote people's self-interest. In the non-human animal world 'reciprocal altruism', as it has been called in evolutionary biology, suggests that evolution has led to animals being programmed to have concern for other animals in proportion to the probability that the other animals will share their genes. In the human world it is the social evolutionary process that has contributed to the development of altruistic considerations in the human psyche.

The concept of 'sympathy', defined widely to include altruism and a capacity to enjoy other people's good fortunes, played a crucial role in the work of Adam Smith and David Hume. Smith's *Theory of Moral*

Sentiments begins with the assertion that, 'How selfish however man be supposed, there are evidently some principles in his nature, which interest him in the fortunes of others, and render their happiness necessary to him, though he derives nothing from it, except the pleasure of seeing it'. Smith was not limiting the concept of 'sympathy' to the more common current usage, which refers to sympathy with the misfortunes of other people. It also included a more general ability to empathise with other people. Sympathy and benevolence also play an important role in Hume's moral and political theory. He wrote that 'No quality of human nature is more remarkable, both in itself and in its consequences, than that propensity we have to sympathise with others, and to receive by communication their inclinations and sentiments, however different from or even contrary to our own'.[10]

In his famous article 'Rational Fools: A Critique of the Behavioural Foundations of Economic Theory', Amartya Sen distinguishes between his concept of 'sympathy' and what he calls 'commitment' (Sen, 1982a). Roughly speaking, sympathy is when you can raise your own welfare by raising somebody else's, and commitment is when you reduce your welfare in order to raise somebody else's. For Sen, 'commitment does involve, in a very real sense, counter-preferential choice, destroying the crucial assumption that a chosen alternative must be better than (or at least as good as) the others for the person choosing it. . . .' (Sen, 1982, p. 93).[11] Whereas sympathy can be regarded as a form of altruism for beginners, or 'elementary altruism', 'commitment' can be regarded as 'advanced altruism' and gives rise to choices that are expected to reduce one's own welfare. In both cases one person's utility function is dependent partly on another's.

However, it is doubtful whether this particular discrepancy between people's choices and their own welfare justifies any intervention in the pattern of consumers' expenditures. The motivations in question – many of which may be highly commendable – do not necessarily detract from the welfare of society as a whole. Nor do they call for any revision of basic economic models of consumer behaviour. They can be seen as being part of the innumerable influences on the position of consumers' demand curves in price–quantity space, without violating the assumption that these curves slope down from left to right in the normal way. It is not obvious that 'commitment' violates this assumption.

Lionel Robbins stressed this point in his famous book, *The Nature and Significance of Economic Science*. In it he argued that that the economic theory of how producers and consumers behave is in no way invalidated by dropping the assumption that *homo economicus* is some totally egoistical creature concerned only with the pursuit of his self-interest. In his book Robbins wrote that '... our economic subjects can be pure egoists, pure altruists, pure ascetics, pure sensualists or – what is much more likely – bundles of all these impulses'. He went on to say that 'Considerations of this sort enable us to deal also with the oft-repeated accusation that Economics assumes a world of economic men concerned only with money-making and self-interest' (Robbins, 1945 edn:95).

Robbins gives the example of a community that had been converted from pure hedonism to the objective of devoting their lives to God. The demand for wine would fall off and the demand for materials to build more churches, synagogues or mosques would rise. These changes in demands and supplies and their consequent changes in relative prices will follow the usual basic laws of economics. The price of wine would fall, and the price of the materials needed to build places of worship would rise. Labour would gradually move out of wine production into the construction industry. Demand and supply would still rule.

Or consider the more mundane case of Mrs X who, out of commitment to the survival of small local shops, goes out of her way to buy apples from a shop near where she lives rather than from a supermarket, which is cheaper and where there is no cat sleeping on the meat-slicer. In terms of a simple demand curve in price–quantity space her demand curve for apples from that particular shop would be further out to the right than would be that of some other customer who does not share her 'commitment'. But it could still slope down from left to right. For example, if the shopkeeper raised the price of his apples she might tend to buy less from him and more from the supermarket, or she may switch from apples to pears. Indeed, if the shop owner raised the price enough Mrs X might decide that she need not carry commitment too far and would stop buying apples from that shop altogether. Thus, commitment does not make her demand curve for apples from that particular supplier slope the wrong way. It merely means that it is further out to the right than it would have been in the absence of this commitment. There are all sorts of reasons why people's demand curves for particular products differ from each other, which are usually ascribed to differences in incomes and 'tastes'. This does not mean that they do not slope downwards from left to right, which has been well-established in a vast amount of empirical research.

5   Conclusions

One of the important limitations on the normative significance of market outcomes is that the choices that people make in the market do not necessarily really reveal their 'true' preferences. And even where they do, their 'true' preferences may not always promote their 'true' welfare. There are various reasons for this, including irrational behaviour, inadequate information and many other psychological influences on choices other than those encompassed in conventional economic analysis. Thus while the assumption that, on the whole, people's choices will promote their objectives in a rational manner is fairly compelling, there are various reasons why these choices may often fail to do so. This weakens the link between choices and people's welfare.

Nevertheless, without the assumption that individuals' preference orderings correspond fairly closely to their welfare orderings, welfare economics would not even get off the ground, let alone fly as far as it has done. For although welfare economics is not very much concerned with changes in the welfare of individuals as such for their own sake, welfare economics does require a criterion of an increase in the welfare of individuals. This is simply because the welfare of society is usually seen as a logical construction from the welfare of individuals. In other words if we use a theoretical model of micro-economics based on the notion of preference satisfaction in order to see under what conditions the market will allocate resources in a way that will best contribute to society's welfare, we have to assume that a key variable in the model – namely an individual's preferences – does have a fairly close correspondence to the individual's welfare.[12] If we just throw up our hands and say 'Oh well, all we are saying is that people are playing this game of making choices and ranking alternatives but these have absolutely nothing to do with their welfare', the moral significance of the outcome of the market transactions could no longer be assessed in terms of its contribution to society's economic welfare.

For various reasons, therefore, the fact that there is strong evidence that, by and large, people behave in a manner predicted by micro-economic theory does not mean that the preferences which give rise to this behaviour reflect their real 'welfare'. No amount of empirical evidence can show that it does, since 'welfare' is not an objective concept. The assumption that people's preferences correspond *approximately* to their welfare may well be justified. But it is important to know why it is not more than an approximation.

Furthermore, some of the welfare that people enjoy comes from their sharing in certain activities or duties or conveying sentiments in a manner for which mere monetary transactions are inadequate. And as has been argued in recent important contributions made by Elizabeth Anderson and Michael Sandel to the problem of the moral limits of the market, this part of their wider welfare can be destroyed, or misrepresented, by excessive marketing of certain goods and services. Sandel emphasizes the manner in which marketing certain goods, such as the sale of blood for medical purposes, diminishes the moral significance that voluntary blood donation gives. Elizabeth Anderson puts more emphasis on the manner in which putting a price on certain social facilities, such as access to parks, restricts their value to the personal values of individuals rather than the social significance of shared facilities. Some marketing procedures – such as Sandel's example of the practice of allowing some prisoners to enjoy special facilities in jail – offend social notions of the equality with which punishment for crimes should be meted out irrespective of a person's financial circumstances.[13]

NOTES

1. Brocas and Carrillo, 2003:xvi.
2. Offer, 2006:49.
3. Kahneman, 2011.
4. See discussion of this point in Aldred, 2009:39–43.
5. Offer, *ibid.*:chs3–5.
6. The case for autonomy has been recently well set out in Conly, 2013. She argues that if Mill had been able to know what modern behavioural psychologists have brought to light he would have taken a different view.
7. Nozick, 1974:ix.
8. Sugden, 2008:226–248.
9. See detailed discussion of this 'nudge' strategy in Thaler and Sunstein, 2008.
10. Hume,1751: sect.2, Pt.1, para.5.
11. See also Sen's later exposition of his distinction between 'sympathy' and 'commitment' in Sen, 2009:188–193.
12. A similar conclusion is reached on the basis of a detailed analysis in Hausman and McPherson, 2009.
13. Anderson, E., *Value in Ethics and Economics.* Harvard University Press, 1953; and Sandel, M., *What Money Can't Buy, The Moral Limits of Markets*, Allen Lane, Penguin Books, 2012.

CHAPTER 6

Fact and Value in Public Policy: Three Examples

1   THE EQUALITY-EFFICIENCY TRADE-OFF

One widely discussed conflict of values, in addition to uncertain positive relationships, is a conflict between equality and productive efficiency, which is what the late Arthur Okun called 'the big trade-off'.[1] In the interests of exposition, I shall defer to Chapters 15 and 16 some of the problems associated with the concept of 'equality'. Here, I shall ignore the question of the criteria by which any particular distribution is to be regarded as 'valuable', or whether equality has intrinsic value or solely instrumental value – for example, is consistent with some concept of 'justice' or is conducive to greater social harmony. And I shall follow the convention in welfare economics of focusing on the distribution of *income* and whether that conflicts with productive efficiency and hence with prosperity.

Of course, some policy measures designed to improve income equality – such as elimination of job discrimination on grounds of race, religion, colour or gender – will tend to improve economic efficiency rather than reduce it. But it is often assumed that there is a conflict between equality and efficiency because some policies designed to increase equality are quite likely to reduce productive efficiency. An obvious example would be redistributive taxes and benefits. It is possible that higher income taxes and benefits would distort people's choices in a way that reduces output below the socially optimal level. For they would drive a wedge between people's willingness to work

© The Author(s) 2017
W. Beckerman, *Economics as Applied Ethics*,
DOI 10.1007/978-3-319-50319-6_6

and the marginal social value of their work. Given the enormous variety of tax and benefit regimes that can be adopted, their possible indirect ramifications are so great that one cannot be certain either about the economic impact or about the precise effect on the equality of income distribution. But it is possible to give some sense of the difficulties involved by considering one specific redistributive economic policy instrument, namely the imposition of minimum wages.

Minimum wage legislation of one kind or another has been widely advocated and implemented on egalitarian grounds. It has even been adopted in such a market-oriented economy as the USA. It does not usually discriminate between poor regions of a country where there may be large pools of workers willing to work for very low wages rather than not work at all, and rich regions where there may be few such workers and where, anyway, many of them may be members of more affluent families. Economic theory would suggest that, compared to, say, family income support, this might be a clumsy and inefficient method of achieving some ethical objectives concerning the welfare of poor people.

But it is a good example of the possible mixture of positive economics and value judgements that may be used to justify the policy, and the manner in which the relevant value judgements may depend on which particular positive propositions are accepted. For example, suppose the proposal is defended by appeal to the positive proposition that the policy would force firms to be more productive and would drive out inefficient firms. There is some evidence (mainly from Scandinavian countries) that although the higher wages for otherwise low-paid workers may mean that some of them will be laid off, it also seems to force inefficient companies out of business. Hence, as long as macro-economic policies maintain a given level of employment, there may be an increase in the 'efficiency' with which resources, including labour, are being used. In other words, greater wage equality could lead to 'creative destruction' of less efficient companies and leave room for the displaced workers to be absorbed, in the end, in more progressive companies.[2] But, we might follow Hume's example and ask 'So what? What is so good about the increase in productive efficiency?' An advocate of the policy would then presumably argue that (i) greater productive efficiency would lead to greater prosperity and (ii) greater prosperity is a top-level intrinsic value.

But suppose the implied positive proposition that the policy would increase overall productivity is challenged? After all, the basic textbook theory of how a *competitive* labour market works suggests that there would be some rise in unemployment among some unskilled workers who could no longer find a job at the new minimum wage who would have been quite willing to work at a lower wage. It is true that there is not much factual support for this view, and some evidence suggests that in Britain there was no significant loss of employment as a result of the introduction of, or increase, in the minimum wage, except perhaps following large increases in the minimum wage in 2001 and 2003.[3] But, for the sake of the argument, let us assume that the rise in (or introduction of) minimum wages does lead to some unemployment and hence some loss of overall prosperity.

This does not, however, mean that the policy should be abandoned. For it could still be defended on the grounds that it would lead to some overall rise in the equality of wage distribution. But we might well ask 'What is so good about that?', to which many people would answer that it is instrumentally valuable since it will lead to greater equality of some higher level intrinsic value, such as greater equality of income distribution among households. This, in turn, might be challenged and might be defended on the grounds that either it is intrinsically valuable in itself, or that it is instrumentally valuable in so far as it promotes some higher-level intrinsic value, such as equality of welfare. Indeed, in popular political debate this defence of the policy has more support than the productivity motivation.

But even if this value judgement is accepted we are still not out of the woods. For if the policy leads to a rise in some wages but also leads to some unemployment, how does one trade-off the rise in wages of some against the loss of income of others? If one is concerned with some overall level of measured equality of low incomes the net effect may be indeterminate. Of course, it is possible that such a policy is not supported out of a concern with 'equality' in general, but out of concern with other value judgements. These might include, notably, a focus on the position of the worst off in society, along the lines of 'prioritarianism' discussed in more detail in Chapters 15 and 16.

Another value judgement that will often motivate support for minimum wage legislation would be the elimination of what one might regard as 'exploitation'. This might provide a justification for minimum wage legislation even if it can be demonstrated that there are better ways of keeping people out of poverty, such as family income support. And some people may support the policy on account of one sort of egalitarianism or another even if it is likely to lead to a loss of productive efficiency and hence prosperity. There cannot be any precise method of weighing up these two conflicting values.

And there is yet another important value that could be brought into the argument. Some 'Libertarians' might object that minimum wage legislation infringes people's right to enter freely into contracts, including contracts concerning the supply of one's own labour. (But how many libertarians would support the right to sell oneself into slavery?)

In short, one is faced with scope for both major differences of opinion concerning the facts of the case and major differences of opinion as to the relevant value judgements. And which facts are relevant depends on what one believes to be the relevant values, and vice versa. An egalitarian would be more interested in the likely effect on overall equality than a prioritarian, who would be more interested in the likely effect on the worst off. If one is a libertarian, what matters is the degree of restraint on the free choices of the workers and the employers. Conversely, if the facts are that the policy would lead to a significant rise in unemployment, what matters is the trade-off of the 'prosperity' value against any egalitarian value – that is, Okun's 'great trade-off'.

In the latter case the optimum policy will then depend on how far we believe that the greater equality will cause less prosperity and the relative strength of our attachment to these two competing values. For example, consider Fig. 6.1 in which we show the indifference curves I_0 and I_1 relating equality to efficiency for Mrs Brown and Mrs Jones. The curves are convex, like ordinary indifference curves, and so show that the greater is the level of equality the more equality one is prepared to sacrifice in order to achieve a given increase in output, and, conversely, the greater is output the more output one is prepared to sacrifice for a given increase in equality. Assume that the two characters are equally egalitarian in the sense that they both attach the same value to equality, so that they have the same indifference curves relating equality to efficiency.

Figure 6.1 also shows two lines, B and J, representing each person's assumption as to the trade-off between equality and efficiency. These represent their assumptions about the positive characteristics of the economy. They are not differences in the relative values they attach to equality, like the indifference curves described earlier. They correspond to the budget lines in ordinary consumer demand theory. Line B represents Mrs Brown's belief, namely that there is a strong conflict

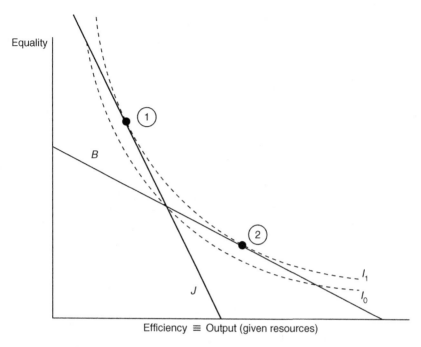

Fig. 6.1 The equality–efficiency trade-off: fact or value?

between efficiency and equality. In other words, she believes that a very great sacrifice of output is required in order to achieve a very small increase in equality. Line J represents Mrs Jones's beliefs that very little sacrifice of output will suffice in order to achieve a very great increase in equality. Consequently, Mrs Jones will prefer a situation that corresponds to more equality and less output than would Mrs Brown. But that is because they have different views as to the positive relationship between equality and efficiency. Their preferred optimum points may seem to indicate that Mrs Jones, at 1, is more egalitarian than Mrs Brown, at 2, when, in fact, this is not the case at all. They just have different views on the degree of conflict between the two objectives, which is a matter of positive economics. It would also be quite possible for both parties to agree on the actual degree of conflict but disagree on the value they attach to the competing objectives. In that case they would have different indifference curves and would finish up at different optimum points that would correctly indicate their different degrees of egalitarianism. Thus we have again an example of the inextricable mix of fact and value in defining an 'optimal' choice.

2   THE PRICE STABILITY OBJECTIVE

Another conflict of policy objectives that is frequently in the news is the conflict between price stability and full employment. Several years ago Martin Wolf published an article in the *Financial Times* headed 'The Fed must weigh inflation against the risk of recession'.[4] He was referring to the difficult choice that the US Central Bank (the Federal Reserve Board) had to make in 2008 between raising interest rates to check the threat of inflation or reducing them to check the threat of a recession. A few months later, in the same newspaper, a column was headed by the announcement that the Governor of the Bank of England 'backs job losses to curb inflation'.

In fact, the conflict between full employment and stable prices has been one of the most perpetual conflicts in economic policy for decades. But is there, in fact, a trade-off between stable prices and full employment, and, if there is, exactly how big is it? This positive relationship has been the subject of an enormous amount of empirical investigation. And why are people so concerned with these two objectives?

The case for full employment is easy to see. High unemployment means an unnecessary loss of output (i.e. a loss of economic efficiency) and hence conflicts with what many people would regard as a basic value, namely the material well-being that enters into 'prudential values'. More importantly, perhaps, it also causes a direct loss of welfare associated with the psychological distress that unemployment – or the fear of it – usually creates.

But how strong is the normative proposition that governments ought to preserve price stability? Few people would regard price stability, *per se*, as a top-level ethical value. A taste for some particular numerical value – namely zero – for one particular statistic, namely the change in the price index, would constitute a strange form of number fetishism. Nevertheless, the aforementioned quotations represent a genuine concern among the public and the authorities. So one has to go back a bit and look for positive relationships between price stability and some other values with which one can more easily sympathise. Links between inflation and more understandable higher-level objectives include the following:

(i) It is believed that inflation causes economic inefficiency in various ways. For inflation might create a more unstable economic environment that could lead to lower investment and hence slower economic growth, and hence less longer-run prosperity. Inflation might also make entrepreneurs devote more attention to speculative factors – such as which of their raw material prices will rise most – than to productive innovations and efficiency. If one asks 'what is so good about greater economic efficiency and its accompanying prosperity?' the answer might be that this will lead, via, say, more expenditure on health, education and personal 'prudential' values, to increased happiness, and this, in the end, is a basic value. Such a sequence is shown in Fig. 6.2. In addition, people may lose welfare on account of having to make more frequent trips to the bank to draw out the minimum cash to satisfy immediate needs (which is why this particular loss of welfare is known in the jargon as 'shoe leather costs'). Both these – and other – effects of inflation are thus linked, by positive economic assumptions, to more prosperity which could be regarded as being either a basic value *per se*, or one that is instrumental in leading to a unique basic value of 'happiness'.

(ii) Inflation is also often believed to increase inequality of income distribution. It is easier for the rich to protect themselves against inflation. For example, they will be able to afford financial advisers, they may be able to spread their assets, they can hold some equities, or gold, or jewellery, or medieval suits of armour, and so on. The poor cannot do these things and wouldn't have anywhere to put the suits of armour anyway. So inflation could increase inequality, which would conflict with a very widely held basic ethical value. Inflation is also likely to affect the distribution of real income between age groups. For it is likely to harm those pensioners whose pensions may not be adequately indexed and benefit younger age groups since the real value of their mortgage liabilities is likely to fall.

Thus the conflict between full employment and price stability seems to boil down to a conflict between, on the one hand, unemployment that reduces happiness both directly and indirectly (via a loss of output), and, on the other hand, the adverse effects of inflation on equality and happiness, either directly or indirectly. Thus an optimal policy would depend partly on the validity of the presumed positive steps in the argument – such as the effect of inflation on equality – and partly on the relative strength of

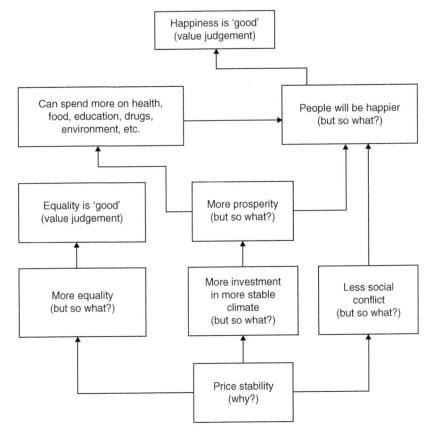

Fig. 6.2 A choice of paths to the ultimate policy goal

the basic values of equality and personal happiness and prosperity. So suppose, for the sake of argument, that some convincing empirical studies are found that show that, in fact, inflation does not make the distribution of income more unequal.

After all, as Sir John Hicks pointed out many decades ago, the operation of the tax system may often mean that profits are hit more than wages at times of inflation. Furthermore, if the inflation is thought to originate from 'wage-push' then, in an internationally competitive environment or in conditions of strict monetary constraint, it may not be possible for firms to pass on the wage increases in prices, so that profit margins will be reduced and there will be a fall in the share of profits in national income. If, then, for one reason or another, some people who had previously been against inflation only because they had believed that inflation added to inequality now discover that, in fact, it did not do so, their opposition to inflation might disappear.

3   THE 'FAIR TRADE' PROBLEM

Another illustration of the inextricable link between ethics and economics and of the influence of the facts on value judgements is the widespread opposition to imports of manufactured goods produced with the aid of child labour. If the contracting partners enter into the trade freely it will often be assumed that both parties benefit. It is true that – for reasons discussed in Chapter 8 concerning the well-known 'Summers memorandum' – this does not mean that *all* the parties involved, including the children and their parents, must benefit from the trade. But suppose that they do. Many people will still oppose the trade on what they believe are 'ethical grounds', such as that we should not profit by the 'exploitation of child labour' (though the opposition will often really be motivated by disguised protectionism). But if the children and their parents do benefit from the trade what is the ethical basis for restricting the imports in question? Suppose the facts are that restricting the trade will not only further impoverish the families in question but also lead to the employment of the children in agriculture under even harsher and less profitable conditions? In that case the optimal ethical policy might be to take steps – such as subsidising child education in the countries in question – that will reduce the pressure on people to put their children to work in manufacturing, rather than erect barriers to the imports in question.

4   CONCLUSIONS

One could go on and on showing how both value judgements and positive propositions must enter, sooner or later, into any specific normative economics prescription. But, hopefully, a few key points have emerged from the previous discussion.

First, however compelling the ethical appeal of certain normative propositions as economic policy is concerned, they will invariably still depend on positive economics.

Second, nevertheless, whatever sequence of arguments is used to justify any normative proposition, at some stage one is driven to introduce some basic value judgement. This is not always a simple matter since different routes that follow different sequences of positive propositions may lead to different value judgements.

Third, even when we have arrived at the relevant value judgement, this is not necessarily the end of the argument, since value judgements are not beyond dispute, even though they are not amenable to 'reasoned' debate in the way described by Hume. For most people have plural values, and some policy problems may require resolving a conflict between incommensurate values.

Thus ethical issues lie at the heart of normative economics. In most cases – such as those entering into the topical economic policy issues discussed above – it may be easy to spot them. But in some policy issues the relevant value judgements are less obvious, and that may impinge on important topical issues, such as the export of polluting activities, environmental protection and distributional policy. If the value judgements relevant to any policy problem are not adequately appreciated some of the valuable achievements of welfare economics can be put to the wrong use. The function of positive economics is to describe and explain economic reality. The function of normative economics is to help improve it. This means taking account of historical experience, of political and institutional considerations, of psychological motivations that are poorly understood, and ethical values that are usually only dimly recognised. Otherwise it becomes a sterile – and possibly harmful – activity.

NOTES

1. Okun, 1975.
2. Research carried out by Rebecca Riley at the National Institute of Economic and Social Research in 2009 also found only a slight influence of the introduction of a minimum wage in Britain in 1999 on the hours worked by low-paid adult males and virtually no influence on employment opportunities for low-paid women, who constitute the majority of low-paid workers.
3. See 2009 Annual Report of the National Institute of Economic and Social Research, p. 13.
4. Wolf, M., *Financial Times*, 26 September 2007:15.

CHAPTER 7

From Economic 'Efficiency' to Economic Welfare

1 COST-BENEFIT ANALYSIS IN WELFARE ECONOMICS

The basic theory of welfare economics enables one to identify how far the market is operating 'efficiently'. This is taken to mean how far the market allocates resources in such a way as to make the maximum contribution – given resources and technical knowledge – to society's economic welfare. Welfare economics provides the criteria necessary for this purpose. This includes the well-known rules that any student of economics would know, such as the relationship between prices and social costs. Satisfaction of these rules is supposed to ensure that society is operating at a point where no reallocation of resources can raise one person's utility without reducing somebody else's utility. Such a point is known as a 'Pareto optimum' point, in honour of the great nineteenth-century Italian sociologist and economist, Vilfredo Pareto.

Before proceeding to examine the criteria of an efficient allocation of resources, however, it should be noted that, as the Nobel Laureate Joseph Stiglitz has put it, 'Unemployment – the inability of the market to generate jobs for so many citizens – is the worst failure of the market, the greatest source of inefficiency. . . .'[1] Since recurrent periods of very high unemployment have characterised developed economies for over a century, it might appear that analysing the 'efficiency' with which resources are allocated, when so many are just not allocated anywhere at all, is a flagrant example of the old warning against swallowing a camel while straining at a gnat. Nevertheless, given the level of resource used at any

© The Author(s) 2017
W. Beckerman, *Economics as Applied Ethics*,
DOI 10.1007/978-3-319-50319-6_7

time – which is a matter of macro-economic policy – there are still innumerable problems of resource allocation to be faced. There is no point in making what may be a bad situation worse by misallocating such resources as are employed. So this book is about the allocation of resources in the market at any point of time.

In practice, of course, there is not just one market. The economy is made up of innumerable markets. There are labour markets, financial markets, second-hand markets, online markets, covered markets, commodity markets, housing markets, and so on. But do these markets all operate in a way that will maximise their potential contribution to society's economic welfare? Most people would say, quite reasonably, that one does not need any fancy theory to conclude that financial markets have been behaving disastrously over the ages. But here we are concerned with other, less 'special' markets. And it is the theory of welfare economics that shows why most markets will generally fail to make the maximum contribution to economic welfare. It is welfare economics that demonstrates that there are likely to be instances of what are known in the jargon as 'market failure' – that is, a failure of markets to make their full potential contribution to society's economic welfare.

There are various well-known forms of market failure. The most widely known include what are known as 'negative externalities': aircraft and trucks can produce a lot of noise, some factories emit poisonous emissions from their chimneys, and so on. Other goods or services may not be produced up to the socially desirable level on account of some monopolistic restriction, or a serious imbalance between the information available to buyers and sellers, or taxes or tariffs. Welfare economics identifies these 'market failures' and the criteria by which the socially 'efficient' level of such activities can be determined.

Thus the basic theory of welfare economics has much to contribute to the promotion of society's economic welfare. When any particular instance of 'market failure' is identified there is often a *prima facie* case for some policies to rectify the matter. Sometimes this may indicate a *prima facie* case for government intervention. But 'government failure' is sometimes likely to be as bad as market failure, if not worse, as when policies are introduced as a result of the influence of particular pressure groups or administrators. Some changes of policy concerning the subsidisation of offshore wind farms, or 'fracking', or investment in 'prestige projects' are modern examples.

And, as everybody will have noticed, governments play a big part in the operation of most markets. All markets are affected by government taxes and subsidies. In the labour market many countries have legal minimum wages or restrictions on the age at which people may be employed. In financial markets, banks are usually subject to certain regulations, though these do not seem to have been very effective lately. Government subsidies to financial institutions by bailing them out when they would otherwise have collapsed may well have helped sustain the instability of financial institutions. In many countries governments are also the main agents in the market for certain goods or services, such as medical services, education, national defence, infrastructure such as transport, and what passes for law and order in our cities. Under what conditions are all such forms of government intervention justified? By what criteria can one judge when the market is not performing well?

Welfare economics helps identify these criteria. And it may also help to identify possible cures. For example, it enables one to identify what tax ought to be imposed on some polluting activity if that is to be the preferred way of ensuring that polluters take account of the full social costs of the activity in question.

2   Cost-Benefit Analysis and 'Franklin's Algebra'

In practice, what is generally known as 'cost-benefit analysis' (CBA) is an essential tool of welfare economics. For it enables one to establish whether the economic benefits of a project exceed the costs and hence whether the conditions of a Pareto-optimising move can be satisfied (leaving aside distributional considerations). In its most general form 'cost-benefit analysis' resembles what Cass Sunstein has called 'Franklin's Algebra', namely a list of all the pros and cons of any particular decision.[2] This decision tool, which was set out in a letter by Benjamin Franklin in 1772, is not necessarily confined to economic considerations or quantifiable inputs. But such economic considerations – including even those that are quantifiable – that enter into a comparison of the pros and cons of any choice are invariably influenced by ethical considerations in two main ways.

First, they influence what factors are included in the economic part of any more general comparisons of the pros and cons of any particular policy. Should the analysis be confined to the 'efficiency' with which resources are allocated in the economy or should account also be taken of the effect of any policy on the distribution of income or the welfare of particular groups within one's country or abroad? For example, consider the provision of health care to poor people, or an appraisal of some trading arrangement such as the export of toxic waste or the protection of domestic agriculture, or industry. How far can beneficence towards poorer groups or countries be taken into account in the analysis?

Second, even when the scope of the CBA has been settled, ethical considerations also affect the prices attached to the relevant costs and benefits. The gap between people's revealed preferences and their welfares that has been discussed in Chapter 5 clearly affects the welfare significance of the pattern of prices on the market. For if people often make choices that do not really reflect their welfares, the market prices may not always correspond to the welfare of the market participants in question. Should one adjust downwards the prices for some items that enter into a CBA if we believe that the goods and services in question are really bad for the people who buy them, or, conversely, are better for the consumers than they know so that they really ought to buy more of them? That is, if the prevailing market price does not adequately reflect the contribution made by the goods or services in question to their welfare.

Third, prices used in a CBA of some facilities can be distorted as a result of the 'commodification' of certain goods and services to which reference was made in Chapter 5. Elizabeth Anderson points out that these prices are often based on surveys of how much people would be prepared to pay for the facilities in question, such as the provision of parks, or improvements in the local environment, or recreational facilities, or improvements in safety.[3] But these prices will usually reflect – mainly or solely – people's desires for the goods and services for their own use, rather than their valuations of them as facilities that are shared by members of society, including perhaps goods that they do not even expect to use themselves. So a CBA based on these prices assumes that the goods in question fulfil only the same indiscriminate want-satisfaction function that is provided by market transactions in ordinary commodities. This also means that the preferences of richer people will have more weight than those of poor people, which may be undesirable for certain categories of goods and services that are publicly provided.

3   PARETO OPTIMALITY AND THE COMPENSATION TEST

As stated earlier, the whole point of an economic CBA is that it shows whether – abstracting from all non-economic considerations and distributional values – the adoption of the project in question would enable somebody to be made economically better off without anybody else being worse off. For if the economic benefits exceed the costs it is *theoretically* possible for some of the benefits to be transferred from the potential beneficiaries of the project to the potential losers and still leave something over for the former. In other words, the beneficiaries could still have gained even if they have fully compensated the losers. Such a move, therefore, would enable the economy to move towards what has been defined previously as a Pareto optimum point. It is called a '*Pareto optimising move*'.

If compensation is actually carried out – that is, the move satisfies what is known as the 'Hicks/Kaldor compensation test' in honour of its originators, John Hicks and Nicholas Kaldor – the move can be judged to have increased the combined utility of all parties concerned without having to make interpersonal comparisons of utility. This is because there is no need to compare how much utility the gainers gain with how much utility the losers lose. For, after compensation, the losers will have lost nothing.

But an excess of benefits over costs only shows that it is *theoretically* possible for the gainers to compensate the losers while remaining better off. Whether the compensation is *actually* carried out or not is another matter. For this reason a distinction is made between a '*potential*' Pareto optimising move and an '*actual*' Pareto optimising move. And the distinction may often be very important, as illustrated in Section 5.

4   PRACTICAL LIMITATIONS ON THE COMPENSATION TEST

To begin with there are various practical difficulties involved in making the transfer from the beneficiaries to the losers. First, the mere act of making the transfers from the gainers to the losers may involve costs – that is, some new kind of losses. If the transfers take the form of taxes and benefits these could, in theory, distort resource allocation as well as incur administrative costs. For example, they may distort people's incentives to work or invest. So total output (and hence prosperity) may be reduced more than is gained by the improved resource allocation.

Second, it may often be impossible to identify who are the gainers and who are the losers from any project. Consider, for example, a CBA of the location of a new airport. In transport studies the name of the game is usually time – that is, time saved. Suppose that the new airport saves time for the airline passengers to reach their final destination. For business travellers this will be a gain to their companies, or their companies' shareholders, who may include some insurance companies who have obligations to pay out pensions to retired people. How is one to track down all the individual pensioners and others who may gain indirectly through the project? Obviously impossible. So who would pick up the bill in the end to compensate the losers, such as the people who may have to put up with environmental damage? The taxpayer, perhaps? But this just creates a new class of uncompensated losers.

Third, the costs and benefits have to be 'cleaned up' to allow for market distortions, such as those mentioned earlier, namely the existence of taxes and benefits, or externalities, or imperfect competition. This adjustment from observable market prices to what are known as 'shadow prices' that are supposed to bear a closer relationship to real social costs and benefits will usually be a highly speculative operation, though in certain circumstances a fairly good approximation can be achieved. However, it does mean that some projects should only be assumed to be desirable if there is a substantial excess of benefits over costs. But, on account of certain theoretical considerations to which we shall now turn, even this is not always a compelling criterion.

5   Pareto Optimality and the Distribution of Incomes

But the biggest limitation on the role of an economic CBA is its neglect of distributional considerations. It is true that, at first sight, a 'Pareto-optimising' move that can make somebody better off without anybody being worse off would seem to be ethically compelling. All that it requires is a little bit of the spirit of beneficence. The trouble is that there are an indeterminate number of Pareto optimal points, corresponding to very different distributions of utility. Consider two people, Smith and Jones, who have been washed up on a desert island. They find that they can manage to catch ten fishes every day (or ten fishes jump out of the sea every day). And let us assume that both like fish. But Smith is a big, tough and selfish person, without a shred of egalitarian or altruistic instincts in him. So every day he eats, with relish, nine of the fish and leaves only one for Jones. But the position is Pareto optimal, since any increase in Jones's share of the fish must mean a reduction in Smith's share of the fish. The same would apply if Smith appropriated eight fish every day, or any number of the fish.

In fact, in this example, there are eleven possible ways in which the fish are shared out, ranging from Smith eating all of them to his eating none of them. All of them would be Pareto optimal points. And in a complex economy with hundreds and thousands of different resources and products there will be a vast indeterminate number of Pareto optimal points, each of which will represent a different distribution of utilities. It is for this reason that Amartya Sen has written that 'a situation may be Pareto optimal but be perfectly disgusting'.[4] So Pareto optimality may not be such a big deal. It is compatible with any degree of inequality in the distribution of utility, which may, in practice, be closely related to the inequality in the distribution of incomes.

Figure 7.1 shows the relationship of the utility of Mrs A up the vertical axis to the maximum utility that can be enjoyed by Mrs B along the horizontal axis, given the economy's resources. It corresponds to the 'budget line' that plays a crucial part in the elementary theory of how a consumer distributes her expenditures between two goods, given their relative prices and the constraint on her total expenditures. In a similar manner, this Utility Possibility Frontier (UPF) indicates how society could distribute utility between individuals or groups A and B, given its resources and technical knowledge.

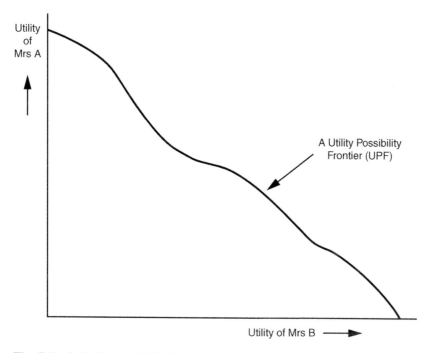

Fig. 7.1 A 'Utility Possibility Frontier'

In the previous diagram, starting from any point on the Utility Possibility Frontier, no move could be justified in terms of the Pareto criterion however much it might mean moving to what society would deem to be a more equitable income distribution. For, by definition of a UPF, somebody must lose by the move. So a point on the UPF at which one agent is very poor and another is very rich is just as Pareto optimal as one where the utilities are shared out more equally. How could society identify which particular point on its UPF corresponds to its optimal choice of how utilities ought to be distributed in society? A method of doing so is analogous to the method used in elementary economic theory to show how an individual consumer chooses her optimal combination of the goods available to her given their prices and her income.

In this theory the consumer selects the optimum distribution of her consumption between various goods (given their prices and her income) in the light of her relative preferences between the goods in question. Diagrammatically, this is shown in a two-good figure as the point at which the budget line representing her constraint is tangential to the highest indifference curve she can reach, given her relative preferences between different combinations of the goods in question. At the level of society's choice between different feasible distributions of utility, what is needed then is to add some function that represents society's preferences between different distributions of the utilities accruing to the various members of society. This is provided by the concept of a 'social welfare function', which will be explained in the next section.

6   INTRODUCING THE 'SOCIAL WELFARE FUNCTION'

The introduction of the concept of a social welfare function seems to provide an escape from the distributional neutrality of the Pareto optimum. It provides a useful analytical tool for clarifying the differences between various value judgements concerning equality, though it is not necessarily confined to this purpose. It can also be invoked in making decisions about any project.

The standard concept of a social welfare function in which the focal variable is consumption has been expressed in the recent Stern *Report on The Economics of Climate Change* as follows:

> The objective of policy is taken to be the maximisation of the sum across individuals of *social* utilities of consumption.... In particular, we consider consumption as involving a broad range of goods and services that includes

education, health and the environment. The relationship between the measure of social wellbeing – the sum of *social* utilities in this argument – and the goods and services consumed by each household, on which it depends, is called the social welfare function . . . (Stern, 2006, p. 30, Box 2.1; my italics)

In order to bring the social welfare function into relation with the two-dimensional utility possibility frontier in a two-person (or group) figure it needs to be in terms of utilities. Thus one way of interpreting a social welfare function is that it indicates the *social* value that one places on the utility, or welfare, accruing to any individual. These values are sometimes referred to as the 'social utilities' of the individuals' consumption. Hence, economists have generally defined social welfare as some function of individuals' utilities, and abbreviated versions of social welfare functions are generally written as

$$SW = W(U_1, U_2, \ldots U_n) \tag{1}$$

where W represents society's total (economic) welfare and U_i represents the social value of the expected utility of the ith individual. As indicated earlier, this is not restricted to the utility an individual derives from his income or his consumption of personal goods, but can include other features of the state of affairs such as the degree of equality. Arrow suggested that an individual's preferences between his own consumption bundles reflect his *tastes*, whereas his preferences between other features of a social state, such as the degree of inequality therein reflect his *values*, though he pointed out that this distinction is by no means clear cut [*loc.cit.* p.18].[5]

The 'social values' attached to individuals' utilities in a social welfare function represent mainly distributional values, though one may not attach a very high social value to some of the ways in which some people derive utility. But for present purposes, we shall focus on the distributional values reflected in a social welfare function. For example, one might attach less *social* value to a marginal increase in the consumption of somebody who started off at a high level of utility than to an equal marginal increase in the consumption of somebody with a relatively low level of utility. In other words, we shall assume that a social welfare function indicates primarily to what extent – other things being equal – one prefers social states that are more equal than others in terms of utilities.

There is, of course, no such thing as 'the' social welfare function. Different people will have different views as to what are the most important variables that characterise any particular social state as well as the degree of inequality in society that should be promoted. For practical policy purposes, the social welfare function that matters will be the social welfare function of the decision makers. If they did not care about the way utilities are distributed and simply wanted to maximise society's total utility they would prefer the following utilitarian social welfare function, in which W is simply the arithmetic sum of individual utilities and the distribution of utilities does not come into it.

$$SW = U_1 + U_2 + \cdots + U_n \qquad (2)$$

But most people do care about the way utilities are distributed among the population. Most people would tend to attach more weight to a unit of utility of a poorer person than to a richer person. This would be the case if one subscribed to some form of egalitarianism (see Chapter 16). In that case they may decide that social welfare has increased even if an increase in the utility of the poor person is accompanied by an equal, or greater, decrease in the utility of the rich person. An egalitarian social welfare function would thus be convex to the origin, rather like an ordinary consumer's indifference curve relating his preferences between, say, apples and pears. Social welfare would depend on the *relative* utilities of people, as well as their *absolute* utilities. Figure 7.2 compares a utilitarian and a mildly egalitarian social welfare function.

In Fig. 7.2, the point at which society reaches its highest social welfare subject to the constraint given by the UPF will, of course, be that point at which the UPF is tangential to the highest attainable SWF. Only at such a point will it appear that we have satisfied the *necessary and sufficient conditions* for maximising social welfare, namely that we are on a UPF – that is, a Pareto optimal position – but also reaching the highest possible SWF. AS indicated earlier, this procedure is analogous to the representation of the optimality of consumers' choice in terms of the tangency between his budget line (the counterpart of the UPF) and his highest possible indifference curves (the counterpart of the SWF). It can be seen from Fig. 7.2 that a mildly egalitarian would prefer a point on the UPF at which the utilities were fairly equally distributed between the two people, A and B. A utilitarian, however, would maximise social welfare at point Y, where there is a very unequal distribution of utility among the agents in question.

For practical policy purposes, however, it is more important to know that a very strong egalitarian might even prefer some points inside a UPF to

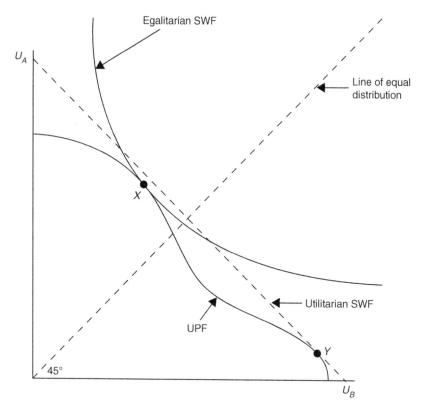

Fig. 7.2 How to reconcile efficiency with social welfare

many points *on* the UPF. Hence, even a Pareto-optimising move (i.e. one that involves no losers) does not necessarily lead to an increase in social welfare. This would be the case, for example, with a move from point I to point II in Fig. 7.3. For in even though B finishes up with slightly more utility than before, A has received far more additional utility. This means that inequality has increased. And given society's strong aversion to inequality – as illustrated by the shape of its SWF – it has actually moved to a lower SWF.

This seems to be precisely what has happened in the Western world over the last two decades or so. As explained in Chapter 15, although even the incomes of the worst off have risen slightly, there has been a much greater increase in the incomes of the richest group in society. The

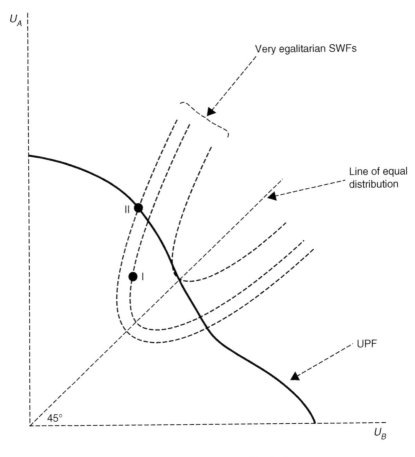

Fig. 7.3 Economic efficiency versus strong egalitarianism

resulting increases in inequality could well have contributed to greater friction and resentment in society.

And conversely, a move from II to I leads to a higher SWF even though it may well fail to satisfy the Pareto optimisation criterion. Thus, for example, a project that led to a slight improvement in the welfare of, say, poor workers (along the horizontal axis) but at considerable loss to rich consumers of their products (along the vertical axis) might be deemed desirable. This might be the case if, say, if poor workers gained a little welfare through more safety in their working environment, but rich consumers in wealthy countries are estimated to lose more through having to pay higher prices for the goods produced as a result of the better safety regulation. In this case the distribution of income has become more equal even after compensating the losers. So, depending on the importance attached to distributional considerations the Pareto optimality criteria is not a sufficient condition for carrying out the project.

7   Conclusions

Overall, therefore, the introduction of the social welfare function enables one to see clearly why, if distributional considerations are taken into account, Pareto optimality is neither a necessary nor a sufficient condition for an improvement in social welfare. In simple terms this means that some egalitarians might be willing to trade off a fall in national income in the interests of greater equality. After all, this is a judgement that most of us are prepared to make in many circumstances and reflects the relative intrinsic value we attach to equality and prosperity.

Of course one should not exaggerate the distributional effects of any project. Quite often these will be negligible as far as the whole society is concerned. But it may often be important in a local context. For example some roads may simply serve to help rich landowners or commuters get back home at night, whereas other roads may help poor farmers get their produce to market. There may well be cases where such distributional considerations will outweigh a narrow comparison between social costs and benefits that took no account of them. What the CBA does is to show roughly how much it will cost in certain circumstances to pursue greater equality. It is then up to society (or the decision makers) to decide whether or not it is acceptable.

Furthermore, in a society in which numerous projects are carried out, it may well be that what some people lose on the swings they can more than gain on the roundabout. This is more likely to be the case if the projects are calculated carefully and correspond correctly to the economic concepts of social costs and benefits.

Finally, it is always open to governments to influence the final distribution of incomes in a more or less equal manner, as it wishes, through the mechanism of fiscal policy. Adjusting project evaluation as a means of achieving one's distributional objectives is not the only means available for pursuing this objective. On the other hand, it cannot always be assumed that any prevailing regime of taxes and benefits is optimal given society's egalitarian values.

However, although the concept of a social welfare function 'is a valuable tool in many areas of public policy, it is also, in turn, subject to its own limitations. These are discussed in the next chapter.

Notes

1. Stiglitz, 2012.
2. Sunstein, 2014.
3. Anderson, 1999.
4. Sen, 1970:22.
5. In the Atkinson measure of the equality of income distribution, the utilities of the individuals are replaced by their incomes so that social utility is a function of these incomes only.

CHAPTER 8

The 'Mindless Society'

1   Is There a ' Society'?

In the last chapter I introduced the concept of the social welfare function –
that is, a function describing what variables contribute to the welfare of
society as a whole. But the British Prime Minister in the 1980s, the late
Baroness Thatcher, is famously misreported as having said that there is no
such thing as 'society'. What she actually said is 'Who is society? There is
no such thing! There are individual men and women and there are
families...'[1] It is not clear what exactly she had in mind. One possibility
is that she was simply referring to the view expressed by Jeremy Bentham
in 1789 that 'the community is a fictitious *body*, composed of the individual persons who are considered as constituting as it were its *members*'.[2]
Alternatively, she may have had in mind *Pareto's* view that it makes more
sense to talk about the welfare *for* society, rather than the welfare *of*
society.[3] Simon Blackburn has suggested that she was reflecting 'the ideology of the self-interested agent in eternal competition with others'.[4]
Another – and more charitable – interpretation is that she was making a
philosophical objection to the metaphysical notion that one can attribute
states of mind to 'society' of the same kind that one can to individuals. It is
not for me to attempt to adjudicate between these various interpretations
and the reader must judge for himself.

But whatever the correct interpretation of the late Baroness
Thatcher's view there is no doubt that it is linked to a serious aggregation problem. This is the problem of how to go from individual

© The Author(s) 2017
W. Beckerman, *Economics as Applied Ethics*,
DOI 10.1007/978-3-319-50319-6_8

preferences to the preferences of society. It is a well-known problem in welfare economics and in political philosophy which we shall discuss in more detail in the next section. The problem arises because the whole edifice of welfare economics is built up on a fairly clearly defined theory of individual choice, some components of which – such as the way consumers respond to changes in prices – has been empirically confirmed. But even if one could assume that these choices correspond to their welfares it is not clear how far one can go from this to a theory of what constitutes the welfare of a group of individuals. How does one weigh together the welfare of individuals to arrive at the welfare of the group?

Another problem, which is less obvious and far less important for practical purposes, follows from the fact that our theory of whether the utility of an individual has risen or fallen is in terms of whether the individual is on a higher or lower 'indifference' curve (or 'behaviour line' as it is sometimes called). Hence, *strictly speaking*, one cannot compare the welfare of societies comprising different people with different indifference curves. This gives rise to what is known as the 'constituency principle', namely that comparisons of welfare are only valid if they refer to identical groups – that is, a 'constituency' of people. But this would even mean that if the GDP of some country were much higher today than yesterday one could not say that its economic welfare had risen. For some people would have died during the previous 24 hours and others would have been born. So we would be comparing societies with different populations, which, *strictly speaking*, is not possible within the framework of economic theory.

But all such limitations on the possibility of passing judgement on the economic welfare of different societies are nonsense, of course. For example, strictly speaking, the constituency principle would exclude our saying that welfare is higher in a country where people are free, well-fed, healthy and happy than in some other country where people are oppressed, hungry and miserable. But we know that this is nonsense.

2   SOCIAL CHOICE THEORY AND THE IMPOSSIBILITY THEOREM

So what do we mean when we talk about the aggregate welfare of 'society'? It is intuitively plausible to assume that society does not have a 'mind' in the ordinary sense of the word so that one cannot attribute to 'society' the sort of mental thought processes that correspond exactly to those that an individual goes through when making choices. This means that, for example, society does not follow thought processes such as those that correspond, ideally, to the rational choice process that an individual would follow. There is no such thing as a 'society' that has a mind that could say to itself, 'Oh dear, silly me! Since I preferred X to Y and Y to Z how stupid of me to prefer Z to X'. This is particularly inconvenient for economists – who are the guardians of 'rational choice' and who like to equate rational choice with the maximisation of something, such as a utility function, or a social welfare function, that respects some criteria of rationality.

One implication of this is that whereas one can make empirically verifiable positive propositions about the preference rankings of any individual, it is not possible to make similar propositions about the collective preference rankings of any *collection* of individuals. For example, if we assert that Jones thinks he prefers situation 1 to situation 2, we are making a positive proposition that could be tested by asking Jones. If he says, 'Yes, I think I prefer 1 to 2', our proposition has been confirmed, unless we have some reason to suspect he is lying. But we cannot make a similar *testable* proposition about the combined preferences of a number of individuals. We can, of course, add up how many prefer one or other of the two options, like in a referendum. But that would simply amount to defining society's preference as being what the majority want.

Or, as in a market economy, we could check the amounts of money that the agents were prepared to pay for the two alternatives and add them up. But to conclude from these that 'society' prefers one situation rather than another merely means that we define the statement that 'society prefers one situation rather than another' in terms of survey results or people's expenditure patterns.[5]

Nevertheless, decisions have to be made all the time about various policies or projects, at all levels of public life. The classic examples are public goods such as national defence, or law and order. These have certain well-known characteristics, namely 'non-excludability' or 'non-rivalry'. Non-excludability means that if the service is provided for one or more persons it is technically impossible, or very difficult, to prevent other people from using it. If we have armed forces to protect the British Royal Family from invasion by the French it is impossible to exclude everybody else in the country from this invasion, however much some of them may have welcomed it. Non-rivalry means that once the service is provided to some people then, within limits, it costs no more to provide it to others.

For example, if one person admires the flowers in a park he does not prevent others from doing so, as he would do if he ate them instead. So his admiration for the flowers imposes no cost on anybody else. In addition, there are services, such as education or health, where there are good reasons for believing that positive externalities or asymmetrical information requires some public provision. And, even where the technical properties of the goods in question may not require public provision there are often cases for some sort of public intervention in the market – for example, to cater for the well-known weak links in the choice-to-welfare chain such as those discussed in Chapter 5.

In addition, there are also the arguments discussed earlier concerning 'the moral limits' of the market. Thus, for various well-known reasons, there is a *prima facie* case for the view that the provision of certain goods or services ought not to be left to the market mechanism, and some other process is needed in order to aggregate individual preferences into some concept of society's choices. Social choice theory is concerned with this aggregation of people's preference rankings between the outcomes – or 'different states of society' – that will follow from different policies. It is concerned with the aggregation of people's preference ranking between different collective choice, such as where to site an incinerator to burn local garbage, or whether to open a new school or shut down some local hospital or build a new road and so on.

This raises the problem of collective – or social – choice theory, to which major contributions have been made since Ken Arrow's seminal work in 1951 set out to answer the question of whether ' . . . it is formally possible to construct a procedure for passing from a set of known individual tastes to a pattern of social decision-making . . . it being assumed, on the way, that individuals' choices are rational'.[6]

Arrow tackled the question of whether it was possible to find a 'constitution' – that is, a set of rules – by which society could rank various social states and that satisfied some apparently appealing ethical axioms, such as no dictatorship, or the weak version of the Pareto principle to the effect that, if everybody prefers situation A to B then A is better than B, or the requirement that rational social choice should respect the same transitivity axiom required of rational choice for an individual.[7] What Arrow did was to prove that no possible rules could be found for reaching such an aggregate ranking in the light of individual rankings without violating one or other of his proposed axioms, all of which have great intuitive appeal. To prove such an 'impossibility' theorem is, of course, a very disconcerting and fundamental result. Although one may question some of the assumptions required to reach this result (such as no interpersonal comparisons of utilities) it was nevertheless an extraordinary achievement to prove that, given these assumptions, '. . . attempts to form social judgments by aggregating individual expressed preferences always lead to the possibility of paradoxes. Thus there cannot be a completely consistent meaning to collective rationality'.[8]

3   An Example: Local Air Pollution

For example, suppose that there is some unpleasant localised air pollution from factories, such as smoke or sulphur dioxide. Consider three methods of dealing with it (apart from just ignoring it). One of them is simple regulation. The other two both recognise the scope for a market in 'property rights'. But these could take the form either of rights to clean unpolluted air that could be given to the potential victims of the pollution, or rights to pollute the air that could be given to the owners of the factories that cause the pollution. There are thus three possibilities, namely:

X = use the market by giving property rights in clean air to the poor people who are the ones usually most affected by the pollution. They would then negotiate to sell some of their rights to clean air to the factory owners at a mutually acceptable price and quantity.

Y = use bureaucratic regulation.

Z = use the market by giving a certain amount of 'air pollution rights' either to the rich owners of the factories who might be willing to reduce their use of clean air in return for suitable compensation, or to the victims of the pollution who might be willing to sell some of their rights to clean air to the factory owners. Both sides could then negotiate a mutually acceptable deal.

A typical bureaucratic way of dealing with such a problem would be to set up a committee, since, as Art Buchwald once put it, committees are places where, for most people, conversation is a substitute for the boredom of work and the loneliness of thought. The committee's remit would be to decide which of these three methods to adopt. This might consist of a pollution expert, a health expert, the owners of the local factories, representatives of the citizens (e.g. local councillors), a lawyer, a moral philosopher and two economists (in order to ensure three opinions). Such a committee would have to begin by agreeing on their decision rules, such as whether the ranking of all the possible alternative decisions should be taken by a simple vote, or by some transferable vote system. Social choice theory is addressed to the rules that the committee would draw up for ranking different possible decisions. Arrow has shown that no rules could satisfy apparently compelling axioms of *collective* rational choice.

The flavour of the argument can, perhaps, be illustrated in the following simplified example, in which the local authorities set up a small sub-committee of only three members, namely:

> Mr LWF-M has left-wing tendencies but is in favour of free markets, up to a point, so wants to promote his distributional judgement that one ought to make income distribution more equal.
>
> Mrs RWF-M, who has right-wing tendencies and also favours free markets, thinks that the pollution rights ought to be given to the factory owners.
>
> Miss BB is a bossy bureaucrat so naturally prefers regulation since it gives her more power and responsibility.

Their preference orderings are likely to be as follows:

> LWFM's preferences are likely to be X > Y > Z.
> RWFM's preferences are likely to be Z > X > Y.
> BB's preferences might be Y > Z > X.

Suppose they vote on the choice between X and Y. Two of them rank X > Y. And if they also vote on the choice between Y and Z, two of them will prefer Y to Z. So it seems that a majority vote would show that X > Z. But if the committee then vote on the choice between X and Z they will find that two of them rank Z > X. So their ranking is X > Y > Z > X!!!! In other words, the democratic procedure of majority voting in this instance does not satisfy the transitivity axiom of rational choice that we met Chapter 4 in connection with individuals' choices. This paradox, to which Arrow referred, is known as the 'Condorcet paradox' in honour of the Marquis de Condorcet who drew attention to it over 200 years ago.

A big industry on social choice theory has developed, of course, since Arrow's pioneering contribution, some of which disputes the significance of Arrow's work. One of the most fundamental critiques was made back in 1954 by Nobel Laureate James Buchanan.[9] He argued that one should not expect a 'social decision rule' to satisfy the same criteria of rationality – notably transitivity – as for a single mind (such as an individual's mind). He argued that 'rationality or irrationality as an attribute of the social group implies the imputation to that group of an organic existence apart from that of its individual components. . . . '

In other words, one might expect that rationality would be the criterion of the preference ordering of a single rational mind. But we cannot go from that to expecting transitivity to be the characteristic of collective preference orderings. Thus Buchanan was not worried by the implications of the result that any decision rule can lead to apparently intransitive orderings, for he regarded this as a necessary feature of democratic decision-making. He argued that 'Correctly speaking, majority decision must be viewed primarily as a device for breaking a stalemate and for allowing some collective action to be taken'.

That is all very well and may even set one's mind at rest. But most of us would have liked to have believed that, if only one could find it, there must surely be some way in which a group could reach decisions that would satisfy our conception of rationality. But Arrow showed that – disconcerting though it may be – this is simply not the case. As he put it ' . . . there are well-known fundamental dilemmas in any concept of social good . . . for reasons that I think are intrinsic to the logic of the subject. The root facts here are the incommensurability and incomplete communicability of human wants and values'.[10]

Thus we have lost our innocence and we now have to abandon our belief in some 'rational' collective choice. According to Partha Dasgupta, 'It seems to me we simply have to live with Arrow's theorem and do the best we can . . . Just as circles can't be squared, ideal voting rules don't exist, ideal markets are a pleasant myth, and ideal governments can't be conjured up because governments are run by people'.[11] One cannot refuse to do anything at all on account of some known ambiguities in the notion of an aggregate, or collective, 'social' welfare. So what do we do? Presumably we eschew referenda on every important decision in the domain of economic policy. Instead we have to fall back on the best approach we have, namely old-fashioned welfare economics, while bearing in mind its limitations.

4   THE WELFARE ECONOMICS APPROACH

The welfare economics approach, as exemplified, for example, in a CBA, is far less ambitious. It is limited to trying to promote the state of affairs that would have been achieved in a free market in the absence of the usual market imperfections, such as monopolistic conditions, taxes, externalities and so on. In this way it might even be able to take some account of the intensity of people's preferences, which is, of course, absent in the social choice approach. As explained in Chapter 5, we know that people's preferences do not always accurately reflect what is good for their welfare. But let us assume, for present purposes, that we are dealing with situations in which this divergence between preference satisfaction and welfare is not very important. How then would conventional welfare economic analysis handle the aforementioned problem of dealing with local air pollution?

In the previous example, two out of the three members of the committee might have preferred solution Y to solution X, but the intensity of the preference of the third person for solution X may have been very great, whereas the intensity of preference of the two members of the committee for solution Y may have been very slight. In ordinary market transactions the intensity of people's preferences is represented by the prices people are prepared to pay for the options open to them.

For example if a vote were to be taken in some office about whether smoking were to be permitted in common areas, there may well be a majority for smoking to be permitted. However, it is possible that the non-smokers would have been prepared to pay a much larger sum for smoking to be prohibited than the smokers would have been prepared to pay for it to have been permitted. In that case, there would have been scope for a mutually satisfactory deal between the smokers and the non-smokers in which some agreed compensation would have been paid by the non-smokers to the smokers that would have left both parties better off. A CBA would have indicated the scope for a Pareto-optimising move.

The welfare economics approach focuses our attention on the causes of market failure in any particular instance and possible ways of rectifying them. One criticism of the cost-benefit approach is that – as mentioned earlier – allowance for the intensity of preferences by taking account of how much they are prepared to pay for different things means giving greater weight to wealthier people's preferences. But a good CBA could take some account of the extent to which costs and benefits are influenced by the distribution of incomes, as well as by other institutional features of society that had a major influence on relative prices.[12]

Thus in the aforementioned example, welfare economics would start by identifying whether there was an externality which established a *prima facie* case for some sort of public intervention. It would then try to establish what would be the optimal amount of the pollution permitted, taking account of the social costs of reducing it and the social damage done by the pollution. (This could make some allowance for the extent to which people's preferences might be biased by incorrect information, etc.) One obvious method for reducing pollution to the optimal amount would be to impose a tax on the pollution equal to the marginal cost or marginal social damage at the point where these two magnitudes are equal.[13] Another method would be to mimic a market system by giving pollution rights to either the victims of the pollution or the factory owners, along the lines indicated in Section 3, and then let them negotiate a price with each other.

The next step would be to go beyond the basic theory of Pareto optimality and to take account of distributional considerations. For example, the victims of the air pollution in the previous example might be mainly poor people, since on the whole, polluting factories tend to be located in poorer neighbourhoods. On the other hand, even if the factories were not located in particularly poor areas they might have employed mainly poor people whose livelihood would be threatened if the pollution charges made their factories uncompetitive. In either case the distributional judgements represented in the social welfare function of the decision makers would come into play and should influence the outcome.

Another subjective judgement that would need to be made would be how far one attached intrinsic value to the consequences of any actions compared to the intrinsic value of the processes by which any particular outcome is achieved and hence of the 'fairness' or 'justice' of these processes. But there are different interpretations of 'consequentialism' and of the extent to which processes ought to be included in the consequences of any action. Standard CBA does not necessarily incorporate information about whether the process leading up to any particular consequences involved violation of anybody's rights. Hence, it tends to be frequently overlooked.

But if the domain of welfare economics is extended to incorporate aspects of processes, such as respect for 'rights', into the assessment of the outcome of any policy, it raises a whole host of other value judgements. In the aforementioned example, judgements would have to include the intrinsic value of 'rights' to the clean air that was being polluted, since this would determine who is to pay and who is to receive the proceeds. For example, if the local residents had lived in the area before the factories had arrived, it might be argued that they enjoyed the property rights in the clean air and so should receive compensation from the factory owners. But if the factories had arrived first their owners might argue that there had been no pollution – in the sense that anybody was actually harmed – before the local residents came to live there. So, it could be argued, it was the arrival of the poor residents who are to blame for causing the pollution. In the words of the old song:

> It's the same the 'ole world over
> It's the poor wot gets the blame
> It's the rich wot gets the pleasure
> Ain't it all a bloomin shame!

Thus, one way or another, although the welfare economics approach avoids the logical problems of arriving at a decision that can be said to represent some 'collective' rational preference ranking, it raises numerous difficult choices between the intrinsic value one attaches to aspects – consequences or processes – of the choices in question. But both welfare economics and collective decisions have crucial roles to play. It is widely accepted that the unfettered market mechanism is unlikely to provide a perfect mechanism for the promotion of society's economic welfare. Hence, there may be room for some form of social intervention. The problem then is what form this should take starting from individuals' preferences. There is no simple algorithm that can tell us how to reach the decisions. Meanwhile, decisions have to be made about policies and projects that will affect the whole of some society.

5   An Example: The 'Summers Memorandum'

It was asserted in the Introduction to this book that, in most practical policy decisions, the basic value judgements implied in welfare economics may often not play as a significant role in decision-making as does the knowledge about the facts. This, it was argued, was because one is never starting from an optimal initial situation. Instead, one is always concerned with relatively small moves from whatever initial situation we happen to have started. But there are often cases where basic value judgements are important.

One well-known example is the memorandum written in 1991 by Larry Summers, who was the chief economist at the World Bank at the time. The memorandum that he wrote to some colleagues soon became famous.[14] This is because he raised the question of whether the export of polluting industries to less-developed countries (LDCs) ought to be encouraged. He outlined the conventional economic case for doing so which was based on certain propositions, notably:

(i) If valued by conventional methods, any economic valuation of morbidity and mortality in such countries would be much lower than in advanced countries.

(ii) In some sparsely populated countries a given amount of air pollution would have a far less serious impact.

(iii) In countries that have much shorter life expectancy anyway, some of the very long-term possible effects of air pollution would be relatively less important.

His famous memorandum has, inevitably, been heavily criticised and scrutinised, and it would be out of place here to rehearse again many of the points made.[15] But it should be pointed out that in the final paragraph of his memorandum Summers did indicate that various objections could be made to this proposal, including objections on moral grounds. And he pointed out that similar objections could be made to many other World Bank proposals for trade liberalisation. He was, therefore, raising a question about consistency in Bank policy rather than making a specific proposal about the export of polluting activities. (It is not his fault that he sometimes raises questions that most people would prefer to leave unasked, presumably because they know that they would not like the answers.)

But it does serve as a particularly good example of five of the weaknesses in Pareto optimality that have been identified earlier (and of which Summers was, of course, perfectly aware, as the final paragraph of his memo indicated). They would be:

(i) The trade in question would be a Pareto-optimising in the sense that both parties would be moving to a preferred position. But it was only the original unequal distribution of endowments that induced poor countries to find it beneficial in spite of its hazards. If they had been much richer the first and third of the aforementioned Summers' points would not have applied.

(ii) The citizens of the LDCs are likely to be very poorly informed about the possible harmful health effects of the polluting activities in question.

(iii) The trades in question are likely to have been negotiated with the authorities of the LDCs, or other powerful interests therein, who, even if they were well informed of the health consequences, may not have worried much about the interests of the population as a whole. In other words, it would be classic example of the agent-principal problem – that is, that certain organisations are often run in the interests of the 'agents' in charge of them instead of the 'principals' who own them or whose interests they are supposed to serve.

(iv) In any case, it is extremely unlikely that the actual victims of the pollution in question would be properly compensated for their loss of welfare (or loss of life in some cases, such as the infamous Bhopal disaster), so that *potential* Pareto optimality would certainly be irrelevant.

(v) How far rich countries ought to take account of the likely loss of welfare of the poor countries raises the issue of how one ought to draw the boundaries around the society whose welfare one is trying to maximise. Thus, in the modern world the most serious problem about what is meant by 'society' is the question of how we draw the boundary around the society the welfare of which (or *for* which) we are seeking to maximise. It is what is often known in moral philosophy discourse as the problem of '*moral distance*'. For example, how far should one take account of distant people or distant generations? Hence, the 'moral distance' problem is examined in greater detail in Chapters 17 and 18 in connection with international and intergenerational justice. It would be nice if welfare economic theory could avoid getting mixed up in this particular value judgement, which is a matter of political philosophy. But this problem has become increasingly important in today's world of globalisation, mass emigration and environmental change.

6   CONCLUSIONS

The way that the value judgements implicit in welfare economics enter into the decision-making process is illustrated in Fig. 3.1 in Chapter 3. Some specific value judgements have already been mentioned – such as the intrinsic value of consumers' freedom to make their own mistakes, or of equality of incomes, or of economic prosperity – and others will be discussed in more detail in later chapters.

It might already appear at this point that welfare economics cannot take us very far in making rational choices among different policy options. But this would be a mistake. Welfare economics and its application in cost-benefit analysis provide a valuable framework and organising principle for taking account of the effect of any economic policy. It clarifies criteria that help to evaluate the relative economic merits of alternative policies and projects. This conceptual framework enables one to identify the value judgements involved so that one can take explicit account of them, rather than to leave them to dwell unacknowledged in some murky background.

This does not mean that decisions become easy to make. For there are probably no clear-cut ethical theories that are in harmony with all our ethical intuitions and attitudes. Insofar as we hold plural values, some of which often conflict, one cannot expect to find an over-riding ethical system that reconciles the different preferences of different people.

On the other hand, as pointed out previously, most policy choices are about *marginal changes* in the allocation of resources, starting from a 'second-best' point. In practice, therefore, what is usually required will be factual information, and there will be little point in wringing one's hands over the normative significance of the starting point. There are many situations where some numerical evaluation of alternative courses of action along cost-benefit lines that take account of distributional considerations will make a useful – if not decisive – contribution to rational decision-making that would be preferable to total reliance on other decision-making processes. An example of this in the UK context is given at the end of Chapter 19, and no doubt innumerable others could be found, not to mention the way some decisions are made in other parts of the world. In most situations the ethical limitations on CBA and its welfare economics underpinning it are small beer compared to the role of uncertain facts, administrative failures, pressure groups and empire-building officials, not to mention downright corruption, so that to jib at the former while accepting the latter is a clear case of swallowing a camel while straining at a gnat.

But, because some of the value judgements implicit in welfare economics are usually only in the background, the extent to which they qualify the whole structure of standard welfare economics is not always adequately appreciated. As a result, the valuable achievements of welfare economics can be put to the wrong use, as is sometimes the case, for example, with bad applications of CBA. The function of normative economics is to help improve the allocation of resources in the economy in the pursuit of its objectives. But this should not take the form of providing ready-made formulae that can be applied mechanically. As far as possible it should take account of the deviations between market prices and costs, on the one hand, and 'social' prices and costs, on the other. It must also take account of historical experience, of psychological motivations that are poorly understood, of political and social circumstances, and of ethical values that are usually only dimly recognised. Otherwise it becomes a sterile – and possibly harmful – activity.

NOTES

1. *Prospect*, May, 2009:35, and Willetts, 2010:279, note 14.
2. Bentham 1789:ch2, para.4.
3. Pareto did not actually use the term 'welfare' (or its French equivalent, 'bien-etre' since he was writing in French) but carefully distinguished between his concept of 'ophelimity' and 'utility', the latter being a much broader concept than the former insofar as it refers to the whole 'property (of something) which makes a thing favourable to the development and well-being of an individual, a community or the whole human species'. See Finer,1966:254 and 99–103.
4. Blackburn, 2009:36.
5. It should not be thought that the economist's device of the 'compensating variation', which owes its origins to the Hicks/Kaldor/Scitovsky compensation tests, overcomes the aggregation problem. For it does not deal with the welfare implications of different distributions of incomes.
6. Arrow, 2nd edn. 1951:2.
7. See Hausman and McPherson, 2006:ch 14, or Hargreaves Heap, 1989:190ff, for more comprehensive expositions of the essential features of social choice theory, including a full enumeration and explanation of Arrow axioms.
8. Arrow, 1974:25. A simple exposition of this feature of social choice theory is Dasgupta, 2007a:ch.9.
9. Buchanan 1954:114–123.
10. Arrow, 1974:24.
11. Dasgupta, 2007a:157.
12. A major pioneering contribution to CBA that indicated how one might take account of distributional considerations was Little and Mirrlees, 1974. A general discussion of this problem and possible methods of dealing with it is in Sugden and Williams, 1978:ch 15.

13. There is not actually a unique optimal point, since different means of reducing the pollution will have different income effects on the parties concerned, which will feed back on the cost and benefit schedules.

14. Quoted in *The Economist*, 8th February 1992:66.

15. A detailed and perceptive discussion of this memorandum is contained in Hausman and McPherson, 2006.

CHAPTER 9

Utilitarianism: The Search for an Overriding Value

1 INTRODUCTION

In Chapter 3 I emphasised the distinction between value judgements, normative propositions and positive propositions. In principle, positive propositions can be confirmed or refuted by facts. But value judgements cannot, though the value judgements that people hold are often influenced by them. But if they are not based on factual evidence, on what are they based? This chapter discusses what is one of the most widespread and compelling moral theories that might form the basis for value judgements, namely Utilitarianism.

Of course, most people do not consciously and explicitly link their views on personal or policy problems to any ethical theory at all. Hardly anybody ever says to himself 'I am in favour of giving equal weight to the interests of future generations because I am a "utilitarian"', or 'I give money to poor people because I am a "prioritarian"'. Most people have never heard of 'Utilitarianism' or 'prioritarianism' or any other ethical theories, but this does not stop their making normative judgements all the time. These judgements may be the product of careful reflection, or intuition, or habit, or a desire to go along with the herd (as with 'political correctness'). And although, in practice, the moral codes that influence the conduct of people in their daily lives are micro-rules of 'moral' conduct in individual situations, such as within a family or a neighbourhood or a firm, they may reflect broader – if unconscious – acceptance of certain higher-level rules of moral behaviour. Exceptionally, at best, appeals to

© The Author(s) 2017
W. Beckerman, *Economics as Applied Ethics*,
DOI 10.1007/978-3-319-50319-6_9

these rules may be made whenever there is some conflict of values, or when one is trying to justify the morality of one's conduct. Nevertheless, although most people arrive at their value judgements in an intuitive and unsystematic way, philosophers have tried throughout the ages to examine whether there are any underlying ethical theories to which one could reasonably appeal as justification for these value judgements.

One of the most appealing moral theories that have emerged from these endeavours has been Utilitarianism. But before giving a brief sketch of the main features of Utilitarianism that are relevant for our purposes it may be helpful to situate its place in the wider area of moral theory.

2   The 'Right' or the 'Good'

Within each of the main classes of ethical theory there are many variations, and the classes tend to overlap or merge into one another at some points. And no serious class of ethical theory would pretend that it could cover every conceivable situation that may arise any more than a body of laws can cater for every conceivable contingency. If it did there would be a lot less need for judges and lawyers. Nevertheless, for purposes of simplification, and at the cost of some violence to the subtleties and variations within each class of ethical theory, it may be said that one can distinguish between those that focus on what is a 'right' action and those that focus on how far an action leads to a 'good' outcome.

The former tend to emphasise the 'rightness' of certain actions independent of their consequences. Theories of this kind, which do not focus on the consequences of any action, are known as *deontological* theories. Probably the oldest form of a deontological moral theory was embodied in the Ten Commandments which simply laid down rules about what was the 'right' thing to do and what was the 'wrong' thing to do. No nonsense about evaluating the consequences and whether they were 'good' or not. God told people what was the 'right' thing to do and that was that.

Deontological theories give priority to what is a 'right' action *even if it fails to maximise the 'good'*, or, more generally, to prohibit what is a 'wrong' action *even if it may promote more good*. Common positive deontological injunctions are that it is always right to keep one's promises or contracts, or to honour one's parents. Examples of negative deontological injunctions would be that it is always wrong to tell lies, or to violate other people's rights such as their right not to be killed or tortured or falsely imprisoned, or to covet one's neighbour's wife (or husband), and so on, *irrespective of the consequences.* Deontological ethics start and finish with the notion of what is the 'right' action.

Thus, *deontological* ethical principles tend to focus on the agent himself and his motives, or on the nature of the action itself, rather than on the consequences of any particular action. Pacifism is a simple example of a deontological injunction that contrasts with utilitarian consequentialism. A dedicated pacifist will object to killing people in a defensive war irrespective of the utility consequences. Similarly, somebody who opposes capital punishment under any circumstances would object to taking a human life irrespective of whether doing so would deter potential murderers and hence, perhaps, save more lives. Society may also take the view that certain sources of utility are inherently evil, such as those that may be derived by a paedophile or a sadist.

By contrast with deontological theories, teleological theories define a 'right' action as one that promotes some notion of the 'good'. The 'good' is defined independently in term of certain value judgements, like 'utility is good', and 'right' actions are defined as those that maximise 'utility'. Thus the focus of teleological theories is on the *consequences* of any action. The good takes priority over the right. Utilitarianism is thus a teleological moral theory in which the *right* action is the one that has the 'good' consequence of promoting utility. There can be many varieties of teleology, depending on how the 'good' that is to be maximised is defined. For example, the 'good' could be defined in terms of happiness, preference satisfaction, capabilities, functionings, peace, rights, prosperity, and so on.

An example of the distinction between deontological and teleological theories is the distinction drawn in Chapter 16 between two types of egalitarian theories. The theory that more equality is desirable because it is instrumental in promoting some desirable consequence, such as greater social stability, is teleological. The theory that equality has some basic intrinsic value, such as being more 'just', is deontological.

3   UTILITARIANISM

Utilitarianism is probably the most popular form of teleological consequentialism. Acts should be judged as right or wrong according to their consequences. And 'good' consequences are those that promote society's utility. From its early days, in the hands of Bentham and Mill, 'utility' has been identified with 'happiness' and happiness is the only thing that is good in itself. Unhappiness is the only thing that is bad in itself.

Everything else is only good or bad according to its tendency to produce happiness or unhappiness.[1]

Bentham began his famous work '*An Introduction to the Principle of Morals and Legislation*' with the words 'Nature has placed mankind under the governments of two sovereign masters, *pain* and *pleasure*' and he goes on to say that 'The principle of utility recognises this subjection, and assumes it for the foundation of that system . . .'.[2] In the next few paragraphs he goes on to explain that utility is the property of any object that tends to produce the happiness or reduce the unhappiness of the party 'whose interest is considered: if that party be the community in general, then the happiness of the community: if a particular individual, then the happiness of that individual'. And in the next paragraph he goes on to make an assertion which is related to the discussion earlier in this book of the concept of a 'society'. This is his statement that

> the interest of the community is one of the most genuine expressions that can occur in the phraseology of morals: no wonder that the meaning of it is often lost. When it has a meaning it is this. The community is a fictitious body, composed of individual persons constituting as it were its members. The interest of the community then is, what? – the sum of the interests of the several members who composed it. It is in vain to talk of the interest of the community, without understanding what is the interest of the individual. A thing is said to promote the interest, or be for the interest, of an individual, when it tends to add to the sum total of his pleasures; or, what comes to the same thing, to diminish the sum total of his pains.[3]

But although Bentham derived the principle of utility from the forces that governed individual behaviour, he was mainly concerned with the aggregate utility of all the people in the 'community' – that is, of society – and its application to public policy and legislation. Utilitarianism did not discriminate between individuals. It did not matter to whom exactly the utility accrued or when it accrued. Thus Utilitarianism was inherently impersonal from the outset.

This has important implications for the discussion in later chapters of whether the society whose welfare we are trying to maximise includes other countries and future generations. And, strangely enough, the impersonal character of Utilitarianism contrasts with the views of David Hume (as explained in the next chapter) in spite of the influence of Hume on Bentham. In a reference to Hume's *Treatise of Human Nature*, Bentham, one of the founding fathers of Utilitarianism, stated that 'that the foundations of all virtue are laid in utility is there demonstrated.... I well remember, no sooner had I read that part of the work that touches on this subject that I felt as if scales had fallen from my eyes'. (The scales to which he was referring included the moral authority of the church or the monarch and the like). He went on to say that, in their place he '...learned to see that *utility* was the test and measure of all virtue; of loyalty as much as any; and that the obligations to minister to general happiness was an obligation paramount to and inclusive of every other'.[4]

4   UTILITARIANISM IN ECONOMICS

The moral rule of maximising utility plays a central role in the behavioural assumptions of economic theory, such as in the notion of 'diminishing marginal utility', as well as in the normative implications of welfare economics. For example, it is incorporated in the economic concept of a 'utility possibility frontier' and its practical application in CBA as explained in Chapter 7. According to one of the pioneering critics of contemporary welfare economics, the late Ian Little: 'For 200 years the concept of utility has been thought of as a cornerstone of normative economics'.[5] In a similar vein, Frank Hahn states that 'the economic theory of public policy is relentlessly utilitarian: policies are ranked by their utility consequences'.[6] The great economist Stanley Jevons wrote back in 1871 that '...the object of economics is to maximise happiness by purchasing pleasure, as it were, at the lowest cost in pain'.[7]

Utilitarianism in one form or another comes naturally to most economists. This is partly because the micro-foundations of economic theory are built on the concept of *maximisation*. Everybody has to be assumed to be maximising something or other. As explained in Chapter 3 this assumption makes it much easier to construct models of how economies operate. Without it basic micro-economic theory would collapse, taking with it much of the mathematical economics used in the analysis of the maximisation of some function or other.

So it is quite natural that economists should be drawn to an ethical theory that is in terms of maximising something, such as total utility, or utility per head (depending on which version of Utilitarianism one prefers). Utilitarianism appeals to economists because it corresponds to their use of the notion of rational choice in the explanation of people's behaviour.[8] This envisages people choosing, on the whole, between the various options open to them – such as choosing leisure over income, or spending rather than saving, or buying this object rather than that object – as a process of rational selection in the pursuit of some given objectives. As Rawls says, 'Teleological theories have a deep intuitive appeal since they seem to embody the idea of rationality. It is natural to think that rationality is maximizing something and that in morals it must be maximizing the good' (Rawls, 1971:24–25).

This maximisation process requires that the options open to people can be ranked in a *comparable* manner. It is easier – though by no means essential – if the options also happen to be *commensurate*. The concept 'commensurate' is taken to mean here that the options can be compared in terms of some relevant *quantitative* metric. And the metric has to be in units of 'utility'.

Quite apart from its obvious appeal to economists, Utilitarianism has the great advantage of resolving conflicts between different deontological moral injunctions. For example, should you tell a dying person that his dependants were provided for even though you know this to be untrue. To do so could violate a deontological moral law that one should always tell the truth, but it would comply with some other deontological law to be kind to people. There may also be conflicts between the 'rightness' of telling the truth and some personal obligation. For example, if some baddies were chasing your friend or brother should you tell them, untruthfully, that 'he went that way' when you know that he went the other way.

The appeal of Utilitarianism is that it appears to provide a way to solve conflicts of values, such as those that may be represented by certain deontological theories. If people have plural incommensurate values, it is far more difficult – and usually impossible – to rank them in a precise and transitive manner. But this inconvenience does not arise for utilitarians. Utilitarians have a view as to what the single ultimate value ought to be, namely utility, and, in theory, all other values can be converted into their contribution to this one basic value.

At a superficial level, Utilitarianism appears to be a beautifully simple system. It appears to replace arbitrary-seeming rules by a morality with a single coherent basis. Acts should be judged right or wrong according to how far they promote society's utility/happiness. This calculating approach to morality is an attempt to make our ethical life more rational and objective. It liberates our moral decisions from any authority (e.g. killing is wrong because that's what some authority, divine or other, declares), and its potentially arbitrary – if not capricious – verdicts. By looking at overall consequences of actions all of us should arrive at the same verdicts about their desirability *provided we all shared the same conception of 'utility' and all contributions to it are commensurate with each other*. But therein lies the snag. Not all people subscribe to the same concept of 'utility', and many people subscribe to values such as kindness, integrity, truth, loyalty, and so on that they find impossible to make commensurate with utility. This is not surprising since it is not even very clear what is meant by 'utility'.

5   What Is 'Utility'?

It was pointed out in Chapter 4 that the concept of 'utility' in modern economics is a far cry from the meaning it had in original Utilitarianism as introduced towards the end of the eighteenth century. Bentham and other early utilitarians defined utility simply in terms of the mental states of pleasures and pains. These either add to, or subtract from, happiness. Utility was thus just the balance between pleasure and pain, though these concepts were defined by Bentham far more widely than is often believed.[9] No distinction was made between different *qualities* of pleasure, though they could differ in terms of duration and intensity. As Bentham famously stated, 'pushpin is as good as poetry' provided due account is taken of duration and intensity. Much later (1862) John Stuart Mill moved away from this simple view of what is conducive to happiness and allowed for different qualities of experience. He distinguished between 'higher' and 'lower' pleasures, which seem to conflict with the notion that units of utility is can simply be added together. However, in Mills' version of Utilitarianism, one can somehow or other translate differences in the quality of different units of utility into corresponding differences in their quantity.[10]

The 'mental state' concept of happiness which is embodied in Utilitarianism and other theories of human motivation is vulnerable to Robert Nozick's well-known 'experience machine' argument (Nozick, 1974, p. 42) His point is that few people would be ready to hook themselves up to some machine that would give them satisfying mental experiences if the price of doing so was the knowledge that they would be sacrificing the freedom to lead their lives as autonomous human beings. In the same way most people would not want to live in a state of happy, drugged stupor even if they could be confident that there would be no harmful side effects.

As explained in Chapter 4 welfare economics is based largely on an alternative theory of what constitutes human welfare, namely the *preference satisfaction* theory. This asserts that people try to choose the option that ranks highest in their preference orderings. Thus this theory is not vulnerable to Nozick's point, for people may prefer to remain autonomous beings rather than sign up to a Faustian bargain of only having pleasurable experiences inside the experience machine. The preferences between which they choose may include preferences for activities or experiences that they would *not* regard as giving 'pleasure' in the Benthamite sense. For example, some activities – writing books, the pursuit of knowledge, aiding a member of one's family, building something, contributing to some charity to reduce poverty in some remote country, and so on – may rank highly in some people's preference ranking even if they seem to require work and sacrifices that cannot conceivably be regarded as 'pleasurable' in the normal sense of the word.

But although the 'preference satisfaction theory' of welfare is generally adopted in welfare economics, most economists know perfectly well that there are several reasons why the satisfaction of preferences is not necessarily the same as the promotion of one's welfare.

6   Main Varieties of Utilitarianism

Over the course of the last two centuries different forms of Utilitarianism have evolved quite apart from increasingly refined concepts of what contributes to people's utility or welfare. First, a distinction needs to be made between *'total'* and *'average'* Utilitarianism. The former refers to the objective of maximising the total utility of any society rather than maximising its utility per head. 'Total' Utilitarianism raises problems, however. For example, how far ought one to approve of an increase in total utility caused by an increase in population so large that it reduced utility per head to an extremely low level, and which Parfit refers to as a 'repugnant conclusion'. But the alternative principle, namely 'average Utilitarianism', has its own problems. Obviously, one of the ways of promoting the maximisation of utility per head would be to cut off a lot of heads, starting with those people who are not very good at maximising utility. So 'average' Utilitarianism would have to be qualified by some form of constraint on the resort to such measures.

Another major distinction within Utilitarianism is between *'rule Utilitarianism'* and *'act Utilitarianism'*. This terminology was not used by Bentham or Mill, and was only introduced by Brandt in 1959.[11] Rule Utilitarianism requires that in any particular situation an individual ought not to try to work out himself which particular choice will maximise utility but should choose to apply the general *rules* of utilitarian morality that are believed have to be followed in order to maximise society's utility, such as 'keep one's promises' or 'do not tell lies'.

By contrast, act Utilitarianism allows an individual freedom to evaluate the morality of *any particular action* in terms of whether he thinks that, on balance, the action will promote society's utility. Both forms of Utilitarianism accept that the morality of any act is determined by its consequences in terms of society's utility. But rule Utilitarianism specifies rules that will achieve this objective rather than leave it up to individuals to judge whether or not the consequences of his action will be to maximise society's utility. For example, a utilitarian rule may be that one should always tell the truth and keep one's promises, but an act-utilitarian might decide, in some particular situation, that the consequences of telling the truth would lead to lower social utility than would telling a lie.

But there are various snags about act Utilitarianism. These include the inability of individuals to assess the full consequences of their choices, either on account of inherent uncertainty, or poor information, or lack of cognitive ability, and so on, as discussed in more detail in Chapter 5. Furthermore, people cannot be trusted to assess impartially what is good for society's utility. All sorts of personal considerations and prejudices will push people towards choices that may be bad for society's utility but that they may be able to rationalise in terms of society's utility. Throughout human history individuals have carried out terrible atrocities while persuading themselves (or having been persuaded) that they were necessary for the long-run good of society. For these, and other, reasons the vast majority of serious philosophers now subscribe to rule Utilitarianism But this has still left plenty of room for debate over which precise form of rule Utilitarianism ought to prevail, and the moral philosophy literature is full of excellent discussions of the relevant positions.[12] After all, no moral theory is expected to cover every possible eventuality that may arise.

One variety of Utilitarianism is '*negative Utilitarianism*' as proposed by the late Karl Popper. The standard understanding of Utilitarianism assumes a symmetry between suffering and happiness (e.g. as explicitly stated by Sidgwick), which implies that the increase of happiness and the reduction of suffering are of equal value when of equal magnitude since they contribute equally towards the maximisation of utility. Negative Utilitarianism denies this symmetry and stresses the moral imperative to relieve suffering. As Popper said, 'I believe that there is, from the ethical point of view, no symmetry between suffering and happiness, or between pain and pleasure . . . In my opinion . . . human suffering makes a direct moral appeal for help, while there is no similar call the increase the happiness of a man who is doing well anyway'.[13] In brief, the message is 'Do not bother about maximising utility; just concentrate on minimising suffering'.

Furthermore, people differ widely in their conception of the good, whereas they differ far less about what constitutes harm or suffering. From the point of view of how the individual formulates his own goals and preference orderings, this philosophy has something in common with that of Max Horkheimer who, while affirming that ' . . . man's striving for happiness is to be recognised as a natural fact requiring no justification', believed that the poorest and most oppressed people in the world were concerned not with the pursuit of some notion of 'happiness' but with relief from suffering (Horkheimer, 1933:34/5 and 44).

According to a leading Utilitarian, a principle of minimising suffering in society as a whole would have to be specified carefully so that it did not lead to the conclusion that the best policy would be to destroy all sentient life painlessly (see Smart, 1973:29). (But perhaps the best policy would be to destroy all sentient life painlessly!) Anyway, even if one does not switch to negative Utilitarianism, the positive version of the theory has been subjected to various criticisms as well as competition from other moral theories. Some of the more important of these criticisms are discussed in the next chapter.

NOTES

1. Glover, 1990:1/2
2. Extract from Bentham's *An Introduction to the `Principles of Morals and Legislation*, in Glover, *op.cit.*:10.
3. Warnock, (ed.), 2003:17–18.
4. Quoted in Warnock (ed.), *ibid.*:6.
5. Little 2002:8.
6. Hahn, 1982:187.
7. Jevons, 1871, 1970 Penguin edition, p. 91.
8. But according to Hausman and McPherson, 'After decades of contempt and neglect, Utilitarianism and consequentialism were virtually reborn in the 1980s, and are now arguably dominant in moral philosophy' (1994:266).
9. For example, in chapter V, of his *An Introduction to the Principles of Morals and Legislation*, Bentham enumerates in some detail different sources of

pleasure including the pleasures of a good name and public respect as well as of benevolence. But, as John Stuart Mill pointed out, these sentiments were valued chiefly as sources of 'pleasure' (including expectation of eventual gain from them) to the person experiencing them, and Bentham still did not go far enough to take account of such objectives that may have a value independently of the satisfactions that they may provide to people who experience them.

10. See an interesting discussion of this problem in Norman, 1983:127–131.
11. Brandt, 1959.
12. It is, perhaps, invidious to select any particular expositions of Utilitarianism but mention might be made of Glover, 1990; Hooker, 2000; and Sen and Williams, (eds), 1982.
13. Popper, 1966 (5th edn.):264,fn.2.

CHAPTER 10

Utilitarianism and Its Constraints

High Heaven rejects the lore of nicely calculated less or more.

– Wordsworth

1   Constraints on Utility Maximisation

Most students of economics will be familiar with the concept of 'constrained maximisation'. It is the bread and butter of students who take an interest in the basic mathematics of economic theory, where they soon encounter the notion of 'constrained maximisation'. For this corresponds to fundamental concepts in economics, such as the notion that consumers maximise something that we shall call utility (for old times' sake and for want of a better word), subject to some constraints including their incomes and the prices of goods. And the difference between Utilitarianism and some competing ethical systems can be seen as being simply all about whether one should just maximise 'some unique intrinsically valuable objective, utility', subject to some constraints or whether, instead, there are other independent intrinsically valuable top-level objectives.

Take a very simple example. Suppose a pretty useless person can be killed in order to use some of his organs to save the lives of several very socially valuable people who are waiting for organ transplants such as kidney transplants. (In fact, in some countries it is suspected that some such process actually has had official approval.) 'But', you might say, 'this would conflict with a rule to respect people's right to life.' 'Ah', says the utilitarian, 'Not really. You just have to deduct the long-term loss of

© The Author(s) 2017
W. Beckerman, *Economics as Applied Ethics,*
DOI 10.1007/978-3-319-50319-6_10

utility that society would incur if such a practice became permissible from the shorter-term gain in utility of the rest of society. Easy. What's the problem?'

After all, in the last chapter, the principle of maximisation of utility *per head*, rather than maximisation of *total* utility, would presumably be subject to the constraint that it should not be promoted by cutting off a lot of heads. So why not just accept that utility maximisation – in which-ever variety – has to be subject to constraints of one kind or another? The literature is full of examples of situations that may crop up in ordinary daily life of possible conflicts between utility maximisation and some other motivation that seems to have strong appeal either in common sense morality or in a more general moral principle, such as justice, or integrity, or loyalty.

One famous example that has given rise to a whole literature on 'trollyology' refers to a situation in which, one day, you may be walking over a bridge over a railway line and you notice that a train (or some big trolley) is coming along the line and five people happen to be tied to the line. If you do nothing they will be killed. But, as often happens, a Fat Man is standing near you on the bridge right over the line in question and you could easily push him over on to the line which would stop the train. What do you do? Maximising utility requires that you push him. But other ethical considerations come into play. For example, if you let the train continue on its route, the death of the five people will not have resulted from any action by you. So perhaps you are not morally responsible for them. Whereas if you push the fat man you are responsible for his death.

True, finding oneself next to a fat man (or woman) is becoming quite a common occurrence these days, but the situation in the above example is still unlikely to happen often. So let us consider a scenario that is more common in these days of international travel, such as the story about the man called Jim, who is walking along minding his own business in South America when he comes upon a group of bandits who are about to shoot twenty innocent people. In these days of globalisation and international travel this could happen to anyone. But in this case Jim is told that if he would shoot one of the twenty, the other nineteen would be set free. Should Jim take up this offer? In this case, in addition to the point made in the Fat Man story about who would be actually moral responsible for the deaths in question, there is also the question of Jim's *integrity*. Can this be simply converted into units of utility that can be weighed against the loss of utility that the certain death of twenty innocent people would entail?

Yet another famous example is the one about the sheriff in some small town in the USA. In this story a man is held in jail awaiting trial. An angry mob gathers outside the jail and tells the sheriff that if he does not hand over the prisoner, who they will hang, they will go on a rampage in the town and kill dozens of innocent people. What should the sheriff do? In this story impersonal utility maximisation would have to be balanced against two conflicting common sense moral intuitions. One is the claim of duty – that is, the duty that the sheriff may feel to his office. But, in addition there is also the claim of justice.

The conflict between utility maximisation and justice has come up already in earlier chapters. For example, in Chapter 6, it was shown that a policy to introduce minimum wages in the interests of what might be regarded as a more 'just' distribution of incomes could conflict with maximising society's output. Similarly, Chapter 7 discusses the way that social welfare functions indicate possible trade-offs between total output and a 'just' distribution of welfare.

Another common feature of examples such as those given above is that certain acts that may maximise utility will constitute acting in a way that conflicts with other basic values, such as certain basic 'rights', notably the right to life. For many people would subscribe to a deontological claim that certain 'rights' are inviolate – for example, right to life, whether of humans or animals. For example, supporters of 'animal rights' would object to the use of animals in medical research even if this impedes medical progress and hence an eventual future reduction in human morbidity or mortality. Other 'rights' that may be claimed to conflict with the reliance on utilitarian maximisation could include property rights, or liberty rights. For example, the opening sentence of Robert Nozick's famous book, *Anarchky State, and Utopia*, is 'Individuals have rights, and there are things no person or group may do to them (without violating their rights)'.[1]

One of the most famous conflicts between the welfare of society and personal sense of duty is Sophocles's *Antigone*, who is faced with a conflict between duty to her dead brother and duty to the laws of the state. It is quite likely that a significant proportion of the world's population believe that 'duty' – such as duty to one's country, to one's family, to one's God, to one's firm (in Japan), to one's pet dog (Britain), or to one's political party – over-rides concern with maximising society's total welfare.

The examples included situations in which certain acts might maximise utility but conflict with the moral obligations and integrity of the person

carrying them out. This is linked to another whole class of possible constraints on impersonal utility maximisation, and one which is far more
common in everyday life. For who has not been faced with a conflict
between doing what could be expected to maximise society's utility and
some personal claim, such as claims of obligations to one's family, or
friends, or community, or country, and so on.

2   'SPECIAL OBLIGATIONS' AND 'AGENT RELATIVE ETHICS'

For this reason one of the most important objections to classical *impersonal* Utilitarianism is an appeal to special obligations that one may have to
particular people or groups – such as the deontological rule that one
should honour one's parents, or fulfill one's duty to one's country. The
appeal to 'special obligations' as a constraint on utility maximisation is
closely related to what it known as 'agent-relative ethics' or 'agent-centred
ethics'. Even David Hume who, as indicated in the previous chapter, was
acknowledged by Bentham as the inspiration of his Utilitarianism, gave a
prominent place to 'special obligations', or 'agent-relative ethics' in his
theory of the evolution of moral conventions (though he did not use these
terms).[2]

For, unlike Bentham, Hume claimed to provide a psychological *explanation* of how moral principles had developed. For he developed at some
length his view that morality is firmly based in human nature. Hume
emphasised that the utility with which people are primarily concerned
originates in agent-relative concerns. For example, he writes, 'A man
naturally loves his children better than his nephews, his nephews better
than his cousins, his cousins better than strangers, where every thing else is
equal. Hence arises our common measures of duty, in preferring the one
to the other. Our sense of duty always follows the common and natural
course of our passions'.[3] Of course, Hume's concept of the 'passions' does
not correspond to its current connotation with its association with obsessions or with extreme romantic sentiments. In brief, passion 'is Hume's
general term for emotion, attitude and desire'.[4]

However, Hume recognised that giving free reign to the natural
instincts of people to pursue their self-interest and that of their family
and friends could prevent the development of social conventions that are
necessary to enable stable societies to flourish and develop. So something
else was needed, even though this would be influenced by expectations of
the advantages that people would derive for themselves and their families

and friends. 'This can be done after no other manner, than by a convention enter'd into by all the members of the society to bestow stability on the possession of those external goods, and leave every one in the peaceable enjoyment of what he may acquire by his fortune and industry'.[5] Hence, over the ages, the societies that survived and flourished were those which successfully developed such conventions. These conventions reflected – if quite unconsciously – not only the direct interests of individuals and their special relations to others but also their indirect long-run interests in the viability of progressive, stable societies. '*Thus self-interest is the original motive to the* establishment *of justice: but a* sympathy *with public interest is the source of the* moral approbation, *which attends that virtue*'[6] (italics in the original).

Hume presented his explanation of how our sense of morality and justice has evolved in a manner that has since been developed in various modern forms, including socio-biology and the well-known 'tit-for-tat' strategy in game theory. (*loc.cit.* sec. II). For example, he writes, 'Nor is the rule concerning the stability of possession the less deriv'd from human conventions, that it arises gradually, and acquires force by a slow progression, and by our repeated experience of the inconveniences of transgressing it'.[7] Indeed, one of the foremost contributors to game theory, Ken Binmore, goes as far as to say that '...a game theorist ought to have recognized from the start that Hume is the original inventor of reciprocal altruism – the first person to recognise that the equilibrium ideas now studied in game theory are vital to an understanding of how human societies work'.[8]

But if our moral intuitions and our sense of justice reflect human nature, which must leave room for agent-relative concerns, why should this give them any irresistible moral status? The answer is that it does not. Hume did not claim that it did. He is famous for deploring the tendency of people to jump from 'is' propositions (such as propositions about human nature) to 'ought' propositions.[9] He only claimed to explain how certain moral principles have developed in society. In a sense Hume had no *a priori* 'moral theory', only a theory of the psychology of how society's moral conventions have evolved. A purely psychological theory cannot be satisfactory for anyone who seeks 'true' moral positions. In Hume's view, however, truth is not a term that can apply to moral beliefs. How far one accepts that moral principles that are anchored in human nature, and hence tend to give priority to 'special obligations' in certain situations, rather than some other impersonal set of principles, such as

Utilitarian or Kantianism, is, of course, a crucial value judgement that plays a major role in certain practical policy issues.

Thus, while Hume can be claimed to be the father of Utilitarianism he differed from classical Utilitarianism in one major respect. This is that his version of Utilitarianism was not so ruthlessly impersonal. He did not subscribe to the view that all that matters is the maximisation of the total utility of society irrespective of the effect on the utility of particular groups in society, such as those to which people would naturally give priority. Nevertheless, as indicated above, he did not believe that prior concern with special obligations of one kind or another and the role that they had played in the early evolution of society's moral conventions should always over-ride 'sympathy' with the rest of our fellow men or with the longer-run interests of our own favoured groups.

There are other 'contractarian' theories of justice that are based on appeals to intelligent self-interest. David Gauthier, for example, has set out in detail the view that our moral values have to be grounded in human nature and that it makes sense for people to eschew blinkered utility maximisation in favour of constrained maximisation that takes account of other people behaving in a similar manner. This leads to a strategy of co-operating with like-minded people and of 'defecting' in dealings with others. Thus, moral constraints make us all better off in terms of our preferences, whatever these may be.[10] If, therefore, we accept (i) the positive proposition that agent-relative/game-theoretic ethics have helped the development of relatively peaceful and prospering societies, and (ii) the value judgement that this development is a 'good' thing, one has some logical basis for the normative conclusion that some form of agent-relative ethics is desirable.

3   PLURAL VALUES AND INCOMMENSURABILITY

Consequentialism, in general, and Utilitarianism, in particular, are very elastic moral theories that can be stretched in all sorts of directions in order to encompass many supposedly non-utilitarian values into the conception of social utility. For example, the utilitarian economist, Harsanyi, wrote that 'any reasonable utilitarian theory must recognise that people assign a non-negligible positive utility to free personal choice, to freedom from unduly burdensome moral standards trying to regulate even the smallest detail of their behaviour' (Harsanyi, 1982:60). Thus if the maximisation of utility appears to violate personal choice this is no problem; one merely has to treat the violation of personal choice as a deduction from the overall net utility that that particular course of action may have yielded.

All of the concerns discussed above – such as justice or special obligations – can be, and sometimes have been, dealt with by simply extending the concept of 'utility' to encompass them. In this case the means adopted to promote some particular consequences – namely a violation of somebody's 'rights' – would be evaluated in utility terms. It would be argued that the value of respect for 'rights' resides only in the contribution that such respect will indirectly make to society's 'utility'. The same sort of argument could be used to incorporate respect for 'special obligations' in the concept of utility.

But if almost every consequence of any choice – however indirect – could be brought under the heading of utility, the scope for differences of opinion about how much any action contributes to the wider concept of utility will be so great that the theory will add very little to our guidance to ethical action. It would mean diluting the concept of utility to homeopathic levels. Everybody will differ in their conception of 'the utility' that is to be maximised. Hence, if the concept of 'utility' is to retain any distinctive meaning that is a helpful guide to policy it has to be defined along reasonably restricted lines, such as the classical definition in terms of some fairly homogeneous concept of 'happiness'. And this has to be distinguished from other values such as freedom, equality, justice, integrity and friendship.

For example, if, say, the government of some country have to weigh up their obligations to promote the welfare of their own citizens against the desire to maximise world utility, it does not help to say 'Oh, that's no problem. Just add the utility of your own citizens to the world utility that you ought to maximise, and then you can simply trade off one against the other'. 'Oh, of course!' explains the politicians, ' How silly of us not to have thought of that at once! But, while you are here, could you please tell us how to determine the weights?' Or suppose the authorities are trying to judge whether, in the interests of freedom, society should permit the dissemination of dangerous propaganda and false information that they believe are extremely likely to reduce society's total utility as conventionally defined. It they are told 'What's the problem? Just redefine "utility" to include the value of freedom and it will all be simple. You could then just trade off one bit of utility against another'. This might not matter if all the values that are brought under the umbrella of 'utility' were commensurate with each other. But they are not. Hence, 'trade-off' would not be an appropriate term for the resolution of the conflict of values. As Steven

Lukes has put it, a more appropriate concept in some contexts would be 'sacrifice' rather than 'trade-off'.[11]

It is the incommensurability that is the crux of the problem. It is this incommensurability of 'plural values' that provides perhaps the main challenge to Utilitarianism, as well as to any attempts to present a unique system of moral theory. If the different values are *incommensurate*, then, whether or not one can put them under the 'utility' label, it cannot be claimed that Utilitarianism still provides a simple and handy means of reconciling conflicting values and the different ethical intuitions that are attached to them. In other words, an attempt simply to stretch 'utility' to encompass incommensurate values would be stretching it beyond breaking point. The concept of 'plural values' refers to basic values that are *incommensurate* with each other and with the classical concept of utility that is identified with 'happiness'. Indeed, one could regard the term 'plural values' as just another term for 'incommensurate values'.

There has been extensive and subtle discussion in the philosophical literature of the concept of *incommensurability* which I shall not attempt to review.[12] But the basic idea is that values (or options of any kind) are 'incommensurate' if they cannot be compared in terms of some common and relevant metric. They are regarded as being *qualitatively* different, so although an increase of any one of these values may add to a 'good life' it will add to a *different* 'good life'. Hence, if some values are fundamentally incommensurate, forcing them into some elastic concept of utility or welfare is an illusion. It merely serves to disguise the fact that where there is some conflict between them – as there frequently is – it cannot be resolved by converting them into some common units of utility and then evaluating the relevant trade-offs.

It is, of course, intellectually attractive to try to force the different kinds of reasons one could advance in favour of one course of action rather than another under one umbrella, namely 'utility'. Sen has recently drawn our attention to the way that 'Adam Smith complained more than two hundred years ago about the tendency of some theorists to look for a single homogeneous virtue in terms of which all values that we can plausibly defend could be explained'.[13] He quotes the passage from Smith's *The Theory of Moral Sentiments* in which Smith refers to ' . . . a propensity, which is natural to all men, but which philosophers in particular are apt to cultivate with a peculiar fondness, as the great means of displaying their ingenuity, the propensity to account for all appearances from as few principles as possible' (ibid.).

4   INCOMMENSURABILITY AND RATIONAL CHOICE

The fact that in personal and public life decisions are made when faced with difficult choices does not mean that, in the end, some precise commensurate numeraire has been found that helps us trade off the conflicting values involved. Sometimes life confronts us with 'tragic choices' where whatever choice we make will lead to violation of some important value and there is no way the alternatives can be compared in quantitative terms. And the fact that some options are strictly *incommensurate* in the sense that they cannot be compared in terms of some relevant metric does not invalidate the economist's concept of rational choice. This is because there is nothing necessarily irrational about ranking options that are fundamentally incommensurate. The axioms of rational choice described in Chapter 4 do not rely on commensurability. Only *comparability* is required. By definition one cannot 'rank' options unless one can 'compare' them. So ranking choices in order of preference only requires *comparability*, not *commensurability*.

True, incommensurability means that CBA cannot be given a decisive role in any practical problem, but we have already reached that conclusion anyway, on other grounds. Rational decision criteria do not have to be expressed in terms of the maximisation of a smooth, continuous, twice-differentiable utility function. Incommensurability thus limits the role of precise mathematical expression of the conditions for optimal choice. It implies that rational choice has to be seen as maximisation of a utility function subject to some constraints, which may be certain values that cannot be pushed kicking and screaming into units of utility and hence incorporated into the utility function that is to be maximised. And, as a rule, these values cannot be quantified in any terms at all, so that the mathematical tools of maximisation of a function subject to constraints that can be quantified are also inappropriate. There are no 'Langrangian multipliers' that can be calculated as part of the maximisation process.

Of course, sometimes it may appear impossible to rank some option as being higher or lower than some other option. In the example given in Chapter 4 some of the characteristics of the career choices facing our student, such as salary, were easily commensurate. But others – such as how interesting would be the work or how satisfying would be the prestige – would not be *commensurate*. But they would be *comparable*. The student would not have to stay undecided for the rest of his life on account of an inability to choose which career he would prefer to follow.

And even if he found that these two features of the options were evenly balanced, some other consideration would eventually occur to him, or turn up, that would push him to choose one or the other. This might be, for example, the discovery of some feature of the location of the two careers, or a desire to placate (or to spite) his parents. In short, several values may be relevant in rational decision-making even if they cannot be incorporated in the precise framework of a numerical CBA. Reason should still play a crucial role in the decisions. It is simply that reason does not imply simple mechanical application of a single basic value.

At the level of public policy, for example, it is unlikely that a strict CBA by a rich country of giving aid to some poor country devastated by an earthquake or storms would be positive. In such cases other, *non-Paretian,* criteria would be invoked, such as humanitarian considerations, or respect for international obligations. Many countries carry out projects in the interests of national prestige, as when they spend money on projects such as building millennium domes or hosting the Olympic Games. In such cases even though costs may exceed the benefits the projects may still deserve to be carried out. The contrasting situation is where some non-economic value could also outweigh a favourable CBA. This would be the case, for example, in connection with the probable favourable CBA of the practice in Ancient Rome of throwing Christians and other troublemakers to the lions.

There are many instances, therefore, where a decision must take account of non-economic and probably incommensurate criteria. The use of CBA in many situations does not mean that it is the only input into the decision-making process. As has often been said, 'CBA is a decision tool, not a decision rule'. It provides some indication of the net cost to society of subscribing to the values in question. For example, if it were found that half of our national income would have to be used in order to avoid the extinction of some particular species of bird in a remote part of the country, one might sacrifice the birds. But at the other extreme, if a small amount of money would prevent the wholesale disappearance of the entire British bird population, most people would be willing to preserve the birds. It should not, however, be thought that concern to preserve a particular species of bird (or beetle or whatever) illustrates a compassionate concern for the birds in question. It is highly unlikely that a bird that is being pursued by a huntsman is likely to suffer more if it thinks it is almost the last surviving member of his species than if it thinks 'Oh, what the hell. There are millions of other birds of my species still around'.

In this bird extinction example one would avoid the extremes and concede that somewhere in between there might be a point at which the decision would be very difficult. This is why economists tend to dislike lexical orderings. We are concerned with identifying marginal costs and benefits as far as is feasible. And the balance to be struck could be the economic costs of saving the birds against some other value that may be difficult or impossible to quantify. But it is an illusion to think that a utilitarian calculus enables the balance can be struck in a precise manner.

5   CONCLUSIONS

Given that Utilitarianism has been the most influential moral theory to have been developed in the Western world over the last two centuries or more, and is still – in one form or another – one of the most widely accepted moral theories, it is inevitable that a vast literature about it has accumulated. Some of this has taken the form of refinements, additions, expositions and defences of one kind or another. And some of it has consisted of criticism.

I shall not attempt to summarise all the main criticisms since many admirable expert critical surveys are available. But for the purposes of its role in economic analysis the most important criticism concerns the utilitarian assumption that all values can be made commensurate with each other and with a unique basic value, 'utility'. If, instead, it is accepted that there are independent plural values – such as freedom, personal integrity, loyalty, truth, personal relationships, duty, and so on – that are incommensurate, Utilitarianism can no longer command a monopolistic position in moral theory. This limits the role in economic theory of the maximisation of utility functions. Instead a place has to be given for other independent intrinsic values such as those mentioned above at various points. As I have emphasised in Chapter 3, such values cannot be confirmed or refuted by any scientific and objective observation.

NOTES

1. Nozick, 1974: *ix*.
2. See, for example, the various contributions to Scheffler, S. [(ed.) 1988], such as those by Nagel, Nozick, Scanlon, Sen, Williams and others, to make a rather random selection. Reference to 'agent-relative' concepts of 'the

good' is also made by Broome, in a carefully articulated discussion of inter-generational justice and discounting, in Broome, 1992:42–43 and *passim*.

3. Hume. 1739:3.2.2.10 and 3.2.11.18. He also gives a detailed account of why we tend to attach less value to distant benefits than to present benefits in *ibid*.3.3.7.2, and why this is a regrettable weakness.

4. Blackburn, 2009:55.

5. Hume, 1739:3.2.2.9.

6. *Ibid.*: 3.2.2.24.

7. For example, *ibid.*:1739:3.2.1.27.

8. Binmore, 2005:ix.

9. However, as some philosophers have argued, it would be wrong to interpret this as meaning that Hume did not attach normative significance to his description of the development of moral beliefs or that he failed to spell out the normative basis for a moral system anchored in human nature. See, for example, Hunter, G. 'Hume on *is* and *ought*', and others in a distinguished collection of contributions on this subject to Hudson (ed.), 1969.

10. See Gauthier, 1986.

11. Lukes, 1997.

12. For a compendium of different views on incommensurability and an extremely helpful and illuminating survey one could hardly do better than begin with Chang, R., (ed.), 1997.

13. Sen, 2009:394.

PART II

Applications

CHAPTER 11

GDP and Friends

1   LIMITATIONS ON THE NATIONAL INCOME CONCEPT

Probably few topics in applied economics are given more attention in the media and in public debate than the growth of 'national income', or two related concepts, namely gross national product (GNP) and gross domestic product (GDP).[1] All three concepts are approximate measures of how much income a country produces each year. Most people will have seen or heard claims about which country has the highest GDP per head, or the fastest growth rate of GDP and so on. At the same time there has been growing criticism of the national income concept as a measure of 'welfare'. In the last five decades or so all the advanced countries of the world experienced historically unprecedented rates of economic growth, so that *per capita* real incomes soon reached levels that were way above those of the prewar period. Yet this remarkable rise in prosperity, as conventionally measured, did not seem to be accompanied by a corresponding rise in people's sense of well-being or 'happiness'.

Over the first two decades after the war the most obvious changes in the quality of life were an increased awareness of environmental pollution. This included air pollution, both local and global. Water pollution also rose sharply – and often visibly – in many places. Noise – particularly noise near airports or motorways – also seemed to be on the increase. At the same time, crimes of violence were increasing in many cities of the world, as were other manifestations of social disorder, in general, or of urban deterioration, in particular.

© The Author(s) 2017
W. Beckerman, *Economics as Applied Ethics,*
DOI 10.1007/978-3-319-50319-6_11

Of course, there had also been many improvements in aspects of welfare that are not directly reflected in GDP, such as advances in medical treatment and a dramatic increase in life expectancy, job security, leisure and the conditions of work and housing for the vast majority of working class people in the more advanced countries. And during the last two or three decades there have been some substantial improvements in local urban pollution in many cities in developed countries as a result of legislation, such as the Clean Air Acts introduced in Britain in the 1950s, and greatly increased public expenditure on methods to reduce harmful effluents into water courses. Nevertheless, people seem to be more conscious of the possible harmful effects of economic growth and ignore the great benefits that it has also brought. Few people take to heart the words of a popular 1940s song:

You gotta accentuate the positive
Eliminate the negative
Latch on to the affirmative
And don't mess with mister in between

2   ECONOMISTS AND THE GDP-WELFARE LINK

The aforementioned developments naturally led many people to question the extent to which the conventional measures of national income provided a good indicator of how much we were really better off and for how much longer could any improvement be sustained. One person whose position of power enabled him to take account of the discrepancy between GDP and 'happiness' was General Surayud Chulanont, the former army chief of Thailand, who was appointed interim prime minister of that country in October 2006 and who proclaimed that 'We won't concentrate so much on the GNP numbers.... We would rather look into the indicators of people's happiness and prosperity'.[2] Indeed, given (i) recent scholarly research that claims to have identified a positive correlation between measures of 'happiness' and the extent to which people enjoyed satisfactory sex lives, and (ii) Thailand's wide reputation – deserved or not – as a country where people lead particularly satisfying sex lives, it is quite possible that the switch of emphasis would raise Thailand's ranking relative to other countries.[3] However, since the scope for technical progress in the activity regarded as being one in which Thailand had a comparative advantage is severely limited, Thailand's growth rate of happiness would probably be reduced relative to other countries. In any case, recent political developments in that country suggest that if variables relating to political institutions could be adequately represented in the 'happiness' index, the result might be unwelcome to its rulers.

Economists are routinely accused of being misled by their alleged subservience to the national income concept. But, in fact, economists have always known that national income was not a good measure of 'welfare' in the wider sense of the word. At best national income as measured has always been recognised as being only a measure of *economic* welfare. The great economist, Pigou, pointed out in 1920 – that is, about fifty years before the critics began to point out that national product was not identical to total welfare – that 'Hence, the range of our inquiry becomes restricted to that part of social welfare that can be brought directly or indirectly into relation with the measuring-rod of money. This part of welfare may be called economic welfare' and '...there is no guarantee that the effects produced on the part of welfare that can be brought into relation with the measuring-rod of money may not be cancelled by effects of a contrary kind brought about in other parts, or aspects, of welfare.... The real objection then is, not that economic welfare is a bad index of total welfare, but that an economic cause may affect non-economic welfare in ways that cancel its effect on economic welfare'.[4]

Much later an eminent American economist, the late Arthur Okun, put the issue very clearly in writing that

> It is hard to understand how anyone could seriously believe that GNP could be converted into a meaningful indicator of total social welfare. Obviously, any number of things could make the Nation better off without raising its real GNP as measured today: we might start the list with peace, equality of opportunity, the elimination of injustice and violence, greater brotherhood among Americans of different racial and ethnic backgrounds, better understanding between parents and children and between husbands and wives, and we could go on endlessly. To suggest that GNP could become *the* indicator of social welfare is to imply that an appropriate price tag could be put on changes in all of these social factors from one year to the next...it is...asking the national income statistician to play the role of a philosopher-king, quantifying and evaluating all changes in the human scene. And it is absurd to suggest that, if the national income statistician can't do that job, the figure for GDP is not interesting. (Okun, 1971)

A few years later an official Australian government report repeated the point at length, stating that '...no one familiar with the construction of estimates of what was then called the G.N.P. would think of attaching to them the significance that was being attached to them by many users'.[5]

3   VALUES IN THE GDP CONCEPT

Quite apart from non-economic elements of total welfare, such as those mentioned by Okun earlier, there are also many technical weaknesses in the measurement of GDP that most economists know about. These include the practical difficulties of accurately measuring certain types of transaction, or the exclusion from the estimates of housewives' services, or the services that people obtain from the consumer durables that they own. Another problem is that a measure of *aggregate* GDP or national income by itself is of no interest. It is only interesting in comparison with GDP in some other period or some other country, after making allowance, of course, for differences in population. And such comparisons only make sense if proper adjustment is made for price differences. But the proper construction of index numbers for purposes of making price comparisons over time or space is also fraught with conceptual and practical difficulties. As the 'Stiglitz Commission' report points out,

> There are now many products whose quality is complex, multi-dimensional and subject to rapid change. This is obvious for goods, like cars, computers, washing machines and the like, but is even truer for services, such as medical services, educational services, information and communication technologies, research activities and financial services. In some countries and some sectors, increasing "output" is more a matter of an increase in the quality of goods produced and consumed than in the quantity.[6]

And there is no fully satisfactory method of adjusting for changes in the quality of some goods, let alone services.

There are other limitations on the welfare implications even of comparisons of aggregate GDP over time or between countries. For they do not show how total national expenditure is distributed, either among different groups of people or between different uses to which the economy's resources are put. For example, the GDP of an economy that devotes an excessive proportion of its resources to the means by which it can kill people – either specific classes of its own citizens or in the course of aggressive wars against foreigners – cannot be a good indicator of welfare of its citizens.

Furthermore, leaving aside comparisons, the measurement of aggregate GDP does not discriminate between people with respect to the differences in the welfare that they obtain from a given unit of income on account of differences in their income levels. A pound sterling accruing to a rich person is counted as having the same value as a pound to a poor person. In an early path-breaking analysis of the value judgements in welfare economics, Graaff went as far as to say we ought to dispense with the time-honoured distinction between the size and the distribution of national income since, he argued, '...we do not know what the size is until we know the distribution' (Graaff, 1967:92).

Another weakness in the link between GDP and economic welfare is the arbitrariness of the boundary line between those productive activities that give rise directly to *final* output (which is a measure of GDP) and those that produce *intermediate* output – that is, goods and services that are not wanted for their own sake but in order to be 'used up' in the course of some subsequent stage in the productive process. For example, some economists would subscribe to the view that a large part of public expenditures, such as general administration, law and order, and so on, are really 'inputs' into the productive system, since without them the whole productive system could not function as it does. Many household expenditures could also be considered to be intermediate products. Many people, for example, have to commute to their work, and this expense can be considered an intermediate cost related to earning a living.[7]

4   'MEASURABLE ECONOMIC WELFARE'

One response to such limitations on national income as a good measure of welfare was the pioneering attempt, by Nordhaus and Tobin in 1972, to estimate what they called 'measurable economic welfare'. For this purpose they excluded 'regrettable necessities', such as defence expenditures, as well as the estimated monetary equivalent of certain disamenities, such as those arising out of environmental damage or urbanisation and congestion. As regards the 'regrettable necessities' Nordhaus and Tobin wrote that '...we see no direct effect of defence expenditures on households' economic welfare. No reasonable country (or household) buys "national defence" for its own sake. If there were no war or risk of war, there would be no need for defence expenditures and no one would be the worse without them'.[8]

Of course, the same sort of reasoning applies to almost any component of GDP. Nobody would want accident and emergency departments in hospitals, or even home first-aid kits, for their own sake. They are only required because of the risk of accidents. Seat belts in automobiles are required not for their own sake, but to prevent injury in accidents. It is not possible to draw logical distinctions of the Nordhaus-Tobin kind between the purposes served by various goods. If they are wanted they are wanted, and that is the end of the matter. If there were no winters, there would be no need for winter woollies or heating expenditure; if one never had toothache there would be no need to visit the dentist. For very poor people, even food, after all, is merely required in order to offset the pain of being hungry and dying of starvation. Surely it is not to be argued that in such cases the food in question (or other similar basic essentials) should *not* be included in GDP and that we should include only the more frivolous inessentials. If so, this runs quite counter to another popular view to the effect that much of the growth of GDP as measured is misleading because it includes so many of the items that we do not really *need*. In other words, some people argue that we should exclude from a welfare-oriented measure of GDP the goods that we do not really need. And others – including, apparently, Nordhaus and Tobin – argue that we should exclude the goods that we *do* really need since these are regrettable necessities.[9]

In fact, Nordhaus and Tobin gave the game away when they wrote 'Maybe all our wants are just regrettable necessities; maybe productive activity does no better than satisfy the wants which it generates; maybe our net welfare is tautologically zero'. Of course, Shakespeare made the same point three centuries earlier when he put into King Lear's mouth the words:

O, reason not the need! Our basest beggars
Are in the poorest thing superfluous.
Allow not nature more than nature needs –
Man's life is cheap as beast's.

(Shakespeare, *King Lear* Act II. Sc. 4)

5   Other Measures of 'Well-Being'

One of the responses to increasing dissatisfaction with GDP as an indicator of well-being has been the development of various alternative measures of well-being or some aspects of it. Instead of attempting to adjust GDP estimates along the Nordhaus/Tobin lines, there have been broadly two alternative approaches. One consists of indices of specific components of well-being – often known as 'social indicators' – such as longevity, or education levels, which may or may not be incorporated in some aggregate index of 'well-being'. The other is based on direct surveys of people's subjective feelings of 'well-being' or '*happiness*'. The latter approach is discussed in the next chapter. Here we shall concentrate on the former approach.

As indicated already, GDP estimates are not expected to encompass many important components of well-being that are not the subject of market activities and that cannot easily be measured as proxies for market activities. These include, for example, literacy, health indicators, standards of housing and access to public facilities, personal relationships, political freedom, leisure, and so on. Consequently various other indicators of components of what the Stiglitz Commission's report calls 'the quality of life' have been constructed.[10] This report points out ' . . . the time is ripe for our measurement system to *shift emphasis from measuring economic production to measuring people's well-being*'. It goes on to say that 'But emphasising well-being is important because there appears to be an increasing gap between the information contained in aggregate GDP data and what counts for common people's well-being'.[11] The report emphasises that ' . . . the information relevant to valuing quality of life goes beyond people's self-reports and perceptions to include measures of their "functionings" and freedoms'. In effect, what really matters are the capabilities of people, which is discussed in more detail in Section 6. Basically, capabilities represent the extent of people's opportunity sets and of their freedom to choose among them the life they value. The choice of relevant functionings and capabilities for any quality of life measure is a value judgement, rather than a technical exercise. But while the precise list of the features affecting quality of life inevitably rests on value judgements, there is a consensus that quality of life depends 'on people's health and education, their everyday activities (which include the right to a decent job and housing), their participation in the political process, the social and natural environment in which they live, and the factors shaping their personal and economic security'.[12]

One of the most widely quoted and most sophisticated index of some concept of well-being is the *Human Development Report*, which has been published annually by the United Nations Development Programme since 1990. These publications contain a wealth of data for most countries on items such as education (including women's access to education), health profiles (including infant mortality rates and life expectancy), environmental conditions, a human poverty index, national income, the labour market and even a 'profile of political life'.

The *Human Development Reports* also show an aggregate 'Human Development Index' (HDI). The construction of this index has changed somewhat over the years, but basically it is a simple average of three sub-indices, namely life expectancy, education, and GDP. But all aggregative indices raise the question 'how should one weight together the constituent items?' With GDP the answer has a clear – if imperfect – conceptual basis. For the weights attached to the various component flows of goods and services entering into the total GDP figure are the prices of the goods and services concerned. And these are supposed to reflect roughly the (marginal) value attached to the goods by consumers. Countries differ with respect to how they want to distribute their expenditures between, say, hospitals, education, the preservation of law and order, the protection of the environment, investment in productive facilities and private consumption. How they choose will depend on their private and social values and the relative costs of the alternatives. GDP estimates combine these choices in a way that indicates, if imperfectly, each society's preferences and relative costs.

There is, of course, no objective basis for weighing together the components of aggregative indices of welfare or human development. The weights must reflect value judgements, which can vary from person to person. There is no objective way of weighing together, say, a change in the environmental conditions associated with a rise in local air pollution, a rise in the literacy rate, and a change in longevity. As pointed out in earlier chapters, the concept of aggregate welfare is open to serious objections if one accepts the incommensurability of plural values. If one person says that GDP constitutes two thirds of welfare, and another says it is only one third, as in the HDI estimates, they are not making positive statements about the real world; they are making statements about their value judgements.

There is also room for much discussion concerning the principles that should govern the choice of the detailed components of aggregates, such as a 'Health Profile'. For example, how far ought they to be related to 'outputs', such as the incidence of various diseases or mortality rates, as well as 'inputs', such as numbers of doctors and nurses relative to the size of the population (particularly since, in some countries, it is very debatable how far more doctors lead to better health). There is no clear conceptual basis for avoiding double-counting as there is in national income estimates.

Nevertheless, many of the individual indicators of specific aspects of human development and welfare that have been developed over the last few decades do fill an important gap in the statistical basis for assessing different countries' levels of welfare and development. The individual indicators are often of great interest in themselves and are valuable supplements to GDP data. Conversely, although GDP may well be a bad measure of total well-being, it is an important component of it. Furthermore in most countries it will still be fairly safe to assume that large changes in 'real' (i.e. adjusted for prices changes) national income will correspond to large changes in economic welfare as well as corresponding changes in various components of GDP, such as consumption of various goods and services, public investment in the economy's infrastructure, the possibilities of devoting resources to innumerable desirable ends, such as health, education, housing and the major constituents of personal consumption, and so on. This is the case even in relatively developed countries, as is illustrated by the following example. In the twenty years following the overthrow of the communist regime in Poland, GDP increased by 78%, and life expectancy increased from 70.7 years to 75.6 years. The direction of causality was certainly not from the latter to the former since most people over the age of 70 no longer contribute to GDP.

6   HUMAN DEVELOPMENT AND 'CAPABILITIES'

Many of the indicators included in the HDI are indicators of the concept of 'capabilities', and vice versa. This concept, which has been developed by Amartya Sen, and to which important contributions have also been made by Martha Nussbaum and others, is applicable to a wide variety of fields, such as development economics, social policy and theories of distributive justice (as discussed in the next chapter). According to the 'Stiglitz Commission' report, the 'capability approach' conceives a person's life as a combination of various 'doings and beings', which Sen calls 'functionings', and of his or her freedom to choose among these functionings, which he calls 'capabilities'. The concept of 'capabilities' can provide a conceptual umbrella for a wide variety of non-monetary indicators that reveal how far people have opportunities to do the things they want to do and to lead the best lives they can lead subject to the constraints on their innate abilities.[13]

A person's 'doings' and 'beings' include working and enjoying leisure activities, and engaging in a rewarding social life. The distinction between these achieved 'functionings' and 'capabilities' is a distinction between the 'doings' or 'beings' that people actually achieve and the effective opportunities open to them to achieve them. Sen summarises the distinction as follows: 'The *capability* of a person reflects the alternative combinations of functionings the person can achieve and from which he or she can choose one collection. The approach is based on a view of living as a combination of various "doings and beings," with quality of life to be assessed in terms of the capability to achieve valuable functionings'.[14] Some of these capabilities may be quite elementary, such as being adequately nourished and escaping premature mortality, while others may be more complex, such as having the literacy required to participate actively in political life.

Some deficiencies in capability may not be socially determined, as, for example, in the case where some disease or food allergy makes a person '...unable to achieve the capability of avoiding nutritional deficiency even with an amount of the food that would suffice for others' (*op.cit.* p. 317). There is no generally agreed precise list of what variables are important in different situations. Indeed, it is generally accepted that the list of capabilities that would be relevant in the analysis of poverty in poor countries would be much more restricted than a list that would be appropriate in wealthy countries. In the former, for example, the capabilities that would be relevant would be those discussed in the operationally important pioneering concept of 'basic needs' developed notably by Paul Streeten and others at the World Bank in the early 1980s.[15] According to Martha Nussbaum, the concept of capabilities goes back even earlier; over 2,000 years earlier in fact, namely to Aristotle (Nussbaum, 2000). (But the same can be said of most contemporary ideas in ethics and political philosophy.)

Sen gives various examples of his concept of capability. One example, which is socially determined and is particularly important in poor countries, is education and basic literacy. In some countries, such as India, lack of both is particularly widespread among women. As a result not only are they deprived of opportunities in the conventional sense – for example, qualifications for certain occupations – but they are inevitably limited in their horizons and their ambitions. They may, as a result, not be as lacking in welfare as would be an educated person because they will not even share the aspirations to achieve their potential as would an educated person. 'For the welfarist, such an illiterate person need not be seen as deprived, but from the point of view of freedom... the positions of the literate and the illiterate persons are not the same'.[16]

Consequently the capability approach contrasts sharply with the subjective measures of self-reported 'happiness' or 'well-being' that have been used in various surveys. For it is quite possible that, in many situations, people may feel more or less content with their life unaware of the possibility of leading a more creative and fulfilling life if they had possessed the capabilities to do so, such as education, or the absence of gender discrimination, or better healthcare and so on. The usual survey data on measures of 'happiness' or 'well-being' are essentially measures of mental states. Sen's concept of capabilities goes beyond that and encompasses some of the aspects of a person's condition that determine the mental state that he can achieve.

The capability approach has spawned a vast literature, explanatory, complementary and critical. Some writers have questioned how far it is operational given the data limitations. Indeed, from a purely conceptual point of view the notion of a 'capability' to perform some functioning is a counterfactual one. It would be difficult to find evidence to prove the causal relationship between certain capabilities and the assumed resulting functionings. In addition to disagreements over certain functionings, people will differ in the importance they would attach to different capabilities. However, further progress will no doubt be made over the years in improving the conceptual basis of the concept and its relationship to empirical data on what aspects of their lives are most valuable to people.

Contrary to the spirit of concepts such as 'capabilities', there have been some attempts to cater for the general predilection for combining social indicators into some aggregative indices that can be used to make simple comparisons between countries or over time. Major differences between countries, or over time, in such indices are probably significant, but one has to be aware of misplaced precision. And one must also be cautious in using some indices that appear to make highly contentious claims.

For example, one frequently quoted index is the 'Happy Planet Index' (HPI).[17] This does not, as the name might suggest, purport to be an index of how happy the planet Earth is by comparison with, say, Mars or other planets. The authors of this index do not attribute to planets sensations of 'happiness' that are normally associated only with sentient creatures, though they get close to it in describing their objectives as 'We work in partnership and put people and the planet first' (presumably meaning that there was a dead heat between the two and that they actually shared first and second place).

This index is actually a ratio, for each country, of its 'Happy Life Years' and its carbon footprint. It is thus presented as a sort of index of the 'efficiency' with which a country uses up the environment in order to achieve its particular level of well-being. The numerator in the ratio, namely the figure of 'Happy Life Years' in each country, is a combination of (i) the responses people make, in four different surveys, to questions about how far the people are more or less satisfied with their lives, and (ii) life expectancy. In principle, this seems to be not a bad idea. But the difficulty – as the authors acknowledge – is that the interpretation of the surveys implies a purely subjective judgement as to what constitutes 'happiness'. The implications of this become very clear when one looks at the results. The latest results covering all the world show that the top country is Costa Rica, and the top ten countries in the index are mainly from Latin America. The highest developed country is The Netherlands, which ranks 43rd. The UK ranks 74th. Yet few people emigrate from the developed countries to the 'happy' Latin American countries, while millions of people – often at great risk to their lives – are constantly trying to emigrate from allegedly happy poor countries to rich – if less happy – countries.

This illustrates one of the psychological points made in connection with variations in 'happiness' that is discussed in more detail in Chapter 12, namely people's capacity for adaptation to their circumstances. People who have immigrated into developed countries learn to put up with the 'bad' features of modern advanced societies, such as the beautiful parks, gardens, buildings, cultural facilities, health facilities, educational facilities, not to mention the material conveniences, and do not hanker for their lost simple life in the primitive sanitary conditions in many cities, the unspoilt environment including the rain forests (and the millions of species of beetles that they contain), that they used to find in their 'happier' countries of origin. They rarely want to return, such is the power of adaptation and 'habituation' as is emphasised in some of the results discussed in the next chapter. But the apparent conflict between the 'Happy Planet Index' and patterns of international migration also highlights the ambiguity of the concept of happiness. For – leaving aside the carbon footprint – it is quite likely that the happiness measured in the numerator of the index is not the only consideration that drives people to choose their location. People also want variety, choice, opportunity and challenges.

7   Is GDP a Useful Concept?

In view of the limitations on the welfare significance of conventional GDP measures, it might be asked 'what is the point of measuring GDP at all?' Alternatives, such as extended accounts or social indicators, may require lots of value judgements, but is GDP so much better that it is worth all the cost of estimating it and all the respect accorded to it? There are three good reasons for persisting with GDP estimates.

First, as long as GDP bears a rough relationship to one 'prudential value', namely *economic* welfare, it is the *only* component of welfare that has a wide coverage and that can be measured at all in a way that bears any clear theoretical relationship to some coherent theory of individual welfare. Hence, those who believe that total welfare is something that one should try to measure – if only approximately – should welcome this measure of one of its ingredients and should not reject it simply because nobody has yet solved the problem of measuring all the others.

Second, there is, of course, always room for improvement from the point of view of the statistical coverage and accuracy with which GDP is measured. For example, there may be a case for trying to take some account, in GDP estimates, of certain ingredients of welfare that have hitherto been regarded as unmeasurable in monetary terms. Work on social indicators is to be welcomed as a supplement to the conventional GDP estimates, but they do not make GDP estimates redundant or even misleading to those who know what these estimates really mean and what the real limitations on them are.

Third, even if GDP cannot measure 'welfare', it still has its uses. As indicated earlier, changes in output have important implications for the state of the economy in general and for certain aspects of it in particular, such as how much can be spent on, say, public transport or education or health, without excessive squeezing of investment or private consumption. GDP provides an indicator of what society has available to promote these, and other, constituents of well-being. Society can choose to use it wisely or badly. Higher GDP makes it easier to spend more on policies, such as mental health, that clearly have a direct effect on happiness. But in other ways it may be badly spent. It may well be that some of the choices made by richer societies are unwise. Increasing affluence leads to greater choice and the demands that this places on people may exceed their capacity to choose wisely (Aldred, 2009; Offer, 2006). On the other hand, freedom of choice is one of the most highly treasured of human values, so that one can make the value judgement that choice is intrinsically desirable. But whether, in fact, the increased choice that higher GDP tends to provide is worthwhile, given the other variables that affect people's 'happiness', is another value judgement that cannot be determined by any amount of measurement.

Finally, some mention must be made of 'sustainability' which is discussed in some detail in the Stiglitz Commission report. The estimates discussed previously refer only to welfare or its constituents (such as GDP) at the present point in time or in the past. But it is also important to have some idea of how far a country's level of welfare is likely to be maintained into the future. A country could enjoy a high or rising level of welfare at the cost of a substantial fall in future welfare. This could be caused by, say, a gradual depletion of its natural resource base that is not offset by increases in the stock of man-made capital and human capital. But the concept of 'sustainable development' is very difficult to pin down. It raises questions such as 'over what time period?' or 'under what circumstances?' Nevertheless, serious research has been carried out to provide some indicators of sustainability, and the Stiglitz Commission report includes a detailed survey of this research, and no attempt will be made in this book to make further comment on this survey.

8   CONCLUSIONS

Economists have always known that national income per head was not a comprehensive measure of welfare. At best it was a measure of only *economic* welfare, and there were many reasons – well-known to economists – why it was not even a flawless measure of that. Hence, the development of measures of other components of welfare has been very constructive. But the incommensurability of values means that the compilation of some aggregate index of welfare raises insuperable conceptual problems. However, social indicators (including those that relate to 'capabilities') and GDP estimates are not competitors. It is still important to work on ways of improving estimates of GDP and, in particular, of the way it changes over time. Hence, as the 'Stiglitz Commission report' points out, 'Despite deficiencies in our measures of production, we know much more about them than about well-being. Changing emphasis does not mean dismissing GDP and production measures. They emerged from concerns about market production and employment; they continue to provide answers to many important questions such as monitoring economic activity'.[18]

NOTES

1. GDP measures the 'product' (i.e. the unduplicated output) in the territory of the designated country, and GNP measures the product accruing to the nationals of that country, the difference being that GNP includes net income from abroad. For many years now the focus has been on GDP, and GNP has now been dropped from official British statistics and replaced by the term 'gross national income' (GNI). 'National income', which is GNI less depreciation of capital assets, is also a common unit of reference, since it is closer to what most people will feel is their actual income (before taxes and benefits). For a full description of the relationship between these and other closely related concepts see the Office of National Statistics, 2008.

2. Reported in the *Financial Times*, 2nd October 2006:6.

3. See Blanchflower and Oswald, 2004.

4. Pigou, A.C., 1932 edn:12.

5. Australian Government Treasury, 1973.

6. This is the *Report by the Commission on the Measurement of Economic Performance and Social Progress*, Paris, 2009:11. This commission, which was set up by the then President of France, comprised Joseph Stiglitz [chair], Amartya Sen and Jean-Paul Fitoussi.

7. See a discussion of these problems in Beckerman, 1980.

8. Nordhaus and Tobin, 1972. This argument implies that, even if it is believed that there is a risk of war, people *would* be worse off without the defence expenditures. Apart from hard-line pacifists, most people would dispute this.

9. See Usher, 1973, for an important critique of the Nordhaus and Tobin adjustments to the US growth rate, and Beckerman, 1978, for a discussion of this and his own estimates of adjusted 'measurable economic welfare' for a number of countries along both the Nordhaus/Tobin lines and the Usher lines.

10. Stiglitz *et al.* 2009.

11. *Ibid*:12.

12. *Ibid*:15.

13. See a list of ten basic capabilities, in Nussbaum, 2000.

14. Sen,1993:31. See also his 'Capability and Well-Being', in Sen and Nussbaum (eds.), 1993.

15. Streeten *et al.*, 1981; Streeten, 1984.

16. Sen, 1984:319.

17. This is produced by the New Economics Foundation.

18. Stiglitz, J., Sen, A., and Fitoussi, J.-P., 2009:para. 21.

CHAPTER 12

Well-Being and Happiness

1   WHY NOT JUST MEASURE 'HAPPINESS'?

In the quotation from David Hume in Chapter 3 of this book, when the man in his example is asked why he wants to earn more money he replies that it is a means by which he can procure more pleasure. In other words it had purely instrumental value to him. And this is no doubt the case for everybody except for a few fetishists who may worship money for its own sake. For many decades now it has been generally assumed that the intrinsic value to which money – or income or GDP – contributes is some wider concept such as 'happiness' or 'well-being'. The implication of this is that 'the benefits of a new policy should now be measured in terms of the impact of the change upon the happiness of the population. This applies whether the policy is a regulation, a tax change, a new expenditure, or a mix of all three. Initially at least, the authors recommend treating total public expenditure as politically chosen, but using evidence to show which pattern of expenditure would yield the most happiness' (World Happiness Report, 2012).

Of course, although there has been a proliferation of studies on the determinants of 'happiness', or some closely related concept, they do not make GDP redundant.[1] After all, insofar as income is suspected of having instrumental value in promoting happiness along the lines of the man in the David Hume example, it is important to know a bit more about how the link works. For example, there is considerable statistical evidence for the very important direct contribution to happiness made by various forms

© The Author(s) 2017

W. Beckerman, *Economics as Applied Ethics*,

DOI 10.1007/978-3-319-50319-6_12

of public expenditure, notably on mental health or public security. The same applies – if often less directly – to features of the tax system. For in view of statistical evidence for the contribution of marriage to happiness, a tax system that favoured married couples would also promote happiness.[2]

In Chapter 3 of this book I proposed that, although meta-ethical reservations have been raised by some philosophers, for the purposes of this book I intend to follow David Hume's distinction between 'value judgements' and 'positive propositions' (though he did not use these terms). So the next section will discuss the value judgement involved in selecting 'happiness' as the intrinsic value to which GDP would be instrumental. This will be followed by a section in which I discuss some of the empirical evidence for positive propositions about what factors are instrumental in promoting the particular conception of happiness used in these studies.

2   But What Is 'Happiness'?[3]

What sort of 'happiness' ought society to promote? What exactly is the value judgement behind the many assertions that 'happiness' ought to be the top-level intrinsic value to which GDP is merely one of the contributing factors? Do the proponents of this view have in mind some Buddhist conception of happiness in which people have learnt not to pursue the usual material and sensual satisfactions of life? I rather doubt it. (Pity, since some governments seem better at reducing economic growth rather than promoting it.) So what sort of happiness do they mean? At least we know what GDP is, more or less. But do we know what happiness is?

Strictly speaking, questions such as 'what is happiness?' are, of course, simply linguistic questions. 'Happiness' isn't anything. Or, to put it differently, there is no clearly identifiable 'thing' that is called 'happiness'. It is not something like the speed of light or the height of Mount Everest. The question 'what is happiness?' is really a way of asking 'how do people interpret the term 'happiness'?" Even if it can be shown that certain measurable physiological changes inside the brain are correlated with certain self-reported states of mind, one can challenge the assumption that self-reported states of mind correspond to the conception of the 'happiness' that ought to be the top-level objective of policy. This applies equally to the concept of 'well-being', which is more commonly used nowadays in statistical analysis since it usually suggests something unambiguously broader and less transitory than 'happiness'.

Nevertheless, although different people will probably interpret happiness or well-being differently, everybody will have some fairly similar idea of what they mean by these terms. After all, some roughly similar concept of happiness probably exists in every language. So the variation in their meaning between individuals or countries is probably not so great that it rules out attempts to discover what causes it. And during the last few years there has been an explosion of interest in the problem of what determines 'happiness' or 'well-being'.

But to carry out these statistical analyses of what factors determine happiness or well-being it has been necessary to settle on some measurable definitions of these concepts. Obviously there is no precise definition that would exactly match everybody's interpretation of the terms or which ones ought to be adopted as the top-level intrinsic value. The best one can hope for is to settle upon some sufficiently acceptable concepts of happiness that can be used in a statistical analysis of their relationship to certain determinants, such as income, health, personal relationships, marital status, age, social stability, freedom, and so on, and other variables that might be found to be correlated with the dependent variable as defined. So what reasonable concepts of happiness or well-being are on the market?

Innumerable definitions of 'happiness' have been in circulation since the early Greek philosophers.[4] In fact, for about 2,000 years or so until the eighteenth century the most widely accepted conceptions of happiness were prescriptive rather than simple descriptions of a particular mental state. To Greek philosophers, such as the Stoics, Plato and Aristotle, happiness corresponded one way or another to their particular conceptions of how a 'good' man should lead his life. This included respect for virtues, such as justice, integrity, courage, knowledge and social responsibility, rather than merely satisfaction of one's own personal desires. It also excluded 'bad' ways of deriving pleasure. For example, to Aristotle, a person who takes pleasure in what he regards as 'bad' activities, such as wanton cruelty or satisfaction of greed, is morally corrupt. This broader conception of happiness, known by the Greek word 'eudaimonia', thus indicates a sense of human fulfilment that goes beyond mere gratification of the senses. *It is a value judgement about what constitutes a 'good' person.*

At the same time the particular forms of behaviour that the Greek philosophers of that time believed to be constituents of their conceptions of 'happiness', such as justice, integrity, courage, and so on, were also believed to be valuable in their own right – like other examples of intrinsic plural values mentioned in earlier chapters of this book. And this plurality of values meant that there could be conflicts between them.

A very different conception of happiness was Bentham's concept of 'utility', which he introduced in the late eighteenth century, inspired – so he said – by his reading of David Hume. Bentham was not really concerned with private morality – that is, how a 'good man' ought to live. The value judgement that he made was about public, not private, morality. He was challenging prevailing ideas of *public* morality, such as 'Natural Law' or some form of 'Social Contract' or religious rules for conduct. He was chiefly interested in providing alternative guidance to legislation and public policy rather than saying how a 'good' person ought to behave. So Bentham's value judgements were very different from Aristotle's. First, it was the 'good' at which *society* ought to aim, not that of the individual. This 'good' was the maximisation of *society's* utility. Second, this was simply the sum of the utility of the individuals in that society. And third, he identified an individual's utility with his happiness, without passing moral judgements on how this utility was obtained.

Bentham's famous 1789 book, *An Introduction to the Principles of Morals and Legislation,* starts with the assertion that 'Nature has placed mankind under the governance of two sovereign masters, pain and pleasure. It is for them alone to point out what we ought to do, as well as to determine what we shall do. On the one hand the standard of right and wrong, on the other, the chain of causes and effects, are fastened to their throne' (i.e. they determined the value which we should promote and the way to do it). And he went on to identify pleasure and pain with 'happiness' when he wrote,

> By utility is meant that property in any object, whereby it tends to produce benefit, advantage, leisure, good, or happiness, (all this in the present case comes to the same thing) or, (what comes again to the same thing) to prevent the happening of mischief, pain, evil, or unhappiness to the party whose interest is considered: if that party be community in general, the happiness of the community: if a particular individual, then the happiness of the individual.[5]

Bentham has been criticised for adopting what is widely regarded as too narrow and undiscriminating a conception of an individual's utility/happiness. True, he did make several distinctions between different *degrees* of utility, such as their duration, intensity, certainty, and so on. But he did not pass moral judgements on the different ways that people derived pleasure. Not surprisingly, therefore, his conception of utility was found to be an inadequate basis for public morality by John Stuart Mill, as well as by most modern authorities (with the notable exception, perhaps, of Richard Layard). Mill is famous for introducing into the concept of an individual's utility the further crucial distinction, namely between higher and lower forms of utility.

This is, of course, generally regarded as essential in deciding what ought to be the proper objective of public policy. For example, Bentham had included in his list of 'The several simple pleasures of which human nature is susceptible.... The pleasures of sense'. And his list of these included 'The pleasure of intoxication.... The pleasure of the sexual sense' and others.[6] And neurological tests have now identified which parts of the brain are responsive to pleasurable or painful sensations. So suppose that it were established that these parts of the brain 'lit up' most when people experienced pleasures derived from drink, drugs or sadistic activities? It is unlikely that we would want the authorities to give priority to policies that promoted such forms of pleasure.

It is true that, apparently, the authorities in ancient Rome sometimes tried to keep the citizens happy by providing legendary 'bread and circuses' or other sources of momentary satisfaction. But a lot of things have changed since Nero died, and even since Bentham died (although this might come as a surprise to any visitor to University College London, who would see him sitting in the entrance hall). Modern democracies would hardly tolerate authorities that concentrated on keeping people momentarily happy by being 'high' on drink or drugs, or whatever is expected to make them momentarily happy. Instead, most people would go along with John Stuart Mill's value judgement, which was a mixture of Bentham and Aristotle. He accepted that the objective for society ought to be to maximise the sum of the utilities of individuals, but he also made the value judgement that some utilities were morally better than others.

And this changed the whole nature of the game. In effect Mill was passing Aristotelian moral judgements on how people should behave.

So are any value judgements implied by the contemporary conceptions of happiness that are used in empirical investigations of what determines it? It seems that they must have implicitly accepted the Benthamite judgement that society's objective ought to be to maximise the sum of individuals' happiness, given its population size. This might seem to be pretty obvious and uncontroversial, except to despots of one kind or another. Otherwise, why go to such trouble to find out what determines it? But it is a value judgement that seems to leave no room for passing judgement on exactly *how* people find happiness. This links to Amartya Sen's critique of what he calls 'welfarism', namely treating society's welfare as being simply the sum of individuals' welfares. So do contemporary happiness studies explicitly endorse the moral significance of any particular ways that individuals are made happier?

Not really. Recent studies – with minor variations and sub-divisions – have tended to focus on two classes of 'subjective' happiness. The first corresponds closely to questions about an individual's short-term emotional state. It can simply refer to the state of mind in some particular short period, such as the previous day, without attaching any moral significance to it. People will obviously vary in the extent to which, in the short term, their 'happiness' will be affected by different experiences, such as spending time with friends or family, sensual experiences, winning some money in a lottery, acquiring a new car, seeing a good film or attending a good concert, having a good day at the beach or the office, eating a particularly good meal, and so on and so forth. This shorter-term concept of happiness is sometimes described as 'hedonism', but is also known as 'emotional well-being'. It is also often broken down into two sub-sections, namely 'positive affect' and 'negative affect', which correspond roughly Bentham's distinction between pleasure and pain.

The second concept of happiness or well-being about which people are asked questions in most happiness surveys refers to a longer-term evaluation, or satisfaction with the way life is – or has been – going as a whole. Again, different people will attach different weights to factors such as personal relationships, work satisfaction, health, security, income, environment, the state of society around them, and so on.

In neither of these two main concepts of happiness are there any *explicit* value judgements about which sources of happiness are morally more commendable than others. But the value judgements are *implicit* in the choice of variables included in the statistical analyses. For example, no attempt is made to measure the contribution to individuals' happiness made by drink, drugs or sadistic practices.

3   THE OVERALL RESULTS[7]

As one would expect, the determinants of the two classes of well-being identified earlier are very different. Short-term emotional well-being is well explained by experiences in the day about which questions are put (usually about the preceding day). It is significant, for example, that people generally feel happier at weekends (though to an extent that depends on the character of their employment). By contrast 'life satisfaction' is much more related to less transitory differences in life circumstances.[8] And it is this that has been the concept of happiness on which most importance is generally attached in both happiness studies and in policy.

One of the most authoritative and detailed surveys of self-reported 'life satisfaction' is that contained in the *World Happiness Reports,* which have been published annually since 2012. These reports give the results of surveys of self-reported well-being, carried out all over the world by the Gallup World Poll, in which people are asked a question that in the English-language version is:

> Please imagine a ladder, with steps numbered from 0 at the bottom to 10 at the top. The top of the ladder represents the best possible life for you and the bottom of the ladder represents the worst possible life for you. On which step of the ladder would you say you personally feel you stand at this time? (This ladder is known as the Cantril ladder in honour of a pioneering study of this problem published by Cantril in 1965.)[9]

The 2015 edition of the World Happiness Report summarised its findings concerning life satisfaction as follows:

> Three-quarters of the differences among countries, and also among regions, are accounted for by differences in six key variables, each of which digs into a different aspect of life. The six factors are GDP per capita, healthy years of life expectancy, social support (as measured by having someone to count on in times of trouble), trust (as measured by a perceived absence of corruption in government and business), perceived freedom to make life decisions, and generosity (as measured by recent donations, adjusted for differences in income). Differences in social support, incomes and healthy life expectancy are the three most important factors, with their relative importance depending on the comparison group chosen. International differences in positive and negative emotions (affect) are much less fully explained by these six factors.

But in a survey by Andrew Oswald limited to industrial countries, GDP is not included among the determinant of happiness. He summarised the factors that contributed to happiness in industrialised countries as consisting of 'High social spending as a percentage of GDP; generous unemployment benefits, as a kind of social safety net; Clean air, namely, low pollution levels; Low unemployment and inflation rates; Low crime and corruption; Openness to trade; And possibly favourable genes (though this is still controversial).'[10]

The last item has to be considered because although several important determinants of international differences in life satisfaction have now been fairly firmly established, they by no means exhaust all these differences. In particular, it has been known – and constantly found in replication studies – that nations like Denmark and the Netherlands regularly head the league table of international life satisfaction, even after allowing for the effect of the usual identified determinants of international differences in happiness. And certain other countries, including high-GDP European countries such as France and Italy, come surprisingly far down in an international ranking after making allowance for the same determinants of happiness.[11]

Proto and Oswald provide evidence for the view that some of the observed differences can even be attributed to genetic differences between populations. They also note that one of the features of the data is that Denmark has an exceptionally low proportion of people who report themselves as being very unhappy. This raises a lot of interesting questions. For example, Proto and Oswald note there may be a significant externality effect at work. That is to say, it is possible that people who are very unhappy not only directly lower the average national level of happiness but also bring down the level of happiness of other people associated with them. Of course, the externality effect could work both ways. That is to say, an increase in happiness of certain individuals may raise the happiness of people who are associated with them one way or another. On the other hand, evidence of 'rivalry' may suggest that the happiness of some people may even reduce the happiness of others!

But, as suggested previously, while the increased attention to happiness in policy analysis in recent years is to be welcomed, the study of incomes and GDP is still relevant. For, as indicated earlier, the studies suggest that differences in average national incomes do contribute to the explanation of differences in happiness up to a certain level. But to what level, and by how much, and to what sort of happiness? The next section briefly surveys some of the findings.

4   DOES MORE INCOME MAKE PEOPLE HAPPIER?

Of course it does; at least for most people in the world. But only up to a point. And the point appears to depend on which of the two main elements of well-being is the dependent variable: life satisfaction or (shorter-term) emotional response. One of the earliest sophisticated studies of the link between incomes and some indicators of 'happiness' was the seminal article by Richard Easterlin in 1974.[12] He did not provide his own definition of the term 'happiness', but was using studies based on questions of the type: 'In general, how happy would you say that you are – very happy, fairly happy, or not very happy?' Almost all the subsequent empirical studies have also been based on individuals' self-reported happiness, but using the ten-point ladder scale described previously. In later articles Easterlin makes it clear that he '...takes the terms "well-being", "utility", "happiness", "life satisfaction", and "welfare" to be interchangeable...' – a Benthamite equivalence that would not nowadays be adopted by most contributors to this topic.

In his 1974 article Easterlin found that variations in self-reported happiness between people *within any country* at any point in time were correlated with their incomes, though the correlation was not very strong. And perhaps the most striking feature of Easterlin's 1974 findings was that, above a certain level, there was even less correlation *over time* between changes in the average income of a country and happiness. In other words, above a certain level of average income, countries that grew richer did not seem to become happier.

The most striking case usually quoted is Japan, where a sixfold rise in average incomes over the last few decades seems to have had no effect on average happiness. And in the USA the rise in incomes over recent decades has actually been accompanied by a decrease in happiness. But research by Blanchflower and Oswald shows the pitfalls of reading too much into aggregate data, since, for example, while average happiness has declined in the USA over the last quarter of a century, the picture is different if one looks at individual groups. The average happiness of Afro-Americans has risen, as has that of males as a group, but the happiness of women seems to have fallen.[13]

Nevertheless, between countries the correlation between reported happiness and incomes seemed to be significant up to about $10,000 per annum, but not above that level.[14] And although not too much significance should be attached to any precise figure, various studies appear to lend support to the so-called 'Easterlin Paradox'. The 'paradox' arises because there would appear to be a conflict between two sets of results. On the one hand, *within* any country, people with high incomes do seem to be happier than people with low incomes. But, on the other hand, above a certain level of income per head, richer countries do not seem to be happier than less rich countries, nor do they get happier as their average income rises even further over the course of time. The latter result suggests that that there is some saturation point at which further increases in income do not lead to increased happiness.

But some studies have disputed Easterlin's original findings. For example, in 2008 Stevenson and Wolfers claimed to have 'established a clear positive link between GDP and average levels of subjective well-being across countries with no evidence of a satiation point beyond which wealthier countries have no further increases in subjective well-being'.[15] They also claim that individual countries exhibit a positive relationship over time between income growth and their reported happiness.

An important contribution to the debate was the 2010 study by Kahneman and Deaton, although this was based only on households in the USA. Two aspects of their study that are particularly relevant here are (i) how the income variable ought to be measured; and (ii) insofar as there is a saturation point does it depend on whether one is talking about shorter-term emotional response or reflective life satisfaction.

As regards the former, they point out that the appropriate variable to use is not income, but the *logarithm* of income. This was because an extra $100 of income would make much more difference to the happiness of a poor man than to a rich income. And they found that, up to a high income level, an equal *proportionate* increase in income – that is, an equal increase in the logarithm of income – would produce a similar proportionate rise in happiness.[16]

But the Kahneman and Deaton findings confirmed that there did seem to be a saturation level of household income as far as short-term *emotional well-being* was concerned. This was still correlated with the log of income up to about $75,000 in the USA in the years 2006 to 2008. But *longer-term life evaluation* continued to rise with a rise in the log of household incomes up to about $120,000 or beyond.

Of course not much significance should be attached to the precise figures. As Kahneman and Deaton indicate in their detailed tables, the margin of error in these estimates is significant. Nor should much significance be attached to the difference between their estimates, which were based on household incomes in the USA at the beginning of this century and those associated with the original study by Easterlin, and which included a variety of cross-country studies a few decades earlier.

Meanwhile, the Easterlin Paradox seems to be alive and kicking – at least as far as emotional well-being is concerned, and possibly even to life satisfaction above a relatively high level of income. As indicated earlier, a

recent authoritative summary of the determinants of happiness in industrialised countries by Andrew Oswald does not even include income.
Consequently, the paradox has given rise to many attempts to explain it.

One of the most popular hypotheses advanced by Easterlin and others is
'the relative income hypothesis' (to use the term coined by James
Duesenberry in a pioneering study of the consumption function back in
1949). This is essentially that people's happiness depends partly on how
they compare themselves to other people. According to this 'rivalry'
hypothesis, what matters most to people is their position relative to other
people. Consequently, above a certain level when all that are regarded as
'essential' components of economic welfare have been more or less satisfied
– a level that will differ between countries, cultures and time periods – if
income continues to rise but relative positions do not change, a further rise
in income will not lead to any further increase in subjective happiness.
Within any country, richer people will always be happier on the whole
than poorer people, and above a certain level, further growth in all their
incomes will not lead to any increase in anybody's happiness.

In Fig. 12.1 two people, Mrs Jones and Mrs Brown, are shown. Mrs
Brown has a much higher level of income than does Mrs Jones. But she
also suffers from a much greater gap between her income and the level to

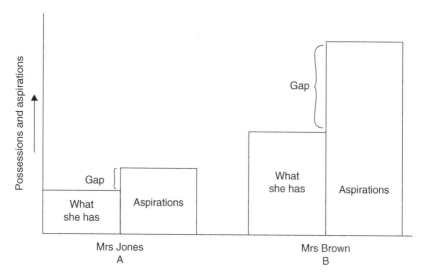

Fig. 12.1   Welfare: what you have and what you would like to have

which she aspires. The former may tend to make her happier and the latter may tend to make her unhappier. Which person would you prefer to be? The answer may be some weighted average of both variables.

In a well-known experiment a number of Harvard students were asked how they would choose between (i) earning $100,000 per annum while others got twice as much, or (ii) earning $50,000 while others got half as much. The majority of students chose the latter. Many other studies have confirmed this relative income hypothesis, such as the study by Clark and Oswald (1996) covering 10,000 British workers, which showed that absolute income had much less effect on happiness than did relative income.[17] It even appears that some people are made unhappier if somebody else in their own family earns a higher income. So much for family love and solidarity!

Another popular hypothesis to explain the Easterlin Paradox is in terms of 'adaptation' or 'habituation'. The idea is that while certain significant changes in one's life – such as winning a big prize or losing one's job – can, for a time, have a big effect on one's reported happiness, after a while people adapt. In the 'hedonic treadmill' version of this hypothesis, 'People adapt to improving economic conditions to the point that no real benefit in terms of higher happiness is attained'.[18] Kahneman and Deaton confirm this observation and report that 'Because of adaptation, the difference in well-being between two random individuals whose income differs by $100,000 is far less impressive than the joy and misery that these individuals would immediately experience were they to trade places'.[19]

This corresponds to a 'set point' theory of human psychology, according to which we are all largely genetically disposed to different levels of happiness, though our early environments may also influence this. For example, a study of twins who had been brought up in different environments indicated that only a small percentage of the differences in life satisfactions could be explained by the usual variables, such as socio-economic status, education, income and marital situation, leaving about 80% to be explained, perhaps, by genetic differences. The idea is that while some events in life may temporarily divert one from one's natural level of happiness, in the end one has a tendency to revert to it. After a while happy people will tend to be happy – up to a point – whatever their circumstances within reason, and unhappy people will tend to be unhappy however rich they are, or so we all like to believe.

And quite apart from adaptation to changes in one's environment, a similar type of behaviour may explain why self-reported happiness is sometimes found to be quite high among poor sections of poor countries if respondents have never experienced higher levels of income.

But the hypothesis that people adapt to changes in their circumstances does not seem to apply to *all* causes of happiness. Some of the identified causes of happiness show that while adaptation and habituation may apply to the influence of income on happiness, this 'set point' hypothesis does not apply – or at least not fully – to some major determinants of happiness, notably health and marital circumstances, as well as others, such as a noisy environment. This has been confirmed in various studies, such as the happiness levels of people who have been victims of accidents, or some other cause of disablement. These studies do not mean that there is *no* adaptation to accidents or serious disease, only that it is not complete. All such findings are very important for policy purposes. For while absolute levels of income may not have a very lasting effects on happiness (though Blanchflower and Oswald's 2004 paper appears to conflict with this view), various other influences on happiness seem to be within the domain of economic policy, as was argued forcibly by Layard in 2003.[20]

5   HAPPINESS AND POLICY

Since income is far from being the only direct determinant of happiness, one must consider how far the instruments of economic policy – notably taxes and public expenditures – ought to take more account of their indirect effects on happiness irrespective of their effects on national income. In other words, economic policy ought to go beyond conventional CBA. For example, mention has already been made of the possible effect of taxation systems on marriage rates, which seem to have significant effects of reported 'happiness'. Layard has placed particular emphasis on the case for greater efforts to deal with mental health, on the grounds that they will directly reduce a major source of unhappiness and increase people's capabilities to lead a fulfilling life. Furthermore, he argues that expenditures on better mental health provision would actually not impose a net economic cost on society, since improved health would reduce long-term unemployment and raise productivity.

Another possible important side effect of tax policy is its effect on people's trade-off between work and leisure. For it seems that, on account of 'rivalry', a general rise in incomes does not make people happier – at least up to a point – whereas more leisure usually does. Hence there is a *prima facie* case for discouraging people from working too much and

encouraging them to spend more time in leisure activities, such as culti-
vating their personal relationships. Furthermore, the 'rivalry' hypothesis
suggests that working harder in order to increase one's income imposes a
negative externality on other people. And, to economists, negative externalities are anathema and so ought to be taxed. (Of course, since incomes
are already taxed in most countries, this does not mean that taxes ought to
be raised everywhere even more than they are already.)[21]

On the other hand, inducing people to work less and take more leisure
will not make all of them happier and may even have the opposite effect.
Not all the people who are discouraged from 'excessive work' will spend
their extra spare time 'enjoying the company of friends and relatives,
writing sonnets and growing bonsai trees'. It is more likely that some of
them would try to achieve prestige and power over others in socially
undesirable ways, such as 'violence, competitive displays of excessive
risk-taking, the tribal rivalries of gangs and soccer hooligans etc.'[22] Some
of them may be simply bored, or fed up with life at home, and prefer the
companionship of a working environment.

And there are certain more general limitations on the so-called 'science
of happiness'. As indicated previously, there is the basic value judgement
as to what constitutes the 'happiness' that policy ought to promote. As
explained in Chapter 7 the social welfare function is usually defined in
terms of individuals' utilities. What some happiness studies attempt to
provide is some concept of happiness that corresponds to these utilities.
But how far these would correspond to the concept of happiness associated with Aristotle's *eudaimonia* or John Stuart Mill's distinction
between higher and lower forms of utility, rather than some more
Benthamite indifference to the sources of an individual's utility, remains
an open question.

Sen's criticism of what he calls 'welfarism' applies equally to 'happiness' as an objective that society ought to maximise. One might not be
so keen on providing incentives to make villains happy. Ought one to
be neutral about the pleasure that some people seem to derive from
watching some people beat each other up in a boxing match, or, far
worse, from the spectacle of a bull being tormented and finally killed
just for their entertainment? And if some activities that make people
happy can be regarded as morally reprehensible, some of the activities
that make people unhappy may be well-deserved. If some people suffer
from envy just because other people have more money it is just too bad
for them. In that case, there is no reason why the negative externality

of making some people envious because others are richer ought to be taxed.

Second, happiness economics cannot take full account of distributional effects. True, CBA aimed at maximising the contribution made by some projects to happiness – rather than to income – will take more account than would a conventional CBA of the fact that an extra £100 would add more to the happiness of a poor man than to the happiness of a rich man. But it would still not allow for the distribution of happiness. And while there are masses of data on the distribution of incomes, some of which are summarised and discussed in Chapter 15, this is not the case, of course, with happiness data. The income distribution data are largely the by-product of the tax system. But it is unlikely that people would be assessed for tax in proportion to their self-reported happiness.

In any case a policy that gives more weight to a reduction in serious unhappiness could be justified in terms of a value judgement to the effect that relief of 'pain' is more important than increase in 'pleasure'. As pointed out earlier, this would correspond to the 'negative Utilitarianism' associated with Karl Popper. As the *World Development Report [2015]* points out '.... how much priority (if any) should be given to reducing misery compared with increasing existing happiness – is ultimately an ethical decision' (p. 7). In this connection the well-known relationship between mental health and happiness is particularly important.

Third, there are also statistical problems in happiness studies as in any problem where there may be a network of inter-connections between variables. For example, health clearly affects happiness but, whereas health will vary between people of similar incomes for all sorts of reasons, it is also likely that wealthier people will also be able to look after their health better. Hence, if you compare two people, one of whom is happier, richer and healthier than the other, it is difficult – in the absence of some other information – to say how far the richer man's happiness is accounted for by his income rather than his health. Of course, the very large samples used in various studies enable the relative influence of different determinants of happiness to be isolated and measured up to a point, but only up to a point.

Another statistical problem is what statisticians call 'selection bias'. This could be the case, for example, with the apparent relationship between happiness and being married, to which reference has been made earlier. For it is quite likely that unhappy people have more trouble finding a spouse than do happy people, or, if they do find one, that the relationship does not last very long. So happy people would be more likely to get married, and stay married, than unhappy people. Thus the direction of causality between happiness and being married is not necessarily from marriage to happiness but from happiness to marriage.

There are probably other reasons to avoid attaching too much significance to the international comparability of responses to questions about happiness. For example the 2015 *World Development Report* ranking of countries in terms of the *life evaluation* concept of happiness shows Mexico ranked one step above the USA. Given that millions of Mexicans have emigrated – and still try to emigrate – to the USA whilst there are no reports of millions of people trying to emigrate from the USA to Mexico, one is forced to have some doubt concerning the reliability of such rankings.

Thus, the goal of maximising some concept of *aggregate* happiness rather than maximising utility is subject to many of the same limitations as is Utilitarianism. It ignores distributional considerations and the way that people obtain utility. Furthermore, it takes no account of minorities' interests and 'rights'. But it would be Utopian to believe that there is some universally agreed single value at which policy ought to aim. Meanwhile, explicit recognition of the link between certain economic policies and happiness can help reduce the danger of pursuing policies that may fail to promote happiness rather than reduce it.

Notes

1. These include the annual [since 2012] *World Happiness Reports,* edited by Helliwell, J.F., Layard, R., and Saches, J., for the Sustainable Development Solutions Network, New York; the OECD *Guidelines....* O'Donnell *et al.* 2014.
2. See Blanchflower and Oswald, 2004, and *World Happiness Report, Special Report,* 2016:18, Table 3.
3. See a wide-ranging discussion of this question in Aldred, 2009., especially chapter 4
4. See Kenny, A. and Kenny, C., 2006, for an overview of ancient and modern concepts of happiness.
5. Bentham, 1789:ch. I, para. 3.
6. Bentham, *ibid*: ch. V, paras: 3 and 4.
7. There are several surveys of the vast literature that has grown up around this topic, many of which contain valuable contributions by the authors, notably those by Aldred, 2009, Kenny and Kenny, *op.cit.*, Frey and Stutzer, 2002, 2008, and the collection of articles in Bruni and Porta, 2005, not to

mention a very wide range of original contributions to the topic by Andrew Oswald, often in conjunction with others.
8. World Happiness Report, 2012:18.
9. Cantril, 1985.
10. Oswald, 2014.
11. Proto and Oswald, forthcoming in the *Economic Journal.*
12. Easterlin, 1974.
13. Blanchflower and Oswald, 2004.
14. For example, Frey and Stutzer, 2002:74–76. See also Aldred, 2009:50–51.
15. Stevenson and Wolfers, 2008.
16. Kahneman and Deaton, 2010:15.
17. Clark and Oswald, 1996:359–381.
18. Frey and Stutzer, 2002:84.
19. Kahneman and Deaton, *op.cit.*
20. Blanchflower and Oswald, 2004; Layard, 2003.
21. In any case, it has even been argued that insofar as people have targets in terms of their *post*-tax incomes, an increase in tax rates makes them work more rather than less.
22. Buiter, 2007.

CHAPTER 13

The Discount Rate

1 INTRODUCTION

The most important price in any CBA in the public domain is invariably the discount rate that is used. For in virtually any CBA in the public sphere, the costs and benefits involved do not usually accrue instantaneously at the point in time at which a particular project in question is carried out. They are usually spread over many years. For example, both the costs and the benefits that are expected from some new transport projects are expected to accrue over several decades. In other projects, major costs are incurred at the end of the project's operation. For example, a major cost in nuclear energy will be the costs of decommissioning and of disposing of the accumulated radioactive waste when the facility in question has reached the end of its useful life after two or three decades.

But the discount rate that society ought to use is an exceptionally value-loaded price. For how far society ought to count a pound's worth of costs or benefits accruing in some distant period of time as having the same utility value to society as a pound's worth of costs or benefits accruing today is largely an ethical question. And it is a crucial one.

For example, with a discount rate of only 3%, a £100 benefit or cost accruing in 20 years time will be worth only about £55, and if the discount rate used is 7% it will be worth less than £26. Thus the choice of the discount rate makes an enormous difference to a CBA of almost every public project. Yet it might appear that this is a purely technical matter, and that the discount rate is just another price and is fixed on the market

© The Author(s) 2017
W. Beckerman, *Economics as Applied Ethics*,
DOI 10.1007/978-3-319-50319-6_13

like any other price. But, in fact, this is not the case. True, there is a discount rate in the market – or, rather, there are hundreds of them in the market. But the trouble is that these are unlikely to correspond to the rate that the public authorities ought to use for public projects if the objective is to maximise society's welfare. And it is not fixed in the same way as are ordinary prices. Why is this the case? The next section discusses this, and the subsequent sections consider what can be done about it.

2   The Market Rate of Discount

In the absence of personal considerations – such as 'sympathy' or friendship or family ties – a utility-maximising individual who had absolutely no preference at all between this year's and next year's consumption would not lend £100 this year for a certain repayment of only £100 next year. For if, say, 5% was the rate of interest he could get in the market for riskless loans, he could invest the £100 this year at 5%, and get £105 back next year. A promise of £100 next year would only be worth £100/1.05 this year, that is, £95.23. In other words, £95.23 is the *present value* to him of a certain receipt of £100 next year. It is all he would need to invest in order to receive £100 next year at the market rate of interest open to him. Five per cent is thus the rate at which he discounts the future.

What determines the market rates of interest open to him – that is, the rate at which he will discount the future? The theory of the determination of market interest rates is part of macro-economic theory and lies outside the scope of this book. But a brief simplified version of it could run something like this. At any point in time the general level of interest rates is determined largely by macro-economic considerations, such as those familiar to any student of economics and that are represented in what is known as the IS/LM framework. This framework encapsulates several variables, including the relationship between national income and the total amount of savings, people's preference for holding money rather than bonds, monetary policy, expected inflation rates, international capital flows and fluctuating and uncertain expectations concerning the future profitability of investment, and so on. As Keynes emphasised 80 years ago the rate of interest is virtually a current phenomenon and its value at any point in time is a poor guide to likely future rates of return on investment.

Nevertheless, the interest rate resulting from the interaction of these variables will still bear some relation to people's willingness to abstain from current consumption – that is, to save – and to the extent to which firms can find it profitable to borrow funds in order to finance investment. As regards the former, although variations in the overall income level in an economy will tend to bring total actual savings into equality with total investment, the level of income at which this equality will be obtained will depend on how willing people are to save at different levels of income and interest rates. If, for example, at any given level of interest rates and income, people were relatively very reluctant to save, the level of income necessary to bring forth a level of aggregate savings that equalled total investment would have to be much higher than if people were very willing to save a lot at any given level of interest rates and income. It might even correspond to a level of income that exceeds the productive capacity of the economy, with a resulting tendency towards inflation or a suboptimal balance of payments.

3   PRIVATE VERSUS SOCIETY'S RATE OF TIME PREFERENCE

Given the macro-economic reasons why the rate of interest is not a price like any other price, and because it is unlikely at any point of time to reflect accurately the future long-term rate of return on investment, it would be unwise to rely on it as a guide to the rate of discount that society should use in allocating resources between consumption and investment or between different investment opportunities.

In addition, there is reason to believe that, even in long-term 'equilibrium' (insofar as it makes sense to talk about 'equilibrium' in this context), market rates of interest will be higher than the rates that would be appropriate for society to use in its public investment decisions. It has been argued earlier that people's choices did not always promote their welfare, so that it might be reasonable to disregard their choices in some cases. But as far as the discount rate is concerned there may be good reason to disregard the market rate of interest (and hence of discount), *not* because people's choices will not correspond to *their own welfares*, but because *their* welfares may not correspond to *society's* welfare. There are various reasons why this may be the case.

First, the risk that savers take into account in deciding how much to save and invest is greater than the risk that society as a whole is facing. For example, one might invest one's savings in a company that fails on account of some superior product being developed by a competitor. In that case the individual who happens to have invested in it may lose all his money. The company that has been put out of business may disappear together with the saver's savings. But society has not necessarily lost much. For example, the company's physical capital and the labour that had been employed in it will not have been wiped off the map in the same way that the saver's capital may have been. They may still be available for other productive uses. In this case, the risk of loss faced by the saver is greater than the risk of loss faced by society. Similarly, suppose that the company is nationalised without adequate compensation. The owners will lose out, but the assets still remain. Yet another ingredient of private risk that the ordinary saver might take into account is that he may not live to reap the rewards of his sacrifice of current consumption. It would be a pity to abstain from some current consumption and then get knocked over and killed by a bus the next day.

Second, in addition to these reasons for why, on the whole, private risk will exceed social risk, the amounts people will be willing to save or invest will be influenced by the existence of taxes. Individuals or companies who expect to pay taxes on the income they will derive from their savings and investments will need a higher rate of return on the investment than they would have done in the absence of the taxes. But from the point of view of society, these taxes are not a cost; they are purely transfer payments, even though they will usually involve some transactions costs.

Third, the market in financial assets is far from being a competitive market. In most countries a few very large financial institutions dominate the market and competition between them rarely takes the form of competitive rates of interest to borrowers. As a result, the market rate of interest is generally likely to be higher than it would be in a fully competitive market.

Fourth, there is probably a discrepancy between people's 'individual preferences' and their 'social preferences'. That is to say, people may prefer that society as a whole should discount the future less than they would do themselves in choices that affect only their personal allocation of resources. Indeed, there will be many policy options where an individual would be willing to contribute to some collective asset if he believed that others would do likewise – what Amartya Sen calls the 'isolation paradox'.[1]

Saving for the future is likely to be one such example of this. Individuals might not think it worthwhile making a sacrifice of their own consumption in order to save for future generations, but if they could assume that others were doing likewise they might be much more willing to do so. Hence, 'It is, for example, perfectly possible that in a society where no one saves anything, everyone might nevertheless be ready to vote for a political proposal requiring each member of the society to save, say, 20 percent of his income for the sake of future generations'.[2]

Fifth, related to this it is likely that, at best, markets only reflect individual preferences over relatively short periods of time. They provide little information about people's preferences over generations, which is important in some areas of public policy, notably climate change.

Sixth, markets cannot properly reflect the interests and preferences of future generations, and some people would argue that society ought to do so, rather than just reflect the preferences of the current generation. As Sen says, 'If democracy means that all the people that are affected by a decision must themselves make the decision (directly or through a representative), then, clearly, there can be no democratic solution to the problem of the "optimum" rate of saving'. But he does go on to add that 'From this it does not, of course, necessarily follow that decisions made by some authoritarian body will be more "fair" to future generations than those made by the present generation voting collectively'.[3] This is another aspect of the general problem of social choice and the more particular value judgement concerning which is the society whose welfare we are seeking to maximise.

Thus, on balance, even in some ideal equilibrium state, market interest rates would generally be higher than the discount rates appropriate to public projects. Hence, there are two possible approaches that can be adopted in order to arrive at an appropriate social discount rate. One is to start with some assumed long-term equilibrium market rate and then to try to adjust it for the excess of private risk over social risk or for the influence of tax rates on the equilibrium market rate. But, of course, the vast amount of information that would be required in order to estimate the whole general equilibrium set of relevant equations is beyond our resources.

The alternative approach is to estimate what the appropriate rate of discount ought to be for society, given the sort of considerations that we think ought to be taken into account by society in fixing a discount rate. One of these will be the extent to which society ought to attach as much importance to the welfare of future generations as to the welfare of current generations. This is clearly an ethical judgement. Consequently, as the *Stern Review* recognises, it is not possible to avoid ethical issues when selecting a discount rate in this context.[4] This second approach has taken the form mainly of a focus on the two parameters in what is known as the 'Ramsey equation', in honour of the genius Frank Ramsey, who published the equation in a rightly famous article in 1928.

4   THE SOCIAL RATE OF DISCOUNT

The Ramsey equation is generally written as

$$r = \delta + \eta g$$

There are differences in the terminology used to define the variables in this equation. We shall define them as follows:

r = the social rate of discount (i.e. the rate that society *ought* to adopt for public projects or policies)[5];
δ (delta) = the 'utility', or 'welfare', discount rate – that is, *'pure time preference'*;
η (eta) = the elasticity of utility with respect to consumption;
g = the expected future growth rate of consumption.

Thus *delta* reflects the extent to which a unit of utility accruing in the future is valued less today than an *equal* unit of utility enjoyed today. And eta reflects the assumption that, on account of the assumed diminishing marginal utility of consumption, the higher is expected future consumption the less utility is derived from a given further increase in consumption. Thus the two parameters together will reflect the extent to which expected future consumption will have less value from today's viewpoint. It will produce less utility and a unit of utility will have less value today. In the above equation, the two parameters, *delta* and *eta,* are often regarded as 'ethical' parameters, although, as argued below, the second of the two is impossible to estimate with any confidence; this is on account of practical difficulties, not ethical considerations.

4.1   The Ethics of Delta

Delta has two components. The first is society's rate of 'pure time preference' and corresponds to what, at the level of the individual, has been described as 'impatience'. The second component allows for the possible extinction of the human race. (To an individual this would correspond to an allowance for the realisation that one is not immortal, and abstract from the satisfaction one might derive from leaving bequests.) Combining these two elements, *delta* is the trade-off that society ought to make between a unit of utility (or welfare) accruing in the future and a unit of utility accruing today. For the sake of the argument let us assume that for practical purposes we can ignore the second component of *delta* so that *delta* is simply equal to the first one. In that case, if one believes that a unit of utility enjoyed by a future generation ought to be valued as much as an equal unit enjoyed by the present generation, *delta* ought to be put at zero. If, however, society ought to value a unit of utility accruing to a future generations below that of an equal unit of utility accruing to the present generation *delta* should be positive. This is clearly a value judgement. And the more society ought to value current utility over future utility, the greater is *delta* and hence the greater the discount rate.

Economists who are under the spell of impersonal Utilitarianism would tend to believe that society ought to adopt a totally *impersonal* approach to the weight that ought to be attached to the utilities accruing to different people. So they would attach equal value to an equal unit of utility (but not consumption) accruing to a member of any generation. Hence – leaving aside the extinction possibility – pure time preference should be zero. This means that the value of *delta* in the Ramsey equation ought to be zero. One authoritative expression of this view is in the *Stern Review*, which states, for example, that 'we take a simple approach in this Review: if a future generation will be present, we suppose that it has the same claim on our ethical attention as the current one'.[6] What sort of ethical principle can justify this equality of valuations of welfare among generations?

It would obviously be the *impersonal* principle that is characteristic of most versions of classical Utilitarianism (Chapter 9). In this approach the goodness of any outcome is measured by the total utility resulting from the actions in question irrespective of who gets the utility or when. The *Stern Review* acknowledges that 'it is, of course, possible that people actually do place less value on the welfare of future generations, simply on the grounds that they are more distant in time. But it is hard to see any ethical justification for this' (p. 31).

The *Stern Review* appeals to some very eminent economists – from Ramsey and Pigou down to contemporary Nobel Laureate Solow – in support of the view that 'the only sound ethical basis for placing less value on the utility (as opposed to consumption) of future generations was the uncertainty over whether or not the world will exist, or whether those generations will be present' (Stern, 2006, p. 45). The quotations from Ramsey, Pigou and Harrod that are routinely quoted in condemnation of pure time preference as representing impatience or 'defective telescopic faculty' are as follows:

Ramsey: '...we do not discount later enjoyments in comparison with earlier ones, a practice which is ethically indefensible and arises merely from the weakness of the imagination...'

Or *Pigou:* ' everybody prefers present pleasures or satisfactions of a given magnitude to future pleasures or satisfactions of equal magnitude, even when the latter are perfectly certain to occur...this preference for present pleasures...implies only that our telescopic faculty is defective'.

Or Harrod: 'Time preference in this sense is a human infirmity...a polite expression for rapacity and the conquest of reason by passion'.

These sentiments may be perfectly justified critiques of the pure time preference exhibited by most individuals *in making choices affecting their own lives*. But they do not seem to have much bearing on time preference *over generations*. As Schelling wrote many years ago, 'That is because the alleged inborn preference for earlier rather than later consumption is exclusively concerned with the consumer's impatience with respect *to his or her own consumption*' (our italics).[7] Schelling went on to say that it is absurd to believe that the virtually universal preference for consumption during one's lifetime by oneself or some member of one's family as compared with consumption by somebody else in 200 years' time can be described as 'impatience' or 'myopia'. And Harrod's frequently quoted apparent disdain for the 'conquest of reason by passion' is very odd since Harrod was certainly familiar with Hume's even more widely quoted assertion that 'reason is, and ought only to be the slave of passions, and can never pretend to any other office than to serve and obey them'.[8] (As pointed out earlier, Hume's concept of 'passion' was a general term for emotion, attitudes and desires, and was not the same as the current connotation of passion in terms of extreme obsessions such as those often associated with romantic sentiments.)

The *impersonal* Utilitarianism espoused by Stern and others in the context of the discount rate can be contrasted with some version of what is sometimes known as 'agent-relative' ethics. This has been discussed in Chapter 10 so it would be superfluous to repeat the main points here. Suffice it to say here that the discounting problem is an extreme example of the general problem of 'moral distance' to which reference has already been made – that is, how far ought we to value the welfare of everybody else, including future generations, on a par with our own welfare. As argued in Chapter 18, there is no clear theory of intergenerational justice to guide us. And Utilitarianism is the only one of the main theories that is able to provide guidance as to the precise value of *delta* in the Ramsey equation. For it requires pure time preference to be valued at zero! It is for this reason, perhaps, that impersonal Utilitarianism may appeal to those economists who die with the word 'maximise' engraved on their hearts, since it provides them with a precise figure to be inserted into a social welfare function extending over time that has to be maximised. But 'agent-relative ethics' or 'special obligations' ought not to be dismissed as lightly as is often the case in the sphere of policies that have very long-term effects.

4.2 The Ethics of 'Eta'

In standard micro-economics most individuals are assumed to have utility functions relating utility to consumption. The functions are generally assumed to be concave, thereby expressing the assumption that the higher their consumption the lower the marginal utility they would derive from a further increment of consumption. The greater the concavity of the func-tion the faster would marginal utility fall off as consumption increases further. And at the level of society as a whole, if one adopts a 'welfarist' utility function such as the social welfare function discussed in Chapter 7, society's utility function resembles that of an individual, so it would attach lower marginal utility to higher levels of consumption. At any point in time, this means that society attaches less utility to a unit of consumption accruing to a rich man than to a poor man. And, if the degree of concavity is represented in the utility function by the coefficient *eta,* the greater is *eta* the greater is the fall in marginal utility attached to higher levels of consumption.[9]

Up to this point in the story, time – and hence discounting – does not enter into it. But if time is brought into the picture, the story changes. For if the overall level of consumption in society is expected to rise over time less value will be attached to future increments of utility. And the greater is *eta,* the faster will marginal utility fall off as consumption increases. Other things being equal, therefore, the more society would discount future consumption, so that less would be saved.

But what about a possible fall in consumption? If we go back to the individual, the greater the curvature of his utility function – that is, the greater is eta – the more utility he would lose from a fall in his consump-tion level. Hence, the greater is *eta* the more risk-averse he would be. For he would expect to lose more utility from a given fall in his consumption level. People differ, of course, with respect to their aversion to risk. At some level of income some people may be gamblers, so that, over the relevant range, they will have convex utility functions.

This means that, when time is brought into the picture, the implications for discounting of different values of *eta* on discounting are mixed, and tend to conflict with each other. On the one hand, if, for example, consumption is expected to rise over time (i.e. a positive value for the coefficient '*g*' in the Ramsey equation) the greater is *eta* the more would society discount future consumption levels. For people would expect to derive less pay-off in terms of utility from future increments of consumption. At the policy level, therefore, a lower level of investment would be justified.

However, if it is believed that there is a risk of some catastrophe – for example, caused by environmental disaster – then it might be necessary to carry out a much higher level of investment in order to reduce the danger of a such a disaster. This appears to imply a lower discount rate – that is, a lower value of *eta*. In short, the *eta* coefficient is expected to do too much work.[10] On the one hand, the more marginal utility is expected to fall off with higher consumption – that is, the greater is *eta* – the more should society discount the future. But the greater is *eta* the greater is risk aversion. So if it is believed that society does face some risk to future consumption levels, the greater should be the level of preventive investment.

But there is nothing particularly 'ethical' about these two ingredients of *eta*. There is no *ethical* reason why the utility functions of individuals or society as a whole should have any particular degree of declining marginal utility of consumption or any particular degree of risk aversion. It is true that the more concave is one's utility function the more one would fear a fall in consumption and hence the more one would prefer a more equal distribution over time of one's own consumption level. But there are two reasons why this hardly translates into an *ethical* judgement about the desirable degree of intergenerational equality.

To begin with, as argued in Chapter 15, it is not obvious that concern with equality at the level of society as a whole is an *ethical* matter, rather than a purely *instrumental* concern with the possible adverse effects of inequality in society. For, if pushed to explain *why* one should value equality, most – and possibly all – people would maintain either that it reduces poverty or that it makes for more harmonious social relationships. For example, it leads to less conflict between people or classes, better health, better labour relationships, and so on. In other words, equality may be believed to be *instrumentally* valuable. But it is not easy to see why equality is also *intrinsically* valuable.[11] It may be possible to justify such a view in the context of some theory of intergenerational justice, but the difficulties that such a view would encounter are discussed in more detail in Chapter 18.

Second, insofar as greater equality at any point in time has the instrumental advantages enumerated earlier, the latter do not seem to apply between non-overlapping generations. For example, better relations or less conflict between people who exist at the same time cannot be claimed to apply also between non-overlapping generations.

In any case, how many proponents of inter-generational equality would object to continued economic growth and deplore the growth that has been achieved over the past, on the grounds that it would lead to, or had led to, greater equality between generations?

So if the value of *eta* is not an ethical question, for which there can be no objective answer, what other basis is there for attaching a figure to it? The *Stern Review* settled on *eta* equal to unity, apparently on the grounds that it corresponds to empirical estimates. But the *Stern Review* also asserts at various points that zero pure time preference would be supported by most people. However the empirical evidence for this view is very shaky. One study restricted to residents in Washington D.C. and Maryland showed that the average respondent would trade off 45 lives in 100 years' time against one life today, and another study in Sweden implied a trade-off over a similar period of 243 lives against one life today.[12] And it seems highly likely that a survey of the whole world's population would give an even higher trade-off. And even if reliable and relevant estimates could be made of people's discount rates, it would be even more difficult to identify how much these rates reflect the 'pure time preference' component of people's discount rates as distinct from the 'eta' parameter in the Ramsey equation.

5   WHICH COUNTRY'S DISCOUNT RATE?

This highlights one of the ethical limitations on welfare economics that we have mentioned at many points in this book, namely the definition of 'the society' whose welfare we want to maximise. Societies are not homogeneous entities. Whatever burdens 'we' ought to bear in order to eliminate the risk of climate-induced worldwide catastrophe depends on who we mean by 'we'. For example, the 'pure rate of time preference' is likely to be much higher in poor countries, where the average expectation of life may be even below 50 years, than in rich countries where it is approaching 80 years.

The same applies to the social opportunity cost of investing in policies that provide a yield over the very long term. For example, Arrow *et al.* suggest that, if account is taken of the higher rates of return on investments in developing countries and an assumed value of 2.0 for the *eta* coefficient, the appropriate discount rate could be between 10% and 16%, in contrast to rates of only about 2–3% in developed countries.[13] In the same report Arrow *et al.* found that 'a review of World Bank projects estimated a real rate of return of 16% at project completion; one study found returns of 26% for primary education in developing countries'.[14] Other examples of very high rates of return in developing countries include estimated rates of return of between 25% and 39%.[15]

Even in developed countries the social opportunity cost appears to be much higher than that to which appeal is often made in discussions of climate change policy. In the OECD countries, until relatively recently, the long-term average yield on equities was over 5% (after corporate and other taxes) for many decades, which is comparable to a pre-tax rate of at least 7%. Even in Britain it has been estimated that the return on 'productive capital' over the long run has been about 4–4.5%.[16] To the extent that public investment directly or indirectly crowds out private investment, the opportunity cost of capital needs to be incorporated into the CBA, so the market rate of interest is relevant here.[17]

Furthermore, the use of different discount rates for different projects is likely to involve a general misallocation of resources. Hence, if it is believed that the ethically correct discount rate is much lower than the prevailing market rate, it ought to be applied across the board – that is, to all investment projects – after due differentiation to take account of externalities and so on. The net result then could be that society would have to sacrifice too much consumption in order to devote an enormous proportion of output to investment. Social welfare is hardly likely to be maximised by such policies. Misallocation of resources could also mean that even future generations will be condemned to a lower consumption level than might otherwise have been available. It may also reduce the ability of future generations to overcome future problems.

6   Conclusions

Previous chapters have identified many ways in which value judgements enter into an appraisal of economic policies and projects. But there is one value judgement that enters into almost all of them. This is the discount rate. For in the field of public policy, decisions have to be taken that will affect costs and benefits over a period of years stretching, in some cases, over generations. And the present value of costs and benefits that are expected to accrue in future years is highly sensitive to the discount rate that is used.

In normal everyday life, the rate at which an individual or a firm will discount the future will be closely related to market rates of interest. However, there are several reasons why this provides a poor guide to the rate at which society ought to discount the future. Consequently, attention has been concentrated on an ethical appraisal of how far society *ought* to value future costs and benefits relative to those that accrue today.

As discussed above, the usual framework for organising an analysis of the basic principles that should determine society's attitudes to future welfare by comparison with today's is based on the 'Ramsey equation'. This equation distinguishes between two crucial parameters. One is the extent to which a future unit of utility (welfare) is regarded as less valuable than an equal unit of utility accruing today. This is known as 'pure time preference'. Only if one is a Utilitarian can one put a figure on this parameter, namely zero. Otherwise one is in the no man's land of unquantifiable value judgements, where all that one can say is that if one cares very little about future welfare one would use what, in most practical applications, would be regarded as a rather high value for this parameter, and vice versa.

The other parameter is more complex and some attempts have even been made to justify a particular numerical value for it on the basis of surveys. But, even leaving aside the many limitations on the reliability of consumer surveys in this field, the problem is that this particular parameter reflects too many influences on human behaviour, some of which affect the parameter in opposite directions. For, on the one hand, it is related to the degree to which income levels in the future are likely to be higher than they are today and the extent to which this will lead to lower marginal utility of future increases in consumption. But this second parameter also reflects attitudes to risk – for example, the risk of some catastrophe in the future that could lead to a very big fall in consumption. Thus while this parameter is sometimes regarded as an 'ethical' parameter, the judgements that enter into it are as much judgements about what human preferences actually are as about what society believes they *ought* to be. It might have been expected that such judgements, like the selection of a parameter to reflect 'pure time preference', could be illuminated by some theory of intergenerational justice. Unfortunately, as will be seen in Chapter 18, this does not provide a very useful solution.

However, as Chapter 18 also points out, justice does not exhaust the whole of morality. For example, the spontaneous manner in which most rich countries help poor countries whenever some natural disaster afflicts them owes little to any conscious theory of justice between nations. It seems that altruism or benevolence has become sufficiently deeply ingrained in the human psyche to become freed from the constraints of the smaller societies in which it was originally cultivated. This appears to apply also to concern with the welfare of future generations. So even though the vast majority of the world's population probably treat inter-generational distribution in an agent-relative manner (i.e. by giving prior-ity to their families, friends and so on down the line), this does not seem to preclude a willingness to make some sacrifice for posterity, even when no advantage can conceivably be expected from it. One does not have to accept 100% *impersonal Utilitarianism* in order to make such a sacrifice.

The economic analysis of the discount rate has made a great con-tribution to bringing out into the open the ethical determinants of society's discount rate and hence to clarifying the ethical intuitions on which they depend. But, as emphasised at various points, ethics is about balancing conflicting intuitions and value judgements, and there is no way this can provide an objective scientific numerical estimate of where the balance lies.

NOTES

1. Sen, 1984:123.
2. Sen, *ibid*:132.
3. Sen, *ibid*:121.
4. Stern, 2008
5. It is also often known as the 'social rate of time preference'.
6. Stern, 2006:31. The same sentiment is repeated on pages 45, 48 and 160 of this report. The view that one cannot logically attribute to unborn people any characteristic, whether it be brown hair or the possession of 'some claim' on anything or anybody (such as those embodied in 'rights') is discussed more fully in Chapter 18.
7. Schelling, T., 1995:396.
8. Hume, 1739: 2.3.3.5.

9. *Eta* is defined as the elasticity of utility with respect to consumption, For example, if the value of *eta* is taken as 2, a 10% increase in consumption would imply a 20% increase in utility.

10. See discussion of this in Beckerman and Hepburn, 2007.

11. See Raz, 1986, and Frankfurt, 2015.

12. Frederick, 2003.

13. Arrow *et al.* 1996:para. 4.2.1.

14. Arrow *et al.*, *ibid*:133.

15. Scott, *et al.* 1976:43–44.

16. Weale, 2009:4.

17. Arrow *et al.*, *ibid*:139.

CHAPTER 14

The Price of Life

1   'LIFE' OR 'RISK TO LIFE'?

There are some things in life that cannot be valued in terms of money. One of these is death. It is true that Hamlet did a CBA of staying alive when he weighed up '...the whips and scorns of time, the pangs of despized love, the laws delay', and so on, against the fear of the awful experiences one might have when one has 'shuffled off this mortal coil'. But he did not try to put a monetary value on the components of his balance sheet.

Yet there is a substantial literature on the monetary valuation of life.[1] For many public agencies, such as those concerned with transport, or medical expenditures, or safety regulations in the workplace, need such an estimate. Some studies of the possible costs of global warming even refer to the monetary value of the lives that could be lost as a result of it. How does one explain this apparent paradox?

To government agencies the answer is simply that the term 'the value of life' is just a convenient shorthand for 'the value of safety or risk to life'. As Sunstein puts it in referring to the extensive use of 'values of statistical lives' (VSAs) in the USA, 'With these values the government is not actually "valuing life." It is valuing the reduction of mortality risk...'.[2] In other words it is important to distinguish between attaching a monetary value to life and attaching a monetary value to *risk* to life, or safety. The two concepts are entirely distinct and there is very little basis for going from one to the other. The difference corresponds to Kant's famous statement

© The Author(s) 2017
W. Beckerman, *Economics as Applied Ethics*,
DOI 10.1007/978-3-319-50319-6_14

that 'In the kingdom of ends everything has either a *price* or a *dignity*. If it has a price something else can be put in its place as an equivalent; if it is exalted above price and so admits of no equivalent, then it has a dignity'.[3] 'Life' is the example, *par excellence*, of something that has a dignity, whereas a given degree of risk to life can have an equivalent and hence can have a 'price'.

Prices are the units in which one can compare the *exchange* value of things. Kilometres are appropriate units for comparing the height of mountains or the distances people are running; kilograms are appropriate units for comparing the weight of baskets of vegetables; hours are appropriate units for measuring how long it takes to read this book. But if prices are the appropriate units for comparing the exchange *value* of things, they are useless if no meaningful comparisons can be made. And no meaningful comparison can be made between being alive with some given amount of money and being dead with a lot more money. In Kant's terms, no 'equivalence' can be established.

For being dead is non-existence, not just an extreme version of existing but with less of something to which one can attach a monetary value, such as an automobile or a certain degree of safety. Being dead is a state in which one can neither have anything to value, nor suffer from being deprived of something, such as the satisfaction of being alive.

If you ask somebody how much he would accept as compensation for giving up his life, his answer would depend on whether or not he is an economist. If he is an economist he would say that the marginal utility to him of money (or anything else for that matter) is zero when he is dead, so that no amount of money, however large, can compensate him for giving up life (for the sake of argument I exclude the bequest option). If he is not an economist he might reasonably answer by saying 'don't ask me stupid questions!'.

But if, instead, you ask him how much money he would accept as compensation for an increase in the *risk* to his life from, say, one in a million to one in half a million over the next year, he might very well be prepared to give you a figure. Why not? He expects to go on living with one or other of the two risks to life he is asked to compare. And if he can compare the living in the two situations he can assess the monetary value of their difference. And if you ask him how much he would be prepared to accept in compensation for an increase in the risk to his life from one in 100,000 to one in 50,000 he might again be willing to give you a figure, which would no doubt be much higher, since most of us will attach more significance to changes in the risk to our lives at high levels of risk than at much lower levels of risk. Thus it does make sense to attach a monetary value to a change in one's safety, because one goes on living with it. Life may be more or less enjoyable with different degrees of safety. And one may be prepared to accept a life that has to be lived with a slightly higher level of risk if one is suitably compensated for it.

This is why risk to life can have a price. And it is this price that is usually the basis of policy decisions that involve risk to life. This is because policy is not generally concerned with attaching a monetary value to the life of an *identified individual*, or group of individuals. Instead, it is concerned with policies or projects that will change the statistical risk to life of unidentified individuals. This is why the central measure used in policy analysis is the '*value of a statistical life*' [VSL]. For example, if it is believed that a particular transport project is likely to reduce deaths from one in 1 million to one in 500,000, the relevant measure of the VSL would be based on an estimate of what monetary value the average person would put on such a reduction in the risk to his life. How this is done is explained in Section 3.

2   THE VALUE OF LIFE TO SOCIETY

The fact that life cannot have a monetary value does not mean that it has no value at all, either to a living person or to society as a whole. For while a person is alive his value to society comprises two elements. One is the value of life to himself, insofar as he does find life worth living. The other is his externality value. This is what he contributes to the rest of society. In turn, this externality value has two components. One of them can be monetised. It is what he contributes, while he is alive, to the rest of society from his output (less his own consumption). The other is the intangible value (hopefully) that other people – notably his near and dear – derive from his existence. And if somebody dies the loss experienced by the society that is left behind is this externality value, the second part of which is not measurable.

The non-measurable component of the loss to society from somebody's death will usually be more important – and in many cases incomparably more important – than the loss of his or her measurable economic contribution to society. But it will be incommensurate with the economic loss. For this component of the value attached to the life of the deceased – like other values identified above such as freedom, integrity, justice and so on – cannot be compared to other values in terms of some relevant metric, such as its price. But society will still have to adopt policy projects that will be judged worthwhile even though they will certainly involve some loss of life, in the same way that many other policy choices will involve conflicts of incommensurate values.[4]

One possible objection to restricting the loss to society of a person's death to this externality value is that this takes no account of the loss of utility by the victim himself. He will usually have wanted to go on living, which means that staying alive gave him utility of one kind or another. Hence, the utility of the society he leaves behind will no longer include the utility he had derived himself when he was alive. Should this not also be included in the loss to society of his death? Most economists would answer 'No'. The society left behind has suffered the 'externality loss' (grief, etc., and possible pecuniary value) resulting from the death. That exhausts its loss. The only other loss of welfare (utility) that society has suffered is the loss suffered by the deceased, assuming that the deceased had enjoyed positive welfare while alive. *But he/she is no longer a member of that post-death society.*

The two components of the externality specified above are clearly recognised in law cases concerning the damages that ought to be paid in the case of an identified individual who has been killed in some accident as a result of somebody's negligence. In such cases judges frequently have to decide what level of compensation should be awarded to the dependants. They may take account of the deceased person's expected lifetime earnings minus his own consumption. This will be the measurable monetary – or 'pecuniary' – component of the externality. For an identified individual the pecuniary effect can be measured in money by his lost income minus his own consumption. Judges also usually add to the pecuniary loss something to compensate for the second component of the externality effect, namely the grief and loss of companionship that the surviving dependents may have to endure.[5] But the judges have recognised that this component of the externality cannot be given a precise monetary value and is largely a matter of social convention. For example, in a representative judgement Lord Diplock stated that

Non-economic loss.... is not susceptible of measurement in money. Any figure at which the assessor of damages arrives cannot be other than artificial and, if the aim is that justice meeted out to all litigants should be even-handed instead of depending on idiosyncrasies of the assessor, whether jury or judge, the figure must be 'basically a conventional figure derived from experience and from awards in comparable cases.[6]

In the same way that the 'net output' of a deceased person can be roughly estimated for an identified individual some estimate could be made of the 'net output' of the average member of society. For society as a whole the counterpart of the measurable component of an identified person's externality effect on the rest of society would be an average person's expected lifetime earnings less his lifetime consumption. This would be the average person's 'net output', which is then a measure of the pecuniary element in the cost to society of a person's death. For this had been what was left over for the rest of society to consume when he was alive and so what measurable loss society will suffer by his death.[7]

But there are several reasons why the average person's 'net output' is not generally used for policy purposes, quite apart from the fact that it does not include the non-pecuniary element in the loss to society from somebody's death. One reason is that it implies that, other things being equal, society ought to make less effort to save the life of old or unemployed people. Indeed, the lives of those who have no *earned* income and actually draw on society's resources have a negative pecuniary value (e.g. retired or incapacitated people who cannot work, or the unemployed).[8] But this would conflict with the main function of society.

This is to protect the lives of its citizens irrespective of their age, let alone their personal situation and net output. This is why the sentence handed out to a person who has been convicted of murder takes no account of the age of the victim, or his expected net output. This primary duty is also why society is concerned with reducing the risk of terrorist activities. Not to do so would be like arguing that the danger of a few dozen people out of many millions being killed in some terrorist outrage would not matter much since it would merely mean a minute reduction in the average expectation of life of citizens as a whole. The prime obligation of society is to protect the lives of its members, not just to prevent a minute reduction in their average expected longevity. This obligation applies to individual identified lives as well as to unidentified lives. But no obligations or counterpart rights are unqualified or unlimited, so that, like any other incommensurate value, one cannot preclude the adoption of policies that have other values even if they involve certain deaths to some members of society.

3   MEASURES OF THE VALUE OF RISK TO LIFE

There are two main methods. One, referred to as the 'contingent valuation' method, consists basically of asking people how much they are willing to pay for some specific policy to reduce risk to life,[9] such as by reducing local air pollution, or how much they would receive as compensation for some policy or project that might increase risk to life, such as certain transport projects.

The second method, referred to as the 'revealed preference' method, consists of observing how much people spend in order to increase safety, such as by spending more on an automobile on account of its extra safety devices, or by observing how much extra salary is required in order to undertake a more dangerous job.

The justification for these methods follows from the seminal articles by Schelling (1968) and Mishan (1971a). They emphasised that we are not concerned with trying to estimate how much it would take to compensate a person for the loss of his life, which would be absurd, but how much people value some change in *risk to life*. This would provide the basis for applying the Hicks/Kaldor compensation test of what would constitute a potential Pareto-optimising move. For if everybody is exposed to some extra risk but is adequately compensated for it, and there is something left over as well, somebody is better off and nobody is worse off. As Mishan put it '...the relevant sums to be subtracted from the benefit side are no longer those which compensate a specific number of persons for their certain death but are those sums which compensate each person in the community for *the additional risk* to which they are to be exposed'.[10]

For example, consider a project that will increase GNP by, say £20 million, but at a cost of some specified increase in risk to lives. And suppose that one can estimate by one means or another that the average person would accept £10 in compensation for the additional risk to his life and that there are one million people in the society in question who face a roughly equal risk. Hence, the total amount of compensation that would be required to pay everybody for this increased risk to their lives would be only £10 million. So the project would satisfy the Hicks/Kaldor compensation test, namely that those who gain from the project could compensate the losers and still remain better off. If everybody shared equally in the gain in national income and in the extra risk, the project would constitute an *actual* Pareto-optimising move without the necessity of any redistribution.

Or consider a project that will reduce risk to life. Consider, for example, a country with a population of five million, all of whom are exposed to an equal risk of being killed in a railway accident. And suppose that a sample survey shows that, on average, people are willing to pay £10 to reduce the annual deaths from rail accidents by one person (e.g. from ten people per year to only nine people per year). If five million people are, on average, prepared to pay £10 to save one life in this manner one can say that the total amount that whole society is willing to pay for the specified reduction in risk to life £50 million. Hence, if the project costs only £40 million it appears to pass a compensation test.[11] It will have cost £40 million but the benefits are worth £50 million in terms of increased safety.

Thus if people can indicate one way or another – for example, in answer to a questionnaire or in their personal expenditure habits – how much they are prepared to accept as compensation for a specific increase in the risk to their lives – that is all one needs to know, as in the above examples. In that case if some policy is adopted that would, indeed, lead to the specified increase in the risk to their lives and if they received the corresponding compensation the policy would be justified on conventional welfare economics grounds. It will satisfy the Hicks/Kaldor criterion of a *potential* Pareto-optimising move. Similarly, suppose that people indicated, one way or another, how much they would be willing to pay in return for some project that would lead to a specific reduction in the risk to their lives. Again, in that case carrying out the project at a cost that did not exceed the indicated amount would also be a good idea and satisfy the Hicks/Kaldor compensation test.

Advocates of this approach emphasise that the estimates are only estimates of how much people are willing to pay for given small marginal changes in risk or safety *in specified circumstances*, and nothing more. Nothing should be read into them as estimates of some 'value of life' in spite of this convenient term being used throughout much of the literature on the subject.

There are, of course, innumerable technical problems with these methods. For example, the contingent value method is open to the well-known objection that that the answers people give in surveys depend very much on the way that the questions are posed, such as whether one is asking how much people are willing to pay for some advantageous project or how much they are willing to accept as compensation for some undesirable project. Answers to such questions are known to be distorted by what are called 'endowment effects'. They are also vulnerable to many of the other weaknesses in people's choices that – as discussed in Chapter 5 – have been fully demonstrated by behavioural psychologists.[12] Some of these weaknesses, such as information gaps, also apply to the 'revealed preferences' method. One of the most widely used of these methods is the study of wage differentials between activities that involve different amounts of risk to life. But employees will generally have little knowledge about the risks involved in different potential forms of employment. And even after they have taken some risky job they are under all sorts of pressures not to give up the job and look for something else.

Thus the authorities are faced with the choice between consumer sovereignty and paternalism discussed in Chapter 5. In particular, people are notoriously ill-informed about choices involving some estimate of the risks. In any case risk aversion will vary from one person to another, and hence the amount of compensation for incurring extra risk to life will vary from person to person. To accept that in this respect, as in many others, the value that society as a whole is prepared to pay for some benefit – whether it is a reduction in the risk to life or defence of the realm – is justified, therefore, is perhaps the price one has to pay for living in the society in question.

For it is a problem that is common to all 'collective goods' – that is, goods such as clean air, which have to be supplied equally to large numbers of people whether or not they want to spend so much on it (indirectly). In general members of the public will differ with respect to how much money they would accept as compensation for experiencing a greater risk to their lives. Some may have wanted far greater compensation for doing so than the average figure esti-mated on the basis of surveys or some 'revealed preference' method. Not only may some people be more risk-averse than others, they may simply be richer. This leads to a major problem in this area, namely how far one should discriminate between different types of risk or the valuations placed on them by different groups of people. This is the 'individuation' problem, discussed in Section 5.

Thus all such estimates raise the question of how far decisions should respect consumer sovereignty rather than what are probably better estimates that the authorities can make of the relevant risks in different situations. But an even more fundamental aspect of the conflict between consumer sovereignty and paternalism is inherent in a fundamental challenge to this whole approach. This is the major challenge made in various publications by the economist-turned-philosopher, John Broome.

4   THE BROOME CHALLENGE

In his publications, Broome has challenged the 'compensation' argument alleged to justify the two main methods used to estimate the value of risk to life. But he explicitly states that he has 'made no fancy claim that the value of life is infinite, but simply pointed out a difficulty in measuring it in monetary terms'.[13] He points out that although, *on his interpretation of the 'costs'*, no projects could pass any compensation test this does not mean that such projects have to be rejected. Indeed, if society never accepted projects that involved the slightest risk to life we would probably still be living in the Stone Age.[14] His point is that for projects involving saving or losing life, the compensation test and the Pareto criterion of what is an optimising move are not relevant.

His argument is that it may be perfectly rational for an individual to maximise an expected utility function in which some various small changes in the risk to his life are accompanied by a compensating change in his financial situation. But Broome points out that the expected utility function faced by the authorities is fundamentally different. It is no longer a question of risk. It is a question of certainty. Consider the case of a project that will lead to an increase in national income but will certainly lead to some loss of life. The authorities know that no amount of money could compensate those who will die, since life cannot have a price, for the reasons given at the beginning of this chapter.

From Broome's perspective the whole object of the operation is not just to give people the compensation for bearing extra risk or to make them pay for some reduction in risk. It is to actually carry out the project that is expected to lead to some loss of life. And from the point of view of society as a whole none of the possible outcomes can be valued in monetary terms, since every one of them involves a certain loss of lives. Projects involving virtually certain loss of lives have to be evaluated, therefore, in the light of other criteria. This appears to weaken the normative significance of estimates that have been made of the VSL. But it does not completely destroy it, and such estimates are widely used. But it cannot be justified in terms of the Hicks/Kaldor compensation test.

The authorities face a dilemma. To simplify the argument consider just the case where if the policy in question is implemented it is virtually certain to lead to the death of a number of people to which no monetary value can be attached. Should they recognise their democratic obligation to respect the preferences of the citizens, or should they accept that their own decision will depend on incommensurate value judgements between some certain loss of life and some other value? A well-known example originally given by James Griffin is of the practice by French authorities to line many major roads with trees on account of their aesthetic value even though it is known that this regularly causes the deaths of some motorists.

So here we have a basic clash of value judgements. From the point of view of the authorities the loss of value to society from the certain death of a number of people – the precise number or the identity of the victims makes no difference – is just as incommensurate as that of a certain identified individual. But if the public is quite happy to accept the change in risk given the estimated compensation, is it not the duty of the authorities to respect that expression of preferences? They are not supposed to be maximising any separate expected utility function. The compensation test may – as Broome argued – be totally irrelevant to some expected utility function that could be attributed to the authorities, but it is the relevance of such a function that is debatable.

5   The 'Individuation' Problem

With an ordinary private divisible good that is sold on the market, whether by a public or a private institution, people buy the goods up to the point where, roughly speaking, their marginal utility corresponds to the price they have to pay for them.[15] People will buy different amounts of any particular commodity, even if its price is more or less the same for all of them, on account of their different preference patterns.

But with a 'collective' good this is not possible. These are goods that have to be supplied equally to a body of people, and from which nobody can be excluded. Radio broadcasts are one such example, though nobody is obliged to listen to them. National defence is another, but differs in that everybody is obliged to share equally in it, irrespective of how much the different people want to spend on it. Since nobody can be excluded from the provision of 'collective goods' everybody loses *some* welfare (except, possibly, some very lucky individuals who happen to be getting just their preferred amount of the good in question).

For example, some people would like to spend more on national defence than is actually spent, and some people would like to spend less. Similarly, within any particular city everybody will have to be more or less equally protected by measures to reduce local air pollution. Usually, poorer people would be better off if less were spent on such measures and, perhaps, more on something else. But it is not usually feasible to give them less protection against local air pollution than is given to people living in wealthier parts of the city. The service of law and order is also an obvious example of likely differences in willingness to pay. Honest folk and people with a lot to protect might have liked greater expenditure on law and order than would burglars and other villains.

Thus in all such collective goods there has to be some loss of welfare, by both those who would have liked to spend more and those who would have liked to spend less. In general in a society in which very many different projects and regulations are implemented, it has to be hoped that what some people will lose on some projects will be roughly offset by what they gain on others.

But the inevitable loss of welfare involved in the supply of collective goods can be reduced to some extent insofar as the amount of any particular collective good supplied – such as greater safety on some particular means of transport – can be adjusted to match the preferences of the people who most use it. For example, one should not use the preferences of the whole population of any society when deciding how much to spend on improving local air quality in big cities. People living in rural areas will not want as much of their money to be spent on improving air quality as those who live in the cities. In the same way, people differ with respect to their fear of different ways of dying. 'All death is one, only the tracks we take to it are different'.[16]

There is a lot of evidence that, even after allowing for income differences, people will be prepared to pay more to reduce risk of dying from cancer or in an aircraft accident than from other causes of death, even when the probability of the former is less than that of the latter. In addition, it is well known that there are racial and cultural differences between different groups of people with respect to their attitudes to different forms of risk to life. In general, therefore, there would be less loss of welfare if the expenditures were to take account of the different values placed on the different forms that risk to life may take and by different groups of people.

And, of course, the most obvious source of differences in how much some groups want to pay for some collective good or service is the difference in their incomes. If the provision of some collective good is based on the average willingness to pay of the whole community poorer people will be buying more it (if only indirectly, of course) than they would have liked, and richer people will not be getting as much of it as they would have liked.

In some cases, however, the differentiation between groups may be perfectly acceptable and justifiable. For example, should medical resources be concentrated on programmes that save lives of younger rather than older people? If so, should society spend more on child care than on geriatric facilities? If policy were to focus on saving *life years* it would mean that older people would have a lower claim than younger people. For example, consider the case where surgeons are faced with a choice between saving the lives of one or other of two people. Assume that in all other relevant respects – such as chances of the operation being successful, or length of time that the patient has been waiting for the operation, and so on – the patients are equal, but one patient is old and the other is young. In this case it would make sense to give priority to the young person if only because, other things being equal, he can be expected to make a greater a contribution to society.

This might look like unfair age discrimination. But insofar as people who live to an old age were also young once, there cannot be any *net* 'discrimination' against them over the whole of their lives, as long as each of their remaining *life years* were valued as much as the *life years* of younger people. The focus on life years would have been in their favour when they were young but against them when they are old. It is true that this argument does not apply if there has been a switch in policy from a focus on *lives* to a focus on *life years*, since older people could complain that they had not had the advantage of the life year focus when they had been young. But since they have survived to old age anyway they do not really have anything to complain about!

But, as with most other ethical problems, there can be no simple solution to the question of how far one should differentiate between different risks or different social or income groups. According to Sunstein, 'Whether the government should use a higher or lower VSL across demographic lines cannot be answered simply. Any judgement about the appropriate VSL, and about individuation, must be heavily pragmatic. It must rest on the human consequences of one or another choice'.[17] For although the limits on how far 'individuation' can allow for differences in groups preferences or in attitudes to different kinds of risk to life are usually technical, there are also social considerations. For example, there would be social objections to discrimination between different incomes, racial or social groups according to how much one thinks that the different groups would like to pay for specific collective goods. As Sunstein goes on to say, '...the question of individuation should be a central part of the next generation of cost benefit analysis; a step beyond the first generation debate about whether to do such analysis'.[18]

Lack of differentiation in the supply of collective good, such as those affecting risk to life, can also be defended – up to a point – on political grounds. For, as discussed earlier in connection with the 'Broome challenge', it may be claimed that people accept that the society in which they live has to make decisions that, in many cases, will not correspond to their preferred optimal allocation of resources, and, in some cases, will affect their life expectancy. Citizens have to decide whether they accept society's decisions in very many collective goods. It is the price they pay to live in a democratic society. As Sunstein puts it, 'Well-functioning constitutional systems are deliberative democracies, not maximization machines...'[19]

The individuation problem might also apply to the analysis of global problems, such as the climate change problem. For one of the possible effects of climate change may be a net loss of life, possibly all over the world. And a monetary estimate of this effect has been discussed in the *Third Report of the International Panel on Climate Change*, and in other sources. If such values are based on national estimates of risk to life as expressed as VSL they would be much lower in poor countries than in rich countries. Sunstein quotes estimates of VSL that range from $1.2 million to $19 million.[20] But we know that the marginal utility of income in poor countries is likely to be much higher than in rich countries and their average longevity much lower. If an average world valuation of loss of life through climate change was to be used the global expenditure on combating combat climate change would be greater than poor countries would have wanted given the other claims on their resources. This is an inescapable problem in the supply of collective goods.

6   CONCLUSIONS

It has been argued at the beginning of this chapter that there is no point in estimating the value of lives lost, since it is inappropriate to put a value on life. Aldred is probably right in asking whether there is much point in such valuations anyway.[21] In many specific instances it may be just as useful to abandon the ambition of welfare maximisation and an attempt to satisfy the criteria of theoretical welfare economics, and to fall back on 'second-best' solutions in which a life is a life and it is misleading to pretend that it can be given a monetary value. If for a reasonably similar expenditure on, say, road improvement, one can save ten lives on one project and fifty lives on another one can dispense with putting value on the lives saved. Of course, not all choices are as simple as this. The criteria used in medical interventions, such as chance of success, length of time that a patient has been on a waiting list, as well as expected life years, are examples of second-best solutions that are valid in the absence of any method of putting a monetary value on life. And they also illustrate the unavoidable conflict between the particular values involved, thereby reinforcing the case for appealing to the Aristotelian virtue of practical wisdom, rather than seeking some precise formula.[22]

7   ANNEX

7.1   Sandel's examples of bad CBAs involving value of life

Some misunderstanding of the way that the valuation of life should be included in a CBA has been highlighted by the two examples of CBA given by Michael Sandel in his lectures on philosophy.

The first example he gives is of some calculations made by the Philip Morris tobacco company concerning the costs and benefits of smoking in Czechoslovakia.

(a) Philip Morris' study of costs and benefits of smoking in Czech Republic

Costs	Benefits
Increased health cost for smokers	Tax revenue from sales of tobacco
	Less health care for those who die prematurely
	Less pension payments to those who die prematurely
	Less housing costs for those who die prematurely

(b) Real costs and benefits to Czech society of smoking

Increased health costs for smokers	Less health care costs for smokers who die prematurely
Loss of output over lives of smokers	
Grief and loss of net output, etc., caused by premature deaths	

The point is that the Philip Morris study is only about the effects of smoking on the expenditures and revenues entering into the government budget. It is nothing to do with a CBA for the society in question. Thus the extra revenue that the government collects from the taxes on tobacco, as well as the savings in pension payments to smokers who die early, are both transfer payments, they do not correspond to change in society's output, they merely transfer claims on that output from some members of society to others.

The real costs and benefits, which are shown in the lower part of the table, include – on the left-hand side – genuine losses of utility to the families and friends of people who die prematurely and who suffer grief, and to society as a whole, since this is deprived of the net contribution (if any) that the smokers may have made to society's output over the rest of their lives. All these items are related to the question of how to value lives in any CBA.

Sandel says, in his public lecture on this topic, that the Philip Morris calculation purports to be '...a cost-benefit analysis of smoking in the Czech Republic'. But, as he points out, it only showed that there was a 'net public finance gain'. This, of course, has nothing to do with whether there is any net welfare gain to the Czech society.

The well-known Ford automobile company study of the costs and benefits of running the risks of death from the Ford Pinto car did at least include, among the costs, some estimate for the monetary value of the lives that might be lost. But the figure they gave for this seems to have been plucked out of thin air. Anyway, it is an example of the error that I discuss at the beginning of this chapter, namely that one cannot place a monetary value on life. The welfare loss to society resulting from a death is an externality, which in most cases will consist mainly of grief and other non-pecuniary and incommensurate losses, which cannot be measured in monetary terms.

Thus neither of these two examples are valid calculations of the effects on the welfare of society as a whole. One is a calculation of the effect on the Czech national budget and the other is based on an estimate of the monetary value of life that can have no theoretical justification. True, there is room for serious debate about how the boundary lines around the society in which we are interested ought to be drawn. But they certainly do not correspond to the costs and benefits to any government budget or some automobile company.

NOTES

1. These include, notably, several important publications by Jones-Lee, 1989; Broome 2009; and Sunstein, 2014.
2. Sunstein, 2014:51.
3. Kant, I. 1785/1964.
4. See important discussion of this aspect of the valuation of life in Lukes, S, 'On Trade-Offs Between Values', in Farina, F, Hahn, F, and Vanncussi, S, *Ethics, Rationality and Economic Behaviour,* pp. 36–49. Clarendon Press, Oxford, 1996.
5. In *Wright versus British Railway Board,* 1983, quoted in *McGregor on Damages,* 16th edition, 1997:1,696,
6. McGregor, *loc.cit.*

7. I am indebted to my colleague at UCL, Hugh Goodacre, for drawing my attention to the fact that William Petty used a similar calculation for the value of a person's life in the 1670s to 1680s, and even employed a discount rate in his method of calculation of 6% in most cases, a rate that would not be unusual in the contemporary world.

8. Incomes that they may derive from, say, interest or dividends or pensions, do not count since they do not add to national income. They are just transfer payments from some members of society to others that are not in exchange for anything that the people in question currently add to society's output.

9. See a full discussion of these methods and of their weaknesses, as well as of Broome's challenge to the usual justification given for them, in Hargreaves Heap, S., *et al.*, 1992, *The Theory of Choice: A Critical Guide*, Blackwell, Oxford.

10. Mishan, 1971a:694.

11. There are numerous surveys of such estimates, notably those in N. Crafts, 2003:42. See also Jones-Lee, 1989. Estimates ranging from $0.7 million to $16.3 million in the USA are reported in Sunstein 2014:131.

12. See, for example, Kahneman, 2011.

13. Broome, 1985:262.

14. Broome, 1978:96. See also Mishan 1981:136, and 1982:82.

15. More accurately, the ratios of the marginal utilities are equal to the ratios of the prices of the goods in question.

16. Satyamurti, 1987:12.

17. Sunstein, *op.cit.*90.

18. Sunstein,Ibid:89.

19. Sunstein, *ibid*:123.

20. Sunstein, *ibid*:104. William Petty's estimates in the 1670s to 1680s are that the 'net output' of an Englishman was about £80 as compared with that of an Irishman of about £60 or even lower in some cases.

21. Aldred, 2009:156ff.

22. This case is forcibly argued in Crisp, 2004.

CHAPTER 15

Equality: 'Fact' or 'Value'?

He would cut up the ceilings of the Veronese into strips so that every one might have a little piece. I don't want everyone to have a little piece of anything, and I have a great horror of that kind of invidious jealousy which is at the bottom of the idea of a redistribution. (Henry James, *The Princess Casamassima*)[1]

1   The Recent Increase in Inequality

There has recently been a spate of important books and reports about the increase over the last two or three decades in the inequality with which incomes are distributed in most developed countries.[2] According to one of the most important contributions to this topic that has been published for many decades

Inequality is now at the forefront of public debate. Much is written about the 1% and the 99%, and people are more aware of the extent of inequality than ever before. . . . When the Pew Research Center's Global Attitudes Project asked respondents in 2014 about the 'greatest danger to the world', it found that in the United States and Europe concerns about inequality trump all other dangers. (Atkinson, 2015, p. 1)

One of the most widely publicised and discussed contributions has been the major study by Thomas Piketty, which, with the aid of a wealth of data

© The Author(s) 2017
W. Beckerman, *Economics as Applied Ethics*,
DOI 10.1007/978-3-319-50319-6_15

going back to the nineteenth century, studied the long-term dynamics of the distribution of income between capital and labour.[3] On the basis of this the author constructs a model that not merely explains the increasing share of income from capital over the last few decades but is also supposed to show that this trend is likely to continue into the future in the absence of certain drastic measures to increase taxes on income from capital assets. The implications of Piketty's model for future changes in the distribution of income between capital and labour has been subject to criticism, of course, but his statistical data for the last few decades match other sources of data in highlighting the increase in inequality that has been taking place during this period.

For example, a recent report by the OECD stated that 'the gap between rich and poor is at its highest level in most OECD countries in 30 years. Today the richest 10% [i.e. the top "decile"] of the population in the OECD area earn 9.5 times more than the poorest 10%. By contrast, in the 1980s the ratio stood at 7.1 times'.[4] It goes on to say that 'The increase in income inequality is evident not just in a widening gap between the top and bottom income deciles, but also in the "Gini coefficient".' (This is a commonly used measure of inequality right across the whole range of the income distribution. Its value varies from zero, where everybody has identical incomes, to 1, where all income goes to only one person.) 'In OECD countries in the mid-1980s, the Gini measure stood at 0.29; by 2011/12, it had increased by 3 points to 0.32. The Gini coefficient increased in 16 out of the 21 OECD countries for which long time series are available, rising by more than 5 points in Finland, Israel, New Zealand, Sweden and the United States and falling slightly only in Greece and Turkey'.

And it should not be thought that the general increase in inequality is confined to the developed countries which are members of the OECD. A recent report from Peking University shows that the Gini coefficient in China rose from about 0.30 in the 1980s to 0.49 in 2012, which is higher than any other country covered by World Bank data except South Africa and Brazil.[5]

In most developed countries the increase in the inequality of incomes over the last three decades represented a break from the preceding decades. For example, in the USA until about 1980 the distribution of (pre-tax) incomes had become more equal and then remained fairly stable, with the Gini coefficient falling from around 0.38 in 1950 to around 0.35 in the 1960s and 1970s. However, around 1980 it began to become more unequal with the Gini coefficient rising to 0.43 by 1993 and continuing to rise thereafter.

A roughly similar pattern emerged in the UK, albeit from a lower level of inequality. In the UK, post-tax and benefit income inequality fell steeply in the post-war period. However the Royal Commission on the Distribution of Income and Wealth attributed much of this to a steep post-war decline in the share of the top 1% because of much higher taxes.[6] The Gini coefficient remained fairly stable at around 0.25 for the period from 1960 to 1980. But inequality rose steeply during the following decades, with the Gini coefficient rising from 0.25 in 1980 to some 0.34 by 1991, and to around 0.36 by 2010. Over the period from 1978 to 2005, the post-tax income share of the top 1% in the UK rose from around 6% to over 14%.[7]

The above data refer to the distribution of incomes of households, not of individuals. Hence, the reasons for the changes in the degree of inequality can represent a multitude of different factors. For example, for many of the early post-war years a significant rise in the proportion of women who went to work helped boost the household income of the poorer sections of the population. This meant that greater inequality of wages was offset to some extent by greater employment amongst female members of households, with a particularly pronounced effect in the USA. However, the overall effect of increased female participation is mixed – women with higher earning power are more likely to work, the single adult in one parent families may be able to earn less, and wives of employed husbands tend to earn more than the wives of the unemployed. And in any case, simple comparisons of household income do not take into account household size, as noted elsewhere. But the general view in the recent literature is that increased female participation reduced inequality in both developed and developing countries.[8]

Another major reason for any discrepancy between trends in the inequality of earnings and trends in the inequality of household incomes *after tax and benefits* is, of course, the incidence of redistributive policies. Atkinson shows that during the early post-war period in Britain the increase in inequality of household incomes was more than offset by the equalising effect of redistributive tax and benefit policies. But this effect went into reverse in the 1980s.[9]

Although the increase in the *post-tax and transfer* Gini coefficient since 1980 has been greatest in the UK (10 percentage points) and the USA (over 7 points), the same trend has occurred in most other OECD countries, such as Finland (5 points), Germany, Spain, Norway and Australia (approaching 4 points), and the Netherlands, Canada and Japan (around 3 points). The only country that seems to have bucked the trend is France, which has seen a two-point reduction in the Gini coefficient since 1980.[10] Nevertheless, on balance, taxes and benefits still have an equalising effect in all OECD countries. A recent authoritative and detailed study by the OECD summarises the situation regarding the impact of transfers (taxes and benefits) as follows:

> Inequality of income before taxes and transfers is mainly driven by the dispersion of labour income and the prevalence of part-time employment and inactivity. Despite their wider dispersion, self-employment and capital income play a smaller role. Tax and transfer systems reduce overall income inequality in all countries. On average across the OECD, three quarters of the reduction in inequality is due to transfers, the rest to direct household taxation.[11]

However, measures of overall inequality, such as the Gini coefficient, are probably not telling the most important part of the story as far as current political and economic problems are concerned. Perhaps what is more important is the position of the worst off sections of society in contrast to the manner in which the top 1% have increased their lead over the rest. A recent article by Martin Wolf in the *Financial Times* is headed 'The economic losers are in revolt against the elites'.[12]

For the USA there is an abundance of analysis based on official statistics compiled by the US Bureau of Labor and the Social Security Administration that documents the failure of typical wage earners in the USA, the largest market economy in the world, to reap the benefits of the overall increase in productivity and output in that country over the last few decades. For example, during the four decades from 1973 to 2013, although the productivity of the economy rose by about 140% the pay of a typical worker rose by only about 9% in real terms. Indeed, during this period in real terms the legal minimum wage actually declined.[13] The counterpart of this is that whereas, in the 1980s, the pay of the chief executive officers of the largest American public companies was about 30 times the earnings of the typical workers in these companies, by the early years of the current decade it was about 270 times as much.[14]

Of course, among wage earners some did share equally in the overall rise in productivity, but the vast majority failed to do so. In fact, even excluding the lowest paid workers, the 'middle class' (defined as those in the middle three-fifths of household incomes) received a much smaller rise in their average incomes than they would have done had the overall level of inequality (measured by the Gini coefficient) not increased over the last few decades. More precisely, in the latter part of the decade 2001–2010 the average household income in this group in the USA was about $76,000, whereas if their incomes had risen in line with overall national income since 1979 it would have been about $94,000.[15]

Although comparable data are not so readily available for other developed counties such data as are available tell a similar story. For example, data provided by the *International Labour Office* show that for the developed countries as a whole real wages rose by only about half of the rise in labour productivity over the last fifteen years. Of course, the picture varies somewhat from country to country. The gap between the rise in productivity and the rise in real wages was greatest in the USA, Germany, Spain and Japan, whereas in many other major developed countries, such as the UK, Australia and Canada, both wages and productivity rose more or less in line.

Given that the overall rise in prosperity in developed countries has been very modest over the last decade it is not surprising that the general failure of the worst off groups in society to share in this meagre overall rise in prosperity has hindered policies to reduce poverty. In the USA there has been little improvement in the poverty rate since the late 1960s.[16] According to a recent report, 'The number of people living in high-poverty ghettos, barrios, and slums has nearly doubled since 2000, rising from 7.2 million to 13.8 million'.[17]

And in the European Union the 'at-risk-of-poverty' rate has risen in recent years so that the *European Union Social Protection Committee* reported in 2014 that there are 6.7 million more people living in poverty or social exclusion since 2008, representing a total of 124.2 million people for the European Union – that is, about one quarter of the population.[18] Furthermore, although the correlation is not very high it does appear that, in fifteen OECD countries for which comparable data were available, higher poverty rates do seem to be accompanied by larger shares of income going to the highest income groups. Indeed, Atkinson's data show that, of the fifteen countries covered, only Switzerland has a below average poverty rate with a higher than average share of income going to the richest groups.[19]

2   POSSIBLE CONSEQUENCES OF INCREASING INEQUALITY?

Everyday life is constantly throwing up instances where the 'justice' or 'fairness' of the distribution or allocation of some goods or entitlements is a real practical problem. As Peyton Young puts it,

> Equity is, after all, an everyday concern. Families try to divide up the household chores equitably among their members. Businesses are sensitive to issues of equity in the salaries and perquisites that they offer to their employees. Public agencies worry about equity when they decide who has access to public housing; how much to charge for basic services such as water, electricity, and public transport; who gets a kidney transplant; and who gets into a nursery school (or a nursing home). (Peyton Young, 1994, pp. xi–xii)

In this book I shall not consider these problems, which are in the domain of what Peyton Young calls 'micro-equity'. Here I am limiting the discussion to the distributive justice of 'macro-equity', such as how incomes are distributed. This is because, as mentioned in Chapter 7, the moral significance of an 'efficient' (i.e. a 'Pareto optimal') allocation of resources in the economy is limited by the macro-distributional features of society. And it is these that are a major source of social and political debate.

In Chapter 6 I discussed the well-known possible conflict between 'efficiency' and 'equality', or what Arthur Okun called 'the Big Trade-off'. It was pointed out that these two objectives may not *always* conflict. For example, if, in the interests of equality, there is less discrimination against women in the labour market, this is likely to lead to an increase in productive efficiency. And, conversely, some policies designed to increase productive efficiency may also increase equality between income groups. This would be the case, for example, with taxes on environmental pollution when their incidence falls mainly on richer people and if they enable taxes on poorer groups to be reduced or welfare benefits to be increased.

But there is a theoretical presumption that, in general, measures to reduce inequality, such as taxes on the rich and benefits to the poor, will reduce productive efficiency. After all, what is known as the 'First Theorem of Welfare Economics' demonstrates that, under certain conditions such as perfect competition, information, no externalities, and so on, any taxes or benefits will tend to reduce the overall productive 'efficiency' with which resources are allocated. Of course, everybody knows that these conditions do not prevail fully. Nevertheless, there is some theoretical and empirical support for the presumption that there is often a conflict between productive efficiency and equality.

According to the OECD study to which reference has been made above,

> Some taxes have a greater adverse effects on economic activity than others. Personal and corporate income taxes are the most distortive taxes as they have sizable negative effects on labour use, productivity and capital accumulation. Shifting the tax mix away from such taxes and towards recurrent taxes on immovable property (the least distortive) and consumption taxes should thus raise living standards. However, there is likely to be a trade-off with the income distribution objective since personal income taxes are progressive while real estate and consumption taxes are at best neutral in a lifetime perspective. Targeted transfers, however, can reduce the severity of this trade-off.[20]

This conflict has always seemed to be important because inequality – beyond a point – was widely believed to be undesirable. There are two classes of reasons for this belief. Many people believe that, beyond a point, inequality is simply 'unfair' or 'unjust' – that is, that equality is *intrinsically* valuable. Many people also believe that rising inequality has undesirable social or political effects – that is, that equality has *instrumental* value. The former view – that is, that beyond a point, inequality is 'unjust', or 'unfair' – that has pre-occupied philosophers for millennia. Unfortunately, as discussed later in this chapter, they have still not been able to reach any agreement about the intrinsic value of equality. At least, not yet. By contrast, much more progress has been made in recent years in establishing the *instrumental* value of equality, as summarised in the next section.

But in Section 4, I return to the theory. And the stagnation of the earnings of the worst off sections of society indicated above happens to correspond to one of the most important contemporary contributions to the theory of justice and 'just' inequalities. This is John Rawls's famous theory of justice, which is discussed at length in Section 4. But before discussing this theory I shall digress briefly to review some of the evidence for the view that economic equality also has instrumental value.

3   THE INSTRUMENTAL VALUE OF EQUALITY

In the last few years several major contributions have been made providing empirical evidence of a link between economic equality and the welfare of society. For example, a recent OECD report states that 'this long-run increase in income inequality not only raises social and political concerns, but also economic ones. It tends to drag down GDP growth, due to the rising distance of the lower 40% from the rest of society'. People on lower incomes have been prevented from realising their human capital potential, which is bad for the economy as a whole.[21] A similar conclusion was reached in a recent IMF staff study. This found that

> ...lower net inequality [i.e. inequality after redistribution via taxes and benefits] is robustly correlated with faster and more durable growth, for a given level of redistribution. These results are highly supportive of our earlier work... redistribution appears generally benign in terms of its impact on growth; only in extreme cases is there some evidence that it may have direct negative effects on growth. Thus the combined direct and indirect effects of redistribution – including the growth effects of the resulting lower inequality – are on average pro-growth.[22]

Inequality also has serious social effects, in addition to its negative effect on growth. These have been eloquently summarised recently by Nobel Laureate Joseph Siglitz, who writes,

> There are two visions of America a half century from now. One is of a society more divided between the haves and the have-nots, a country in which the rich live in gated communities, send their children to expensive schools, and have access to first-rate medical care. Meanwhile, the rest live in a world marked by insecurity, at best mediocre education, and in effect rationed health care—they hope and pray they don't get seriously sick. At the bottom are millions of young people alienated and without hope. I have seen that picture in many developing countries; economists have given it a name, a dual economy, two societies living side by side, but hardly knowing each other, hardly imagining what life is like for the other. Whether we will fall to the depths of some countries, where the gates grow higher and the societies split farther and farther apart, I do not know. It is, however, the nightmare towards which we are slowly marching.... Of all the costs imposed on our society by the top 1 percent, perhaps the greatest is this: the erosion of our sense of identity in which fair play, equality of opportunity, and a sense of community are so important.[23]

It is true that Stiglitz's vision is of a possible future US society, but trends in the USA tend to be followed in other developed countries without much of a time lag.

Still at a general social and political level, beyond a point inequality has been alleged to have serious social and political consequences on account of its negative effect on a society's sense of cohesion. For example, Robert Reich, in a wide-ranging study of inequality trends, maintains that a thriving democracy depends on trust, and this depends, in turn, on the belief that the organisation of society is basically 'fair'. Hence, if growing inequality creates a general belief that society is operating only for the benefit of the few, not the many, this undermines a general respect for the legitimacy of capitalist democracy [24] Furthermore, it is increasingly difficult to ignore the extent to which great wealth distorts the political process since it enables some of it to influence elections one way or another, through mechanisms such as control of the media.

One well-documented effect of inequality is its harmful effect on the health – both mental and physical – of people who are lower down in 'the social hierarchy'. For example, pioneering surveys by Sir Michael Marmot and others found that the lowest grades of Whitehall civil servants were about four times more likely to die during a given period than those in the highest grades. They were also more likely to suffer from heart problems, depression and back pain. This was after full allowance had been made for other variables, such as smoking and poor diet, and was not because they were impoverished. Among the civil servants, those at the top of the hierarchy – who, presumably, have more stressful jobs – have better health than those at the bottom.[25] (In fact, there are even studies that show that similar relationships exist in the animal world, for example in rhesus monkeys, where there is no need to adjust for other variables, such as smoking!)

Richard Wilkinson and Kate Pickett have also convincingly confirmed the conclusions of Marmot's work.[26] They showed that 'health gets worse at every step down the social ladder, so that the poor are less healthy than those in the middle, who in turn are less healthy than those further up'. In other words, it is not just those near the bottom of the social ladder whose health is affected.

Thus there is strong empirical evidence for the proposition that greater equality of certain variables, such as income or wealth, is simply desirable because it makes society a happier place, irrespective of any theories of distributive justice. For example, it can be argued that greater equality of wealth or income reduces envy, or increases community solidarity, or enhances the dignity of the poorer groups in society, or leads to better industrial relations, and so on.

Of course, greater equality might also reduce the pleasure that some people may obtain from their possession of certain goods or services, known as 'positional goods', that give pleasure to their possessors on account of their rarity in addition to their intrinsic value. For example, much of the satisfaction of wearing a Dior dress or expensive jewels may come from the knowledge that most other women cannot wear the same things. If *perfect* replica Dior dresses could be worn by all the ladies their appeal to the wealthy would diminish. And if most young ladies wore bikinis hand-painted by Picasso others would probably regard them as rather vulgar (especially since one can guess what Picasso would have painted on them!).

4   The Intrinsic Value of Equality and the Stagnation of Earnings of the 'Worst-Off'

As indicated in Section 1, one of the most striking features of the last two or three decades in some developed countries has been the stagnation of the 'real' incomes of the lowest paid members of society. It is likely that this has added to an increased dissatisfaction with the current state of society and resentment against the well-known increasing wealth of the richest members of society. And it is not surprising that this trend is regarded as politically dangerous. For it can obviously provide a culture in which populist extremist views the can easily take root and flourish. And, as Martin Wolf points out in the article mentioned above, 'Native populists must not win. We know that story and it ends very badly indeed'.[27]

Thus, although there appear to be good reasons to believe that inequality in general has harmful social and political effects, it is probably not the general increase in inequality that has been most important in recent decades in creating a sense that society is, somehow or other, 'unjust'. For the vast majority of people have never heard of a 'Gini' coefficient, or of 'decile values' and other widely used measures of general inequality in society. But most people are aware of how well-off they are and whether their economic position has been improving or not. And those on the lower rungs of the social and economic ladder will know that over the last two or three decades their position has stagnated. Furthermore, the media and the cult of celebrity means that they are probably also well aware of the growth in the incomes of those on the top rungs. This contrast will inevitably create a feeling that while the economy as a whole may be growing, they are not getting a 'fair' share in it and all the benefits are going to the rich.

But what principles of justice would justify such a reaction and how would they relate to 'fairness'? An answer to this question happens to be a crucial ingredient in the most important contemporary contribution to the theory of justice, namely the Rawlsian theory of justice. For, roughly speaking, a central ingredient of Rawls's theory is that everybody, including the least well-off, should get *some* share in any increase in the general prosperity and stability of their society to which they contribute in however a modest way. And, as shown in Section 1, this has manifestly not always been the case over the last two or three decades.

But most people who believe that some particular degree of inequality is 'unjust' would do so on purely intuitive grounds without explicitly deriving this from some prior coherent theory of justice. In his great book, *A Theory of Justice* (1971), Rawls tried to rescue sympathy for certain principles of justice, including dislike of considerable inequalities in society, from being purely intuitive or *ad hoc*, and to provide them with firmer and explicit logical foundations. His rejection of utilitarianism – and indeed of any teleological framework aimed to maximising some 'good' without reflecting the relationships between individuals – also corresponds to his emphasis on the function that principles of justice play in enabling people to live together peacefully in spite of different interests and beliefs. No philosophical publication in the last few decades has spawned such a vast literature as has this book. Naturally, given the subtlety, the vast scope, the originality and the ambition of Rawls's project, even Rawls's sternest critics find it difficult to discuss political philosophy without starting from Rawls.

Rawls constructed a theory that helped reconcile two apparently conflicting conceptions of justice, namely justice as *mutual advantage*, and justice as *fairness*, which is closely linked to the concept of justice as *impartiality*. Justice as mutual advantage is in a long and honourable contractarian tradition, going back to Hobbes, Locke, Hume and Rousseau – though each formulated their theories in very different ways and drew different conclusions. In this tradition a contract is 'just' if it is a freely negotiated contract by parties who have reached some agreement in the light of their own self-interest. According to Rawls, 'Justice as fairness is an example of what I have called a contract theory'.

How did Rawls manage to combine a contractarian theory of justice with his emphasis on justice as fairness or impartiality? His ingenious solution was to conceive of a hypothetical contract as being drawn up *not* by actual people who knew what their particular situation in life happened to be, but by notional people in what he called the 'original position', behind a 'veil of ignorance'. In such a situation 'no one knows his situation in society nor his natural assets, and therefore no one is in a position to tailor principles to his advantage'. This appears to be an ingenious way of combining contractarianism with justice as fairness.

Since they would have no axe to grind the parties to the contract would be perfectly impartial. The 'original position' device suggests the image of a group of people drawing up rules for playing some game – like football or bridge – without knowing in advance what particular abilities or disabilities they will have when the game begins – for example, whether one will be fleet of foot, or possess good hand-eye coordination or quick thinking, or be good at mental arithmetic, or whatever. But since they agreed on the rules in question none of them could have cause to complain that the rules were 'unfair' if, when the game commences, some of them discover that the rules did not favour the particular skills that they possessed.

The principles of justice that would emerge from 'the original position' would depend on how the original position is characterised. Rawls assumed that the participants in the original position would not suffer from envy, but they would be risk averse. So they would not want to run the risk of being condemned to lives of poverty or oppression. He also assumed that they would be rational and that '... each tries as best he can to advance his interests'.[28] Given the characterisation of the original position as one in which participants would not know what position they would come to occupy, the principles of justice that emerge from it will be 'fair' in the sense that they emerge as a result of totally impartial negotiations over these principles. The glue that binds *actual* people to principles of justice, whatever position they happen to occupy, has to be stronger than self-interest and include respect for their manifest 'fairness'.

To what basic principles of justice would the participants in the Rawlsian original position agree? Rawls argued that the notional participants in the original position would agree to the following two basic principles:-

(a) Each person has an equal right to a fully adequate scheme of equal basic liberties, which is compatible with a similar scheme of liberties for all.

(b) Social and economic inequalities are to satisfy two conditions. First, they must be attached to offices and positions open to all under conditions of fair equality of opportunity; and second, they are to be to the greatest benefit of the least-advantaged members of society (this is what he called 'the difference principle').[29]

Of course, as they stand these two principles raise a host of questions concerning their precise interpretation and justification, and whether they are even consistent with each other. It is to these that Rawls devoted a substantial part of his 1971 book and his later (2001) clarifications and amendments. But I am only concerned here with some of the implications of his guiding principles. In 2001 he reformulated them slightly to make more explicit the point that inequalities should work to the benefit of the least well-off members of society.[30]

The idea is that even the least fortunate groups in society will accept certain economic inequalities as 'just' as long as they believe that the system of rewards necessary for social cohesion and increased economic progress benefits them as well as everybody else. In simple terms, they accept the 'trickle down' theory and believe that it justifies their relatively low position. The details of what it is that is to be distributed equally or unequally are spelt out in detail by Rawls, but basically they are social 'primary goods', which include rights and liberties, opportunities and powers, income and wealth, and the basis for self-respect, which he suggests may be the most important primary good.[31]

One way of appreciating the distributive principle is to go back to the problem that is supposed to have been first formulated by Plato, concerning what to do with a flute. Who has the greatest claim to it? The person who made it, or the person who would derive the most pleasure from it, or the person who would be the most skilful performer with it? Of course if we are talking about a single good, such as one flute, one can hardly cut it up and share out the pieces to the different people who have a claim. But the person who made the flute presumably has *some* claim, so he should be rewarded somehow or other, such as a nice Greek vase to put on his mantelpiece.

And in an economy in which a vast number of different goods and services are produced, there is no technical difficulty in giving some appropriate reward to everybody who has made some contribution, however modest, to the viability and progress of that economy. Their 'right' to this reward would be one of the principles of justice that would be enshrined in the contract drawn up by people in the 'original position'. So, if some members of society today feel that they are getting nothing out of the peaceful functioning and progress of their society, Rawls provided them – with extraordinary prescience – with a theoretical justification for their resentment at being victims of an injustice.

In conclusion, in addition to the *instrumental* value of equality set out in the last section, it seems that a strong case can also be made out for it also having *intrinsic* value by virtue of its part in a theory of justice.

5   The Libertarian Critique of Egalitarianism

Of course, one would not expect such a position to go unchallenged. And Rawls's theory of justice has been challenged from opposite directions. From one side it can be challenged as being insufficiently egalitarian, for one reason or another.

But the most common challenges have come from those who maintain that Rawls is *too* egalitarian. One of the most important of these has been the late Robert Nozick's theory of entitlements, set out in his scintillating and seminal 1974 book, *Anarchy, State, and Utopia*. Many years later he wrote that the view he expressed in that book was ' . . . one that now seems seriously inadequate to me'.[32] But one of the basic themes of the book, which is still commonly regarded as expressing the essence of 'libertarianism', was, as mentioned earlier in Chapter 10, that 'Individuals have rights, and there are things no person or group may do to them (without violating their rights). So strong and far-reaching are those rights that they raise the question of what, if anything, the state and its officials may do' (Nozick 1974, ix).

The essence of Nozick's theory is that, as long one has acquired one's assets legitimately, it does not matter – within reason – what particular pattern of distribution of assets then emerges from the exercise of freedom to do what one likes with them. This is not so much a critique of egalitarianism *per se* as a criticism of the enforcement of a particular pattern of distribution since this may conflict with certain rights, notably rights to property that had been acquired by legitimate means.

In an important respect he shares with Rawls the rejection of the utilitarian neglect of the rights of the individual. But Rawls and Nozick differ, however, on the question of which rights are most important. To oversimplify, we can say that for Rawls, one of the most important distributional rights is a right to a share of society's output. For Nozick, on the other hand, the most important rights are rights over oneself – the rights which constitute 'self-ownership'.[33] There is obviously no objective way of comparing the intrinsic value of these conflicting 'rights'.

Starting from the rights over oneself, Nozick went on to develop – rather as did John Locke in 1690 – an 'entitlement' theory of property rights to the effect that everybody has an equal natural right to dispose of their property in any way that they please, provided that this does not infringe on other people's rights and that the property in question has been acquired as a result of freely negotiated transactions. To take away any property that has been acquired legitimately would, therefore, violate a 'negative' right, in other words the right not to have certain things done *to* you, such as deprive you of your property or liberty, by contrast with a 'positive' right to have certain things done *for* you, such as provide you with a job or a house and so on. Nozick made the point that certain principles of 'justice', such as that everybody has a 'right' to something or other, '... treat objects as if they appeared from nowhere, out of nothing'.[34] In other words, it seems to avoid the problem that the goods or services in question belonged to somebody who had acquired them 'legitimately'. In the absence of a theory that justified this violation of property rights this would rule out many – and perhaps all – of the 'positive' rights that are commonly claimed today in many spheres of social organisation and that one eloquent exponent of libertarianism, Anthony de Jasay, describes as '... the obligatory buzzwords in any political theory aspiring to modernity'.[35]

6   THE 'LEVELLING DOWN' CRITIQUE OF EGALITARIANISM

A more general and well-known philosophical objection to the intrinsic value of egalitarianism is what Derek Parfit called 'The Leveling-Down Objection'.[36] This is the objection that equality cannot be *intrinsically* valuable since, if it were, it would make sense to promote it by reducing the particular 'good' (whatever it happens to be) of those who happen to have most of it even if this did not lead to any increase in the amount of the 'good' received by the worst off.

Thus, consider a change that results purely in greater equality but in which the worse off do not receive any of the 'good' taken away from the better off. And exclude, for the time being, cases where the reduction in the inequality of the 'good' increases society's welfare indirectly. Many people would believe that such 'pure' levelling down would not make sense. If we achieved greater equality of incomes, for example, simply by taking some away from the rich even though none of it would go to the poor (e.g. it would all get lost through reduced incentives, bureaucratic procedures, etc., that Okun referred to as the 'leaky bucket') few people would approve an increase in equality achieved this way on the grounds of its intrinsic value. Some of those who did so may be motivated largely by envy, which has no moral significance.

Why should we believe that levelling down without improving the welfare of the worse off has no moral force? One reason would be that many people would subscribe – without, presumably, being aware of it – to what is known among philosophers as the 'Person-Affecting Claim' (to use the terminology of Parfit, who first demonstrated fully the power and implications of this claim), or what Temkin has called, more conveniently, 'The Slogan'.[37] Temkin defines 'the Slogan' as follows: *'One situation cannot be worse (or better) than another if there is no one for whom it is worse (or better)'.*[38] Thus a more equal society cannot be 'better' than a less equal society if nobody is better off in it. Consequently, if reducing the G (i.e. the 'good') of the better off does not improve anybody else's G then the new situation cannot be better than the old one. It has nothing to do with what we take to be G. Whether it is utility, or welfare, or resources, or opportunities for any of these things, or for anything else, the notion that we should equalise G by reducing the amount of G of those who have most of it without increasing the G of anybody else does not seem appealing. Nevertheless, some political philosophers would assert that 'fairness' has an intrinsic value, so that, even if nobody is better off as a result of some levelling down, it could still be justified on 'fairness' grounds provided the reduction in overall G is not excessive.

Whether the elimination of 'unfair' inequalities even if nobody is actually made better off has the intrinsic value that Temkin and some others claim is, of course, a major value judgement. As Roger Crisp once said to me, 'Even if there is a kind of goodness that is not good for any being, why should we care about it?' In other words, what is so 'good' about it?

7   PRIORITARIANISM

As I have suggested above, the theoretical concept of social justice probably plays very little part in the way that most people see the problem of distribution. As well as some intuitive feeling about what constitutes an injustice most people are probably motivated also by sentiments of 'sympathy' of the kind set out by Adam Smith and David Hume. This would take the form of a desire to relieve obvious poverty or deprivation. One proponent of the view that equality should not be the focus of our concern is Harry Frankfurt, who argued that

> Inequality is a purely formal relationship, from which nothing whatever follows as to the desirability or value of any of the unequal terms. The egalitarian condemnation of inequality as inherently bad loses much of its force, I believe, when we recognize that those who are doing considerably worse than others may nonetheless be doing rather well. Surely what is of genuine moral concern is whether people have good lives, and not how their lives compare with the lives of others.[39]

In similar vein, Raz writes that '... wherever one turns it is revealed that what makes us care about various inequalities is not the inequality but the concern identified by the underlying principle. It is the hunger of the hungry, the need of the needy, the suffering of the ill, and so on'.[40] In other words, it is argued, most people – egalitarians included – do not seem to be much concerned with equality per se, although they are genuinely concerned with equality as a means of reducing some 'bad'.[41]

Even the argument advanced by Nagel in favour of the intrinsic value of egalitarianism is essentially an argument in favour of giving priority to those in greater need. He argues that 'egalitarianism... establishes an order of priority among needs and gives preference to the most urgent...'.[42] He defends this on the grounds that, faced with several options, as a matter of basic principle society ought to choose between options the one that is least unacceptable to the person to whom it is most unacceptable. And, he argues, 'A radically egalitarian policy of giving absolute priority to the worst off, regardless of numbers, would result from always choosing the least unacceptable alternative, in this sense' (*op. cit.*, p. 123).[43]

These views might appear to resemble Rawlsian concern that the gains from social and economic cooperation in a society be shared out in a way that benefits the worst off members of that society. But there is an important difference. The Frankfurt and Raz views are more akin to what is known as 'sufficiency' or 'prioritarianism'. For, unlike the Rawlsian principle, this does not take account of people's *relative* position. For Rawls, the worst off are those who are worse off relative to everybody else. In 'prioritarianism' the worst off are those who are the most badly off compared to how they would be under a different distribution, not compared to how badly off, or well off, they are compared to other people.[44]

In other words, the distinctively moral case for giving priority to benefits to the worst off is that what is bad about people being badly off is simply that they are badly off in *absolute* terms. The criterion of an improved distribution is not that it reduces inequality it is that it benefits most the people who – from society's point of view – would obtain the most benefit.[45] Of course, comparisons have to be made: by definition the term 'priority' implies comparisons. But what is compared is not the relative starting position of the people in question but a comparison of who – in the eyes of society – would benefit most from a different distribution.

In practice, of course, it will usually make little difference whether society gives priority to those who it believes will benefit most or gives priority to those whose increase in welfare will contribute most to equality. As a rule, the two groups would coincide. But one can imagine theoretical scenarios where this is not the case.[46] This is why the qualifying clause 'in the eyes of society' is essential in this theory since it rules out redistribution to the rich in cases where they might gain more utility from having more caviar and fine wines than would the poor from more basic needs. Thus a prioritarian social welfare function would still be in terms of the benefits to the worst off, as valued by society, not by the beneficiaries. This also implies that the recipients of the benefit may not appreciate or anticipate the extent of their benefit. This might be the case for example, if the 'capabilities' of the worst off are increased in a way that expands their horizons and the scope for realising more fully their potentialities.

A common example would be education, where people who had been deprived of it were unaware of the way that it could enrich their lives. One theoretical advantage of the prioritarian view is that it is not vulnerable to the 'levelling down objection' to egalitarianism that we have discussed above. For egalitarians there is some merit – up to a point – in reducing the welfare of the better-off even if the worse off receive nothing as a result, since it would still increase equality, which can be set off against the loss in total welfare. To a prioritarian, if the worse off gain nothing such 'levelling down' has no merit at all.

Some people would go further than simple prioritarianism and prefer an amended version of the Priority view, which, as described by Roger Crisp, incorporates a threshold. According to this view, we should give priority to people below a certain threshold of welfare, but, apart from that, we need not care much about the distribution of welfare among the rest of the population.[47]

However some people might like to qualify prioritarianism – like most other egalitarian principles – by a widespread intuition that there is no moral obligation to help people who are in some sense responsible for being badly off. For example, Arneson proposes what he calls 'responsibility-catering prioritarianism', about which he says that 'Roughly stated, the idea is that justice requires us to maximize a function of human well-being that gives priority to improving the well-being of those who are badly off and of those who, if badly off, are not substantially responsible for their condition in virtue of their prior conduct'[48] (Arneson, 2000, p. 340). This would correspond to the tendency that Atkinson says is prevalent in recent economic literature to separate the determinants of economic outcomes into those 'due to circumstances that are beyond personal control, such as family background, and "effort" for which an individual can be responsible'.[49] However whether it is possible to make moral distinctions between lucky people who have inherited genes that gave them more brains or athletic talent or self-discipline and capacity for hard work, and people who did not have any such luck, is an interesting subject for speculation.

To summarise, therefore, one can distinguish various types of 'egalitarianism' and 'prioritarianism'.

(i) Straightforward egalitarianism focuses on relativities right across the board.

(ii) Rawlsian egalitarianism focuses on the worst off group in society, and tolerates inequalities provided they are to the benefit of that group.

(iii) Prioritarianism focuses on those who would gain the most absolute benefit, whatever their position relative to others ('benefits' being judged by society, not by the recipient).

(iv) Threshold prioritarianism focuses on those who are below some specific, absolute threshold and ignores the distribution of welfare above them.

(v) Responsibility–catering prioritarianism takes into account how far people are regarded as morally responsible for their plight.

Of course, the above beliefs are not mutually exclusive. One can, for example, believe that there are good reasons – instrumental or intrinsic – for believing that overall equality is a desirable objective, while still believing that policy ought to focus on helping the poorest members of society or curbing the potential power of the richest.

Notes

1. Penguin Classics edition, 1987:396/7.
2. These include books by Atkinson, A.B.; Deaton, A.; Marmot, M.; Wilkinson, R., and Pickett, K.; Piketty, T., Reich, R.B.; Stiglitz, J.; and reports by the OECD and the World Bank.
3. Piketty, 2014.
4. OECD, 2014.
5. Wildaum and Mitchell, *Financial Times*, 14 January, 2016.
6. Royal Commission on the Distribution of Income and Wealth [RCDIW] 1979, [Cmnd. 7595]:17. The World Top Incomes Database estimates suggest that the post-tax income share of the top 1% in the UK fell from around 12% in 1945 to just over 8% in 1960.
7. Atkinson, Piketty and Saez, 2011: 41, Figure 8.
8. Using Luxembourg Income Survey (LIS) data for 17 industrialised countries, Harkness (2010) has explored in detail the link between female participation and inequality, while Sobhee (2011) has demonstrated the importance of changes in female employment in a variety of developing countries in Latin America and Sub-Saharan Africa.
9. Atkinson, 2015:66.
10. Atkinson, 2015:82, Figure 2.7.
11. OECD, 2012:3.
12. *Financial Times*, 26 January, 2016.
13. Mishel, Gould and Bivens [EPI] 2015: Figures 2 and 8
14. Mishel *et al.*, *ibid.*: Figure 7.
15. Mishel *et al.*, *ibid.*: Figure 1.
16. Atkinson, 2015:24.
17. Jarowsky, *Financial Times*, August 7th, 2015.
18. Atkinson, *ibid.*
19. Atkinson, *ibid.*: Figure 1.4.
20. OECD, 2012:10.
21. http://www.oecd.org/social/in-it-together-why-less-inequality-benefits-all-9789264235120-en.htm
22. Ostry *et al.*, 2014.
23. Stiglitz, 2012 and 2015.
24. Reich, 2015.
25. Marmot, 2004 and 2015.

26. Wilkinson and Pickett, 2009 and 2011.
27. Wolf, M., Financial Times, 26 September 2007:15.
28. Rawls, 1971:142.
29. Rawls,1993. The principles as set out in 2001 [in *Political Liberalism*] and reproduced here differ slightly from those originally set out in 1971, p2. 50, but it would be out of place here – and irrelevant to the main argument – to embark on an analysis of the differences.
30. This was, of course, implicit in his earlier 1971 formulation which required that social and economic inequalities be 'reasonably expected to be to everyone's advantage' (1971:60) and was made explicit at numerous points in the book, such as '... the higher expectations of those better situated are just if and only if they work as part of a scheme which improves the expectations of the least advantaged members of society' (*loc. cit*:75).
31. For example, Rawls,1971:440.
32. Nozick,1989:17.
33. Kymlicka., 2002:108.
34. Nozick, 1974:160.
35. de Jasay, 2010a:8. See also his provocative dissection of the concept of 'rights' in de Jasay, 2010b.
36. Parfit,1991:17–18 and passim.
37. This corresponds to what Broome calls 'the principal of personal good' in Broome, 1991:ch.8.
38. Temkin, 1993:248.
39. Frankfurt, 1997. See also a much later re-statement of his views in Frankfurt, 2015.
40. Raz, 1986:240.
41. On prioritarianism, see also Parfit, 1991; Broome,1991; Fleurbaey, 2006.
42. Nagel, 1979:116–117.
43. Strictly speaking, one ought to distinguish between three concepts, namely (i) being the worst off; (ii) having greatest needs; and (iii) deriving the most benefit from redistributive policies. But for purposes of the point made here it is assumed that all three are sufficiently closely correlated.
44. See e.g. Parfit, 1991:22; Brighouse and Swift, 2006:fn.2
45. Before the concept of 'prioritarianism' came into widespread use it was discussed by Broome as an 'additively separable utility function', in Broome, 1991:179ff.
46. For example, as shown in Broome, 1991:185; or Brown, Campbell, 2005.
47. Crisp, 2003: 757.
48. See also Arneson, 2000.
49. Atkinson, 2015:9.

CHAPTER 16

Equality of What?

1 DIFFERENT CONCEPTS OF EQUALITY: CONFLICTING OR COMPLEMENTARY?

Anybody who advocates greater equality of, say, wealth or income, would normally be regarded as an 'egalitarian'. And they would normally regard themselves as egalitarian. But there is a little logical problem about claiming to be an egalitarian by appealing to the desirability of equality in one or another particular 'space' or 'focal variable', such as income or opportunity. For – as Amartya Sen has emphasised – greater equality in one or other 'space' may lead to greater inequality in some other 'space' (Sen, 1992). This is on account of basic human diversity taken together with the variety of possible 'spaces' in which equality can be conceived. So you could be an egalitarian in one space but anti-egalitarian in another.

For example, equality of opportunity is likely to lead to unequal distributions of income since people differ in their ability to take advantage of their opportunities. But an equal distribution of income would lead to an unequal distribution of welfare since people have different needs and tastes. Similarly, redistribution policies designed to increase equality in incomes are likely to require some restrictions on people's freedom to dispose of their assets freely, thereby leading to inequalities in the space of 'rights'. In other words, if you are in favour of greater equality in some 'evaluative space' you will usually have to condone greater inequality in some other space. So are you an egalitarian or not? It is not possible to be an egalitarian in all of them.

© The Author(s) 2017
W. Beckerman, *Economics as Applied Ethics*,
DOI 10.1007/978-3-319-50319-6_16

In fact, since 'to make people equal in one respect can make them unequal in another...we cannot simply assume without further clarification that we know what an equal society would be like' (J. Wolff).[1] Nevertheless, there is room for major differences of opinion as to which 'evaluative space' is the most important. Before marrying somebody one might take account of the prospective spouse's age, good looks, IQ, wealth, income, cooking abilities, musical tastes, congenial parents and even whether the person is already married. But most people will regard some of these evaluative spaces as more important – perhaps crucially – than others. To attach importance to one criterion does not make the others totally irrelevant, except perhaps marital status. Indeed, many of the focal variables can be complementary in some circumstances. The same applies to the choice of the appropriate focal variable in the equality debate. For example, greater equality of incomes is more likely than not to lead to greater equality of welfare. But this may not be true for all the commonly cited focal variables, including welfare, opportunity, resources, income, capabilities or rights.

Many of these variables will be complementary, so that it would not matter much which ones should be promoted, or even which ones are the most important. Anyway, it is difficult to see by what criteria one could justify concentrating on one of these variables rather than another. Presumably one has to treat them as either top-level intrinsic values that are incommensurable, or as being simply *instrumentally* valuable in promoting some higher-level intrinsic value, such as 'happiness', and then test – on the basis of empirical data – which ones are most conducive to that value. Unfortunately, even ignoring the problem of reaching some generally agreed definition of 'happiness' and serious statistical difficulties, there would still be the problem of how far happiness itself is equally distributed. For, as indicated in the *World Happiness Reports* discussed in Chapter 12, it cannot be assumed that the aggregate happiness of a given society is all that matters irrespective of its distribution.

For example, suppose you are faced with two societies which, to simplify the argument, have equal populations. In the first society people are equally happy, but on a happiness scale of zero to ten, each person's happiness is only three. In the second society individual happiness ranges from four to ten. So in terms of happiness it is a much more unequal society (it is assumed that each person's happiness takes account of the degree of inequality in that society). In the second society there is more inequality but everybody's happiness is higher than everybody's happiness in the first society. Which society do you prefer? And does some modification of the figures make any difference? For example, would you choose the second society if the happiness levels therein ranged only from, say, four to five, so that average happiness would not be much greater in the second society than in the first? If so, you are attaching some intrinsic value to the equality with which happiness is distributed even though it does not increase the happiness of any of the individuals concerned. So you have to answer the question posed at the end of the last chapter, namely what is so good about this greater equality even though it is no good for anybody.

Thus we seem to be driven to the conclusion that it is difficult to identify which particular concept of equality is most important in the sense that it is the most *instrumentally* effective in promoting some higher-level *intrinsically* valuable concept of equality.

2   EQUALITY OF WELFARE

As explained in Chapter 7 the focal variable in a conventional textbook social welfare function is the 'utility' of the individuals to which the function refers. Subjective judgements about the distribution among people of utility/welfare is what a social welfare function is supposed to help us take into account in choosing between different distributions of utility/welfare.

Unfortunately equality of welfare is difficult to measure, though considerable progress has been made in measuring 'happiness' over the last few decades. Nevertheless economists have tended so far to concentrate on the distribution of the relatively measurable concepts of income or wealth. But people differ with respect to their ability to convert incomes into welfare. For example, on the whole, people who are physically disabled, or have expensive tastes, or gloomy dispositions, would experience less welfare than other people with the same income. Yet, society would usually regard remedial action as appropriate for some of these reasons but not for others. For example, most people would accept that it is 'unfair' for people to suffer on account of some physical disability, but not on account of expensive or perverse tastes. Loss of welfare on account of gloomy dispositions might be on the borderline. After all, society does devote a lot of resources to mental therapy and anti-depression drugs. So, either directly or indirectly, attempts to iron out major differences in capacity to convert incomes into welfare will often entail inequalities in the resources devoted to different people.

Furthermore, many people believe that differences in welfare that reflect differences in 'merit' are perfectly legitimate and the state has no business to mitigate such differences. The 'merit' criterion of an equitable distribution of something or other has a distinguished pedigree, going back to Aristotle's assertion that 'Everybody agrees that justice in distribution must be in accordance with merit in some sense, but they do not all mean the same kind of merit...'[2] This seemed to be only slightly less true over 2,000 years later, since many people now dissent from the merit criterion.

For example, according to Hayek the term 'merit' is used in a wide and vague sense, and he describes his own usage of the term to denote '...the attributes of conduct that make it deserving of praise, that is, the moral character of the action and not the value of the achievement' and in this sense

> ...the value that the performance or the capacity of a person has to his fellows has no necessary connection with its ascertainable merit. The inborn as well as the acquired gifts of a person clearly have a value to his fellows that does not depend on any credit due to him for possessing them. There is little a man can do to alter the fact that his special talents are very common or exceedingly rare. A good mind or a fine voice, a beautiful face or a skilful hand, and a ready wit or an attractive personality are in a large measure as independent of a person's efforts as the opportunities or the experiences he has had' (Hayek, 1960, p. 94)

Hayek concludes from this that '...in a free society it is neither desirable nor practicable that material rewards should be made generally to correspond to what men recognise as merit and...an individual's position should not necessarily depend on the views that his fellows hold about the merit he has acquired'.[3]

He goes on to argue that a society '...in which it was generally presumed that a high income was a proof of merit and a low income a lack of it...in which there was no other road to success than the approval of one's conduct by the majority of one's fellows, would probably be much more unbearable to the unsuccessful ones than one in which it was frankly recognised that there was no necessary connection between merit and success' (Hayek, op. cit., p. 98).

Nevertheless, although it would no longer be true that 'everybody' subscribes to Aristotle's merit criterion, most people probably do so. In that case, inequalities of welfare that correspond to inequalities of 'merit' would be widely accepted as 'just'. This is closely related to the goal of 'equality of opportunity' as we shall now see.

3 EQUALITY OF OPPORTUNITY[4]

Equality of opportunity is probably the focal variable that enjoys the most widespread support. Many people identify this with their notion of 'fairness', which they may regard as corresponding to their concept of 'justice'.[5] They simply believe that it is 'unfair' that, say, people from poor backgrounds do not have the same chance in life of prospering or achieving their life's goals as do people from privileged backgrounds. The 'fairness' justification for equality of opportunity (in some sense or other) is thus a top-level value judgement and, as indicated earlier, corresponds to the widespread view that people ought to be rewarded according to their merit. This would differ in some respects from Rawls's concept of 'justice as fairness'. As explained in Chapter 15, Rawls's concept of fairness corresponds to the hypothetical contract that people would have made behind a veil of ignorance in which they did not know which position in society they would occupy. This contract would not, however, be designed to iron out inequalities between people's welfare that arise on account of their choices in matters over which they had control. It would, nevertheless, respect the principle of redress, which Rawls defines as 'the principle that undeserved inequalities call for redress, and since inequalities of birth and natural endowment are undeserved, these inequalities are to be somehow compensated for.... The idea is to redress the bias in contingencies in the direction of equality'.[6] But, in addition to equal access to positions of advantage in society, what matters in Rawlsian theory is access to 'primary goods'. How far people fail to convert these into welfare as a result, say, of lack of motivation, is their responsibility, and the state has no obligation to iron out the resulting inequality of welfare.

In addition, equality of opportunity may often promote greater productive efficiency, or other tangible benefits. For example, it is often claimed that, if children from deprived backgrounds do not have an equal chance of getting higher education, society is squandering a potential pool of ability. The same would apply to discrimination against people on grounds of sex, or colour, or religion, since this, too, would prevent an economy from making the most efficient use of its human resources. A recent official study in Britain estimated that the gap between the employment rates for ethnic minorities and the population as a whole costs the economy £8.6 billion per annum and that this is largely the result of ethnic discrimination.[7]

If certain policies to promote equality of opportunity promote economic efficiency they would be equalising policies that do not lead to the conflict that is usually assumed to exist between such policies and efficiency. This conflict arises chiefly in connection with certain policies designed to promote equality of incomes. For it is presumed that measures to reduce inequality of incomes (or wealth) by means of, say, progressive rates of taxation, reduce some people's incentives to work harder and earn more. This is because it is widely assumed that both benefit recipients and higher tax payers will be less likely to work as much as they could. Also redistributive measures require unavoidable administrative costs. But the evidence for this is weak, which may be because many people are more concerned with some target level of post-tax income, so if they have to pay more in taxes they will simply try to increase their pre-tax income. And how far benefit recipients prefer a life of idleness to the various social satisfactions of work depends very much on the way that the benefit system is organised.

People subscribe to different conceptions of 'equal opportunity'. For there are many, such as (i) the best person should always get the job (meritocracy); (ii) everybody should start in the same position or enjoy the same chance of success; (iii) something narrower, such as the view that certain specific variables, like race or sex, ought not to influence allocations; or (iv) something wider, such as that everybody should have the same opportunity to achieve their full potential to enjoy a satisfying and creative life.

For example, if one wants equality of opportunity only on the instrumental grounds that it promotes productive efficiency one might limit oneself to the view that employers ought not to discriminate against people on grounds such as colour or gender or social class. This *minimal*, or *formal*, equality of opportunity has obvious origins in the needs of societies to develop and has been accentuated in the course of the growth of competitive market economies. But it is limited from the point of view of both fairness and efficiency. Having the relevant qualifications for a job or a University education is not enough insofar as people have unequal chances of acquiring the relevant qualifications. If the only candidates for a post or decent education are the children of the wealthy then *formal* equality of opportunity may not be enough.

For this reason, many people subscribe to a wider and more *conventional* interpretation of equality of opportunity which is some combination of (i) and (ii) – for example, one may believe that best person should get the job but that everybody should have an equal chance of becoming the best person. This could be on both intrinsic 'fairness' grounds as well as instrumental grounds. For there is little doubt that failure to provide equal educational opportunities to poor children will prevent many of them becoming equally attractive to potential employers or achieving their full productive potential even if there is no discrimination on grounds of sex, colour, religion, and so on. It will generally be felt 'unfair' if a talented person is unable to exploit his potential on account of a deprived background, irrespective of how far his potential raises his income and adds to the productive efficiency of his society. This more *conventional* interpretation of equality of opportunity requires some correction for social disadvantages, notably one's family background. It corresponds to the widely held intuition that it is unfair if people suffer from some disadvantage that is no fault of their own. The corollary of this is the belief that one's achievements should depend only on one's natural abilities and the choices one makes (e.g. to work hard, or take it easy).

Because some philosophers accept that people cannot be held morally responsible for their inborn characteristics – good or bad – many of them believe that even the *conventional* concept of equality of opportunity does not go far enough. For if it is believed that it is 'unfair' for people to be worse off through no fault of their own then it would be unfair for people to be worse off because they were born 'intellectually challenged' and lacking in any other special marketable skills, such as some outstanding sporting or artistic ability. The distribution of talents is, after all, morally arbitrary. Talented people are lucky, and if it is unfair for people to be worse off through no fault of their own – that is they are just unlucky – they ought to be compensated. This would provide a case for a *radical* interpretation of equality of opportunity that aims to correct for natural disadvantages as well as social disadvantages. A form of focal variable that comes close to such a radical interpretation of equality of opportunity is 'equality of resources', to which we now turn.

4 Equality of Resources[8]

Ronald Dworkin, rather like Rawls, maintained that people's achievements in life should reflect only their choices, and not their inherited characteristics, let alone their family circumstances.[9] For this purpose he advocates a radical form of equality of opportunity that would be created by equalising the allocation of 'resources' in society when resources are defined widely to include native talents. But since native abilities cannot be redistributed, people who lack talents should be compensated for this as much as people who lack initial social advantages, such as being born into an unfavourable environment. People may be unfortunate in their choice of their parents in many respects. Not only may their parents be poor, or be in the wrong country at the wrong time, but they may also be unable to pass on valuable genes to their offspring. If the effect of all inherited advantages or disadvantages could be cancelled out it *might* be right to say that differences in the degree to which people achieve their goals in life depend only on their choices – notably whether to work hard or take risks, and so on. This conserves the role of personal responsibility in determining the inequality of outcomes and limits the responsibility of society to promote equality of outcomes.

Hence differences in achievements that result from a person's choices ought not to be rectified by redistributive taxation. But taxes ought to be levied on those whose wealth does not appear to be the reward of their own choices, and may reflect, instead greater innate talent, which is morally arbitrary. And benefits ought to be given to those who are deemed to be deprived on account of lack of talent or other inherited advantages rather than lack of ambition and determination.

Thus Dworkin's approach would attempt to mitigate inequalities that have their origins in inherited material resources or income-enhancing genes or sheer 'brute luck', so that the only remaining inequalities would be those that reflected people's choices. The notion that people are ultimately responsible for their choices and that these are not the result of their genetic inheritance or their environment raises the whole question of free will versus determinism, which lies well outside the scope of this book. Dworkin writes that 'I make no assumption that people choose their convictions or preferences, or their personality more generally, any more than they choose their race or physical or mental abilities. But I do assume an ethics which supposes – as almost all of us in our own lives do suppose – that we are responsible for the consequences of the choices we make out of those convictions or preferences or personality' (Dworkin, 2000, p. 7). But one may ask whether the first sentence is consistent with the second. Perhaps even Dworkin does not go far enough and allowance ought to be made for how much innate talent people have for choosing wisely and how much they have inherited an inclination to work hard.

The problem of the dependence of people's choices and ambitions and energies on their innate abilities is addressed by Rawls in his section on 'Legitimate Expectations and Moral Desert'.[10] In it he argues that theories of 'just' rewards in terms of moral worth contrast with his contractarian theory of justice. What people are entitled to according to such a contract 'is not proportional to nor dependent upon their intrinsic worth' (p. 311). And later he adds that ' . . . it seems clear that the effort a person is willing to make is influenced by his natural abilities and skills and the alternatives open to him. The better endowed are more likely, other things equal, to strive conscientiously, and there seems to be no way to discount for their greater good fortune The idea of rewarding 'desert' is impracticable' (p. 312). In this view, he is, of course, echoing Hayek.

5   EQUALITY OF 'CAPABILITIES'

One of the focal variables that lies somewhere between equality of goods and equality of outcome or welfare, which is another form of equality of opportunity, is Amartya Sen's concept of '*capabilities*'. The central idea is the importance of the 'freedom' that people ought to have to achieve certain '*functionings*'. Sen defines these as follows: '*Functionings* represent parts of the state of a person – in particular the various things that he or she manages to do or be in leading a life . . . Some functionings are very elementary, such as being adequately nourished, being in good health, etc . . . Others may be more complex, but still widely valued, such as achieving self-respect or being socially integrated' (Sen, 1993, p. 31). People with the same capabilities may achieve different levels of welfare insofar as they fail or succeed in taking advantages of the capabilities that their own abilities and social conditions provide. What matters, therefore, is the freedom that they enjoyed to pursue their own individual goals.

Obviously the measurement of capabilities raises numerous problems of definition and comparability. But over the years considerable progress has been made in tackling these problems, as well as the correlation between measures of functionings and capabilities, on the one hand, and measures of self-reported happiness on the other. The 'Stiglitz Commission' report contains detailed information and analysis concerning the many different indicators of particular capabilities and functionings that have been developed over the last few decades, which I shall not summarise here, as well as some indices that reflect some aggregation of indicators in various concepts of overall well-being or development. But the concept of capabilities brings into sharp focus the question of how far one should judge welfare in terms of capabilities rather than in terms of actual levels of welfare, or in terms of the shortfall between the two. The choice becomes particularly difficult if, as is likely to be the case, greater capabilities lead to higher aspirations – that is, a greater knowledge of what is possible may induce many people to aspire to a higher level of welfare. There can be little doubt that, as pointed out in Chapter 12, the happiness of most people depends on their perceived relationship to other people.

6   POLITICAL EQUALITY

So far we have discussed focal variables that have a strong economic content or relationship. But many people would argue that these are all heavily dependent on equality in political status. It is argued that economic equality, in whatever form one prefers, can only be achieved if there is political equality. Consequently, one of the most time-honoured claims for greater equality has been in terms of *equal treatment as citizens*. Equal treatment of people as citizens means that the state ought to treat all its citizens with equal concern and respect, whatever their colour, race, gender, religion, or social or economic status. Historically this has been a most important ideal in the struggle against unequal political and social rights for, say, women, or ethnic minorities, or people born into what were regarded as 'lower' social groups. And it is still an ideal today, even in many developed countries, where equality of status and recognition is claimed on behalf of gays and lesbians, disabled people, old people, and even – still – women.

This form of 'equality' is not about 'equality' at all in the sense that is of direct interest to economists. This is because how far everybody is equally entitled to vote, or own property, or stand for electoral office, and so on, does not necessarily depend on equality in the distribution of the stock of some finite, scarce resources. The vote can be extended to groups of people who were hitherto excluded from it without necessarily taking away the right to vote from anybody else. Principles such as 'everybody has an equal right to vote', or 'everybody has an equal right to stand for elective office' imply that everybody has the right in question irrespective of how many people there are. As Raz, Parfit and others have pointed out, in such principles, which are 'entitlement' principles, the qualifying adjective 'equal' is often superfluous.[11] And in economics we are naturally primarily concerned with the distribution between people of some scarce resources. So we are primarily concerned with what Raz suggests is the characteristic form of egalitarian principle, namely 'If there are x people each person is entitled to $1/x$ of all the G that is available'.

Nevertheless, there is little doubt that inequality in the space of certain political or social rights is closely linked to inequality in the space of some 'good' that is in limited supply, such as wealth, are mutually related. And the chain of causation may go both ways. It is usually impossible to guarantee higher-level values such as legal, political or social equality if there are large disparities in incomes. Rich people, for example, can afford more powerful and expensive lawyers, or education. And one only has to observe the importance attached to fund-raising for political parties – especially in the USA – to appreciate that more money confers more political influence. Unequal wealth leads to social and political inequality.

To some philosophers, it is this latter form of equality that really matters. Elizabeth Anderson writes that

> Recent egalitarian writing has come to be dominated by the view that the fundamental aim of equality is to compensate people for undeserved bad luck – being born with poor native endowments, bad parents, and disagreeable personalities, suffering from accidents and illness, and so forth. I shall argue that in focusing on correcting a supposed cosmic injustice, recent egalitarian writing has lost sight of the distinctively political aims of egalitarianism. The proper negative aim of egalitarian justice is not to eliminate the impact of brute luck from human affairs, but to end oppression, which by definition is socially imposed.[12]

But most people today – like almost all political philosophers – probably accept what has been called an *'egalitarian plateau'*, namely that members of a political community should be treated as equals. As pointed out earlier, it is not a *distributive* ideal about the proper distribution of some scarce resource. The ideal of 'equal treatment as citizens' refers to the relationship of people to the state and their political relationships to each other. But, as Swift puts it – echoing a remark by Aristotle – while 'Nearly all agree with the principle that members of a political community should be treated as equals, that the state should treat its citizens with equal concern and respect. What they disagree about is what "treatment as an equal" amounts to' (Swift, 2001, p. 93). For example, there can be big differences in practice between 'formal' and 'effective' equality of treatment. This is exemplified in two of the most important aspects of equality of treatment, namely (i) equality before the law and (ii) equality of citizenship.

As regards the former, this can be interpreted in ways that have less or more radical distributive implications. The less radical interpretation is simply that the law applies to all people without exception. There is not one law for the rich, another for the poor, one for women, another for men. This is a 'thin' or 'formal' notion of equality before the law. More radically, it can mean that inequalities in the resources available to people should not affect their standing in relation to the legal process as a whole. So, it might mean support for legal aid, for example. A relevant common distinction is between 'formal freedom', which means absence of interference, and 'effective freedom', which means having the power or capacity to act in a certain way. So, legal aid would give more 'effective freedom' to those who might otherwise have had only 'formal freedom' to go to law, but could not afford it.

As regards equal citizenship, this, too, could call for different degrees of equality in some resources according to how it is interpreted. A purely formal, minimal, interpretation could mean that all citizens have the right to vote, stand for public office, and so on. More radically, equal citizenship could mean that *effective* freedom ought to be facilitated by ensuring that all citizens have some kind of basic minimum of certain goods that are relevant to the proper performance of their role of the role of citizen. Equal citizenship could mean providing education. As Disraeli said after the 1880s legislation extended the right to vote to most adult men, 'We must now educate our masters'. Even more radically, equal citizenship could mean that the fact that you are rich should not give you more political influence. Thus, for example, equality of citizenship could mean putting a cap on the amount that individuals or parties could spend on political activities.

Thus while 'democratic equality' does not directly imply equality in the distribution of any scarce resources, and hence is more in the field of political philosophy than economics, the form of political equality one seeks to attain will influence how far scarce resources are allocated to the promotion of democratic equality. Historically, the real reason why certain classes or groups – such as whites, males, aristocrats, tyrants – tended to cling on to power is much more likely to have been in order to preserve their material advantages rather than any faith in their superior morals or wisdom.

But it is the distribution of some scarce 'good' that is our main concern here for reasons given earlier. This is not simply on account of the limited scope of this book, however. It is also on account of data limitations. Of course, data are available on some of the components of all of the different concepts of equality discussed previously. There are data on literacy rates, educational attainments, occupational structures, nutritional intakes, IQs, medical conditions, and so on. But none of the concepts of equality that would incorporate such variables – such as welfare, opportunities or capabilities – is yet measurable in any systematic manner in the same way as are data on the distribution of economic variables, such as wages, incomes, consumption, and – up to a point –wealth. It is to the most common of these, namely incomes, therefore, that we shall now turn.[13] However, concentration on the distribution of incomes still leaves us with a very large choice of 'focal variables' that are candidates for equal distribution.

7 WHICH ECONOMIC VARIABLE?

7.1 *Whose Income?*

After the subtleties of the distinctions that different philosophers make between their preferred focal variables and rival versions, it might seem that when we move on to economic variables we shall be on less contentious and firmer ground. But this is far from the case, and, as the saying goes, 'you ain't seen nuffin yet'. This is because even if we limit our analysis to the equality of income, many value judgements still have to be made in deciding which particular concept of income should be the focus of our concern. To begin with, should we be interested in the distribution of incomes between individuals, or families, or households? Which income units should we prefer? This will make a big difference to the measures. For example, distribution among individuals would be far more unequal than among families or households. This is because the larger the unit the less the inequality, since variations among individuals will tend to be cancelled out to some extent.

Also, how far should we allow for household size? On the whole larger households will tend to have bigger incomes. One could just divide total household income by the number of people in it to get income per head and measure the extent to which these are distributed equally. This would then show a distribution of the population in terms of the numbers of people who are in households with different per capita incomes. But this would not allow for economies of scale. For example, two people in a household with total annual income of £20,000, giving £10,000 per head, would probably have higher levels of *per capita* economic welfare *all other things being equal* than if they had been living separately on £10,000 each. So the usual method in income distribution statistics is to convert the raw data to what are known as 'adult equivalent scales', which adjust families or households of different sizes according to assumed degree of economies of scale in larger families or households. But even these adjustments cannot capture the effect of relationships within households since standard available statistics cannot indicate how income – or at least consumption – is shared out among different members of a household.

The effect of household size on the distribution of incomes has implications for comparisons of income distribution between countries or over time. First, it underlines the importance of comparing like with like, especially when making comparisons between different countries, or over long periods of time, insofar as the estimates relating to any particular country or time period may have been based on different methods and assumptions. Thus although considerable progress has been made in this direction over the course of the last few decades, international comparisons of equality of income have to be scrutinised very carefully before passing to judgement on them.

Second, over the course of the last century in Britain – and no doubt in most of the developed world – an important influence on measures of the equality of measured income per head has been changes in family size. For example, there was a big fall in the first half of the twentieth century in the number of families who were poor but very large, with the result that they had very low incomes *per head*. This sharp decline in the proportion of such poor, but large, families during the course of the twentieth century, especially in the first half of the century, tended to reduce the measured inequality of per capita incomes. However, in the last two decades or so the demographic and social trends would have tended to have the opposite effect and have led to more inequality of incomes. This is because of the much greater proportion of single-person families on low incomes. This is particularly striking in Britain where the average household size is one of the smallest in the world.

In a recent discussion of intergenerational inequality David Willetts correctly points out that 'a key difference between more equal and less equal societies is that by and large more equal societies have bigger households' (Willetts, 2010, p. 29). To some extent this has been the result of free choice – for example, more old people not wanting to live with their children, or young people preferring independence even if expensive. To the extent that it reflects their own choices, one may not think that this necessarily implies a worsening of their welfare, any more than does the poverty of a young person who sacrifices immediate gains in the interests of greater gains later on. But it has also meant a lot of poverty among single or single-parent families.[14]

7.2   Annual Income or Lifetime Income?

This question has become increasingly important on account of the rise in longevity and hence the steady increase in the proportion of old people in society. What principles, if any, ought to guide our attitude to inequality between people on account of age differences? Even if everybody had identical incomes over the whole of their lives, variations in their incomes over the course their lives, would show that in any given year the income distribution would be unequal. Some people would be in a low-earning phase and others would be in a high-earning phase. In general, people receive relatively low incomes when they are young and reach peak incomes nearer middle age, at which point their incomes usually fall off, particularly after they retire. Hence, a comparison of the distribution at any point of time would show significant inequality of incomes that could reflect purely age differences. What light do egalitarian theories shed on how far younger people should be prepared to make transfers to older people?

The answer is 'not a lot'. For, most established egalitarian theories are about equality of well-being between people's *complete* lives. Nevertheless, certain features of mainstream theories of justice would seem to provide a basis for a theory that encompassed differences between overlapping generations. For example, in the contractarian tradition, Gauthier claims that *implicit* contracts – notably between parents and children – provide the basis for 'mutually beneficial co-operation' between persons of different but overlapping generations'[15] However, a persuasive criticism of this rather particular application of the contractarian approach was provided by the late Peter Laslett in the course of which he argued that ' . . . what is done for children by those who bring them into the world is entirely spontaneous, proferred without expectation of return at the time or thereafter and done as an end in itself'.[16] But this objection would not apply to a contractarian theory of justice of the Rawlsian type since Rawls's famous 'difference principle' is about maintaining and increasing the position of the 'worst off' groups in society, which could correspond to – or at least include – old people. It is highly likely and that the participants in the contract drawn up in the 'original position' would have in mind the distribution problem created by the existence of old people in society.

Perhaps the only appealing and convenient philosophy in this case – as in many others – would be simple reliance on Adam Smiths 'beneficence'. For in a world in which longevity is consistently increasing, there is no way of avoiding the fact that each succeeding generation will include a higher proportion of people with relatively low incomes. This means that, in the absence of a persistent increase in the productivity of the employed population, each succeeding generation would have a continuous fall in incomes per head. So far, increasing productivity has more than offset the rising proportion of low (or zero) incomes people in society so that the transfer from the working population to retired people has not yet become intolerably high. And it is unlikely that it ever would since, even excluding societies that attach particular respect for old people, most people are aware that they, too, will become old some day, so that they are well disposed to policies that help old people.

Meanwhile, from the practical point of view of what data are relevant, the question is 'what is your welfare function?' Or, to be more precise, do you think that what matters is the distribution of the quality of people's lives over their whole lifetime, to which lifetime income might be the most closely related, or only the quality of their lives in some shorter period, such as a year, or some combination of both? And suppose there are two groups of people; some are content to be very poor for a while during their training as brain surgeons or plumbers (or whatever) in order to become very rich later as a result. The others prefer a higher income earlier in life, even if this means little increase in income later on. But the observed data on annual incomes will show inequality at any point in time between these incomes. Do you think this ought to be corrected in the interests of egalitarianism? Do you really worry about the lower incomes of people earlier in life when they may be voluntarily accepting some temporary sacrifice, or when they have not yet acquired the skill, training and experience necessary to aspire to higher earning. And do you worry about the poverty of the people late in life who had been rich when young but who spent it all on wine, women (or men) and song? If not, then perhaps one ought complement data on annual income distribution by data on the equality of lifetime incomes, which would show much less inequality? Of course, such data would be very difficult to obtain.

7.3 What Income?

There is still a further question of what particular definition of income ought to be used as the focus of concern. For example, should one use pre-tax, post-tax, pre-tax and benefits, or post tax and benefits income? In other words, there is no obviously compelling simple answer to the question of which, out of a very wide range of different concepts of income, one ought to choose. This reinforces the caution with which one must treat any international comparisons of equality of income distribution that fail to adjust to standard international concepts.

NOTES

1. Wolff, J., 1998:98
2. *Ethics,* Book V, Section 4.
3. Hayek, 1960:95.
4. A detailed analysis of the concept of equality of opportunity is Cavanagh, 2002 A brief, yet comprehensive, review of different concepts of equality is in Swift, 2001.
5. 'Justice as Fairness' is probably the most common brief description of one of the most widespread conceptions of 'justice', but it leaves room for a wide variety of views as to what constitutes 'fairness'.
6. Rawls, 1971:100–101.
7. A study by the National Audit Office, reported in the *Financial Times,* 1st February 2008.
8. See various recent introductory expositions of the Dworkin approach in Swift, 2001:68–71; Little, 2002:65–60; Kymlicka, 2002:75–87, as well as a review of Dworkin's book by Kenneth Appiah, 2001.
9. Dworkin, 2000.
10. Rawls, 1971:310ff.
11. For example, Raz, 1986:ch. 8. In the same connection Parfit remarks that 'Though these kinds of equality are of great importance, they are not my subject. I am concerned with people's being *equally well off*' (Parfit, 1991:3).
12. Anderson, 1999:288.
13. Some estimates have been made of the distribution of wealth (i.e. capital assets in any form), but since most people do not make regular declarations to the authorities of their wealth, reliable official statistics of wealth distributions are not as easily and regularly available in most countries as are data on income distributions. Yet it is quite likely that it is the distribution of wealth rather than the distribution of incomes that really matters from the point of

view of the command over society's resources that people enjoy. Somebody with large capital assets but no income is still able to acquire and consume a larger amount of society's resources than somebody with a modest income and no capital assets.

14. See Willetts, 2010:26–28, for a non-technical but authoritative account of the way that family break-up in Britain in the last few decades has led to an increase in the inequality of family incomes and in the number of very low-income families.

15. Gauthier, 1986:299ff. See also a detailed analysis of the problem of inequality between overlapping generations in McKerlie, 2013.

16. Laslett, in Laslett and Fishkin (eds.), 1992:29.

CHAPTER 17

The Boundary in Space: International Justice

1   WHY IS THERE A PROBLEM?

In various forms an example that originated with Milton Friedman has been used to illustrate the problem of how far any one society ought to take account of the interests of another society. My own formulation of the example is as follows. Imagine an island in which the land is rather rocky and infertile, and the climate is harsh, so that the average standard of living is low. But the inhabitants don't complain, at least not much. They are under the impression that they are the only human beings in the world, so they do not know any better.

But one day one of their fishing vessels gets blown off course and finishes up sheltering in the bay of some other island the existence of which had hitherto been unknown to them. And it turns out that this island is inhabited by other human beings who make the crew of the vessel very welcome. The visitors soon realise that the standard of living in this island is far higher than in their own. And they can see that this is the result of more fertile land, a better climate and an abundance of natural assets including lots of tasty edible species, such as fish and fowl.

But the day comes when, like Odysseus, they decide that they must forsake this delightful and unexpected holiday and return home. When they get back they tell everybody about this other island where the land is more fertile, the climate is better, and there is a greater abundance of various natural resources and edible species. (Somehow or other they forgot to mention that the women were also more beautiful.)

© The Author(s) 2017
W. Beckerman, *Economics as Applied Ethics*,
DOI 10.1007/978-3-319-50319-6_17

This aroused everybody's indignation. 'It isn't fair!' the people cried. And before long a new populist political party dedicated to the single issue of rectifying this alleged injustice had swept to power and started preparations to invade and occupy the other island. This was a pity because the people in the other island had just started debating whether some theory of justice, or the demands of 'sympathy', required that they start sending aid to the poorer island, the existence of which had hitherto been unknown to them. Unfortunately their philosophers were unable to reach rapid agreement on this issue. If they had done so in time they might have been able to help the poorer island before the latter embarked on a disastrous policy.

What took them so long? The answer is that their philosophers faced a new and very complex problem to which only some politicians believe there are simple answers. But, as philosophers know better than anybody, simple answers to complex problems are always wrong. They thought up different plausible but competing theories of international justice and their corresponding obligations to the other island. Even today, many years later, our philosophers have still not yet reached full agreement on which theory – if any – is the best.

And this is still a great pity. For there is even more need for it now. In the past the problem of international justice had fewer ramifications than it does today. Historically, justice in international relations had been confined largely to the problem of peace and war between nations, or respect for treaties or – in earlier times – for informal understandings between often far-flung traders and merchants engaged in international trade. It ignored distributive justice. The idea that this might apply between countries as well as between people within a country is relatively new. There are two main reasons for this.

One is the increasing interdependence of different economies, which had been proceeding for centuries, of course, but at a slower pace. The acceleration of this process has led to much controversy about the harmful effects of globalisation on some countries, or groups within countries. This includes the problem of 'unfair' trade, by which is often meant trade that enables richer countries to buy goods produced very cheaply in countries where the minimum age of employees, wages and general working and living conditions are not up to the standards that people in the richer countries would regard as acceptable.

The other reason for our increasing concern with international justice is that we are now much better informed about the appalling inequalities between peoples and nations, so we ask ourselves whether we have any obligations to help the poor wherever they may be, and on what principles such obligations may be founded.

The implications of this for welfare economics are clear. For welfare economics only tells us – at best – how to maximise the economic welfare of some given society. But it does not tell us exactly where we ought to draw the boundaries – in space or in time – of the society whose welfare we are trying to maximise. This chapter will focus on the boundary in *space* – that is, whether the society whose economic welfare one is trying to promote can be restricted to the citizens of any particular country. The next chapter will focus on the boundary in *time*, which has become increasingly important now that we are faced with the threat of climate change that will have consequences over generations.

In this chapter I shall attempt merely to give the flavour of the main theories of 'global justice'. In the Annex to this chapter I shall turn to the practical policy question of how the burden of combating man-made climate change ought to be shared out equitably among countries. International cooperative action is also required to tackle this and other global environmental problems, so that we may ask what would be 'just' terms for ensuring this cooperation.

In the interests of simplification and at the cost of ignoring many varieties between – and within – them, I shall adopt a threefold classification of the main current conceptions of justice between sovereign states, or 'global justice'. These are (i) *'communitarianism'*; (ii) a 'political' – or *'contractarian'* – conception of justice and (iii) a *'cosmopolitan'* conception of justice.

2   COMMUNITARIANISM

Although there is a very wide range of different conceptions of communitarianism, they have in common the view that there are no principles of justice that are universal in the sense that they ought to be followed in all societies. In other words, there are no principles of justice that reasonable people ought to adopt irrespective of their histories, religions, languages or social structures. The appropriate principles of justice are specific to different communities and have to be located within some community in which people share certain traditions and have developed their own particular moral norms. To some extent communitarianism can be seen as a reaction against an impression given by Rawls's *A Theory of Justice*, in

1971 which could be read as implying that the principles of justice that would emerge from his original position had some universal validity and ought to be adopted by *any* society. Rawls's apparently logical deductions of the way that rational individuals in 'the original position' would arrive at some mutually satisfactory contract defining the rights and obligations that should be adopted in any society, certainly seemed to leave no room for differences in the principles of justice that would be adopted in different societies. But in later publications Rawls explained that he made no such claim.

Naturally, communitarians differ among themselves on many points. According to Adam Swift 'community' is very much in fashion. It is warm, caring and nobody knows what it means. And he goes on to say that 'communitarianism' really is unusually ill-defined, even by the standards of other 'isms'.[1] But, on the whole, communitarians believe that within specific societies, language, history and culture come together closely enough to create some sort of collective understanding of what sort of principles of justice ought to regulate the rights and duties of the citizens of that society. Thus they believe that the idea of distributive justice presupposes a bounded world of a political community and the idea of *international* justice is based on the illusion that there exist principles that are shared between different nations and cultures.

3   'CONTRACTARIANISM' AND THE 'POLITICAL' CONCEPTION OF JUSTICE

Although communitarianism is concerned mainly with the variation between societies in legitimate conceptions of 'just' relationships between members of any given society, it has some affinity with the much older tradition of '*contractarianism*'. This goes back a few centuries and is associated most notably with Hobbes, Locke and Rousseau. It is the view that the principles of justice are the principles that govern the rights and corresponding duties in a community, or society, that is organised in such a way that these rights and duties can be enforced.

This raises one of the central issues in theories of justice, namely the relationship between justice and authority. More explicitly, this is the issue of whether the concept of justice has any relevance outside some society in which there is an authority that is able to enforce certain rules of behaviour.

The nature and origins of the contract differ significantly from one contractarian philosopher to another. But they share a common element, namely that there is some sort of contract among people that justifies, or requires, or has led to, the establishment and toleration of some authority. This authority has to ensure the protection of, and respect for, their rights – that is, to enforce the contract. As long as the requisite international authority did not exist there would still be no room for 'global justice'. Thus the 'political' contractarian conception of justice rules out the applicability of the concept of justice *between* sovereign states, except insofar as they have surrendered important specific features of their sovereignty to some authority, of which the European Union is perhaps the most obvious example.

The contractarian conception of justice has had its most important modern expression in John Rawls's theory of justice, some elements of which have been discussed in Chapter 15, in connection with distributive justice *within* any society. Its international implication is that since Rawls believed that justice is the first virtue of social institutions it presupposes a society. Hence, he excluded distributive justice – and hence the 'difference principle' – from his theory of *international* justice because he did not believe that there was an international society that had sufficient institutions and powers for it to make sense to talk about *distributive* justice between states. After all, while there may be enough of an international society to have promoted some rules of international behaviour – for example, outlawing aggression, enforcing treaties, and so on – there may not be enough of an international society to provide the basis for any rules of *international distributive* justice.

In short, Rawls begins with the classical contractarian notion that society is a cooperative venture for mutual advantage among members of a given society. Indeed, Rawls's 1971 treatment of international justice was rather cursory. He thought that 'the principles for the law of nations may require different principles arrived at in a somewhat different way. I shall be satisfied if it is possible to formulate a reasonable conception of justice for the basic structure of society conceived for the time being as a *closed system isolated from other societies*' (Rawls, 1971, p. 8; our italics). In a series of lectures in Oxford (1993), he returned to the principles of international justice and made a far more detailed study of what such principles should consist of. In his 1993 *Political Liberalism* Rawls presented his theory of justice 'as culture and sphere-specific'. He still used the procedural device of an original position, in which notional delegates of democratic 'peoples' would agree on principles of international justice behind a 'veil of ignorance'.

But although he then articulated the basis for his conclusions in much greater detail, they did not change substantially. In his last published views on the matter in 2001 he repeated that he was ' . . . concerned for the most part with the nature and content of justice for a well-ordered society' and that 'justice as fairness is a political conception of justice for the special case of the basic structure of a modern democratic society'.[2] In other words, it did not apply between one society and another.

4   COSMOPOLITANISM

4.1   International Distributive Justice and 'Impartiality'

Since nation states are being increasingly forced to cooperate in a number of spheres of activity it is arguable that the world of nation states increasingly resembles the Rawlsian depiction of a society in which principles of justice lay down some rules that enable the members to cooperate in order to maximise their collective welfare. These principles include some rules for sharing out the fruits of this cooperation.

But although increased relations between countries may have provided the necessary conditions for the emergence of principles of global justice, in the absence of some international authority they fail to provide the sufficient conditions. Progress in this direction has, of course, been made. The development of regional institutions, of which the European Union is an outstanding example, and the proliferation of international institutions, such as the International Monetary Fund, the World Trade Organisation or the International Labour Office, represent steps along the road to international authority in certain specific areas.

While such developments are welcome they do not help answer our central question 'how ought we incorporate distributive concerns in our conception of the society whose economic welfare we seek to maximise?' Yet, at the same time, we are now much more aware of the appalling inequalities in welfare throughout the world and of the dire poverty suffered by billions of people. For example, in 2007 the average per capita income of the seventeen richest countries in the world was about thirty times as high as the average per capita income of the eleven poorest countries, which was less than $3 per day.[3] And if one looks at direct indicators of major components of human well-being, such as average expectation of life, or rates of malnutrition, and so on, the comparison is just as disturbing. For example, Beitz draws attention to the fact that the infant mortality rate in the 'low-income countries' (as defined by the World Bank) is about 20 times as great as in the 'high-income countries'.[4] Why agonise about inequalities within rich countries, where they pale by comparison with those that can be found between poor countries and rich countries today? Does this not amount to 'straining at a gnat while swallowing a camel?'

Increased awareness of the conditions in the 'Third World' stimulated the emergence of '*cosmopolitanism*', the two central notions of which are that (i) individuals should be the focus of our concern, not states or races or any other grouping, and (ii) this concern ought to apply to individuals all over the world, not just those within any particular national boundary. Thus there is a moral obligation to apply to everybody in the world the same principles of *moral equivalence* and *impartiality* that are central to most theories of justice within any society.

What exactly these consist of is a matter of legitimate controversy. The cosmopolitan view is that citizenship is just as much an irrelevant contingency of a person's existence as is, for example, race, religion or sex. Cosmopolitans would thus extend the notion of impartiality to our dealings with everybody in the world.

This view seems to be embodied in 'The Preamble to the United Nations Universal Declaration of Human Rights', which states that 'Whereas the peoples of the United Nations have in the Charter reaffirmed their faith in fundamental human rights, in the dignity and worth of the human person and in the equal rights of men and women and have determined to promote social progress and betters standards of life in larger freedom . . . '. Following this preamble Article 2 of the document begins by saying that 'Everyone is entitled to all the rights and freedoms set forth in this Declaration . . . ' The specific rights are then set out in some detail in the subsequent Articles. But a 'right' imposes an obligation on somebody or on some institution. So the universal rights set out in this Declaration impose an obligation on everybody in the world to respect these rights for all individuals, whatever their nationality or location. According to the Declaration the unit of allegiance and concern can no longer be one's own nation but has to encompass the whole of humanity.

Some critics of such declarations would share de Jasay's view that 'no notice was taken of the fact that these putative rights had no practical effect beyond raising false expectations if the corresponding obligations to provide food, shelter, education and employment were not imposed on those able to provide them' (de Jasay, A., 2010a, p. 8). Furthermore, it is far from clear how these international proclamations on the rights of individuals can be made compatible with the widely accepted 'rights' of nations to be sovereign as regards their internal affairs.

4.2   The Utilitarian Route to Cosmopolitanism

Cosmopolitanism encompasses a wide range of views on the principles of justice within societies. It could include the prioritarian or egalitarian views mentioned in Chapter 15, and even be acceptable to some libertarian defenders of laissez faire. But perhaps the best-known school of thought that has direct relevance to cosmopolitanism is Utilitarianism. As discussed in Chapter 9, Utilitarianism attaches no *intrinsic* value to distributional considerations. Greater equality can have only *instrumental* value as a means to the maximisation of utility in the world. Thus, a utilitarian ethic implies that if some redistribution of wealth from people in rich countries to people in poor countries is likely to raise total world utility it ought to be carried out. Sacrifices for the sake of the needy that would increase total utility are morally obligatory in the utilitarian system.

Chapter 10 lists various objections that have been levelled to Utilitarianism. One is that it attaches no intrinsic and independent value to 'special obligations' (such as those represented in 'agent-relative' ethics), including those that people may have to members of their own families, communities, nations and so on.[5] This is particularly relevant in the international context.

One leading Utilitarian philosopher, Peter Singer, defends an obligation to increase international redistribution of wealth that, in one sense, is less extreme than straight Utilitarianism but, in another sense, is more extreme. It is less extreme in that instead of advocating redistribution aimed at maximising total world *utility* he concentrates on relief of *poverty*, which he hopes will also appeal to non-utilitarians, especially prioritarians. As mentioned in Chapter 10 this view resembles Karl Popper's 'negative Utilitarianism', according to which we should minimise suffering rather than maximise happiness. But in one respect Singer's concept of Utilitarianism is more extreme in that he condemns a failure to do everything in our power to relieve poverty as morally totally unacceptable.

In his *Practical Ethics*, Singer postulated the following two premises: (i) If we can prevent something 'bad' without sacrificing anything of comparable significance, we are morally obliged to do so, and (ii) absolute poverty is 'bad', and this may be defined (following the definition adopted by Robert McNamara, who was the President of the World Bank) as 'a condition of life so characterized by malnutrition, illiteracy, diseases, squalid surroundings, high infant mortality and low life expectancy as to be beneath any reasonable definition of human decency'.[6]

From these two premises it follows that if, for example, one is faced with a choice between spending money on saving lives of poor people anywhere in the world or spending it on something that cannot be judged to be of 'comparable significance' one is morally obliged to choose the former. Singer writes that 'If, then, allowing someone to die is not intrinsically different from killing someone, it would seem that we are all murderers'.[7]

This is, of course, a big 'if'. It raises the age-old question of the relative moral status of acts of omission and acts of commission. Is it just as immoral to fail to send money to Oxfam as to send poor people a parcel containing poisoned food? Most people would think not. Of course one can easily dream up all sorts of hypothetical situations where the distinction is not so sharp. For example, is someone who deliberately fails to give a life-saving medicine to his parent from whom he hopes to obtain a large inheritance guilty of a sin of omission or commission?

But many people would find that wherever we draw the line between sins of commission and sins of omission, the whole utilitarian ethic, pushed to its extreme, is simply far too demanding and wildly utopian. For a worldwide redistribution on utilitarian grounds designed to maximise world utility would, of course, require enormous sacrifices by the wealthier countries which would not be forthcoming by any stretch of the imagination. It would require moral heroism and demand that we all be saints. And the consequences of it would be totally unpredictable and possibly catastrophic.

The problem is that most – and possibly all – ethical rules leave scope for conflicting values, and none claims to cover all possible contingencies. For example, one of Kant's 'categorical imperatives' is that one must always tell the truth, whatever the circumstances. Simon Blackburn gives the classic example of 'lying to the mad axeman who asks you where your children are sleeping' where the normal reaction to the Kantian injunction against lying in any circumstances would be 'To heck with that. If *that's* what morality demands then I'm opting out'.[8] Even in less dramatic circumstances, one might be forgiven for not telling a friend that his work is rubbish, his clothes show very poor taste, and he is ugly. Instead most people would go along with the views of the hero/antihero of Albert Camus's novel 'The Fall' in which he says 'Above all, don't believe your friends when they ask you to be sincere with them. All they really want is that you will confirm them in the good idea that they have of themselves.... If, then, you find yourself in this situation, don't hesitate: promise to tell the truth and lie as much as possible'.[9]

A far more general conflict of values could be said to apply to Singer's particular application of Utilitarianism to the problem of international distributive justice. Joshi and Skidelsky point out that Singer's utilitarian approach completely ignores the claims and moral obligations arising out of 'special relationships', such as those of family, community or nation.[10]

And, as with other moral dilemmas that we have discussed earlier, much also depends on the facts. Vijay Joshi and Robert Skidelsky also question Singer's assumption that greater aid will reach the poor in poor countries and will promote 'reliant self-development'. They argue that, since an increasing proportion of the world's poor is located in failed states in sub-Sahara Africa, where bad governance is the chief obstacle to the relief of poverty, Singer's proposals may not promote the well-being of the poorest members of the global community. It is also well-known that some transfers to poor countries can be counterproductive by undermining the efforts of their own producers to increase output.[11]

5   OTHER THEORIES OF INTERNATIONAL DISTRIBUTIVE JUSTICE

During the last two or three decades theories of international distributive justice have emerged that, up to a point, are intermediate between traditional 'political' or 'contractarian' theories, on the one hand, and outright 'cosmopolitanism', on the other. Because of the dominating position of Rawls in the analysis of theories of justice much of this has taken the form of an attempt to extend Rawlsian theory in a cosmopolitan direction. This has not always taken the form of an abandonment of Rawls' contractarian framework. Instead, it sometimes takes the form of an attempt to derive different conclusions as to what sort of principles of justice would emerge if the participants in the original position took account of the vast disparities in incomes between countries. For Rawls's entire scheme of establishing the principles of distributive justice applies to society as a 'cooperative venture for mutual advantage', and the modern globalised world faces serious global problems – economic and environmental – which call for cooperative solutions on a global scale.

Therefore, in the same way that the need for – and scope for – social cooperation provides a basis for *domestic* distributive justice, so international cooperation should provide a basis for *global* distributive justice. In other words, perhaps one should apply Rawls's procedural device of the 'original position' as a framework for investigating how, in fact, the participants in such a position would have wanted to adopt principles that would nullify the contingencies of an unequal distribution of natural assets internationally. Such principles could be designed both to ensure a fair distribution of the fruits of cooperation between countries and also remedy unacceptable inequalities caused by the endowments with which countries start and hence the varying degrees to which they are able to contribute to overall welfare.

Political philosophers, such as the late Brian Barry, Charles Beitz and Thomas Pogge, start from the fact that being born in a rich country or a poor country is as much a matter of luck as being born with talent or in desirable home circumstances, and so on. Hence, the unequal international distribution of resources is just as arbitrary from a moral point of view as is the distribution of talents.

Imagine the participants in an 'original' position deciding whether they would prefer (i) to be born in a world, where the probability of being born in a country with widespread malnutrition and high infant mortality is roughly as great as that of being born in a rich country, or (ii) to be born in a world in which the average income level was lower but in which the gap between the rich and the poor nations was also lower thanks to international redistribution? Up to a point depending on the precise numbers involved, if they were risk-averse and rational – as assumed in the Rawlsian theory – they might choose the second. It follows that in some 'original position' they might opt for some rules for international redistribution.

Following this line of argument, participants in an '*international* original position' should take account of the fact that the situation of the worst-off people in the world will be maximised not through the application of the difference principle *within* countries but through its global application. '. . . from the standpoint of the "original position" the question of distribution between societies dwarfs into relative insignificance any question of distribution within societies. There is no conceivable internal redistribution of income that would make a noticeable improvement to the nutrition of the worst-fed in India or resourceless African states like Dahomey, Niger or Upper Volta.'[12]

Of course, in the real world the most binding limit on international aid has been the reluctance of governments in democratic donor countries to sacrifice other demands by their electorates. And in recipient countries political systems frequently prevent citizens from obtaining corresponding benefits from such aid as their governments may obtain. This weakens the claim of many countries for more respect for their 'rights'. As Stanley Hoffman points out

> ... states are not divinities, their rights are rooted in the presumption of a fit between them and their people; and this does put a kind of damper on the demands of the Third World governments for absolute sovereignty, for impermeable state rights. We may feel that we have a duty to share some of our wealth with them, but only if that wealth is used toward justice for those communities of people. This also means that equity claims presented by Third World states are in a sense conditional on their doing something for their people.[13]

An independent judiciary Hoffman adds that although 'it may sound like blackmail, but in blackmail cases one of the actors is doing something illegitimate or selfish' (*op.cit.*, p. 181). It is significant, for example, that candidates to join the European Union and hence benefit from the economic assistance that they could then expect are obliged to demonstrate that they satisfy certain political conditions, such as the effective rule of law, and independent judiciary, and other criteria of a functioning and effective democracy before their membership can be seriously negotiated.

6   Conclusions

In Chapter 15 I characterised the Rawlsian conception of justice as being a set of principles according to which a given political society allocates rights and obligations among members of that society that are accepted by them as being, on the whole, a 'fair' way of sharing out the fruits of their mutual collaboration in promoting the well-being of that society. These principles provide a framework that enables people to resolve their conflicting interests peacefully by reference to the accepted rights and obligations of that society. An authority is needed (i) to fulfil the function of being the body that interprets the rights and obligations and so can adjudicate differences of opinion about them, and (ii) where necessary, to enforce their observance and punish violations.

Much of the debate about different conceptions of global justice that we have very briefly sketched out earlier is about whether some corresponding rights and obligations can be found that apply on an international scale between different sovereign states. Should the rights and obligations to which *states* can appeal in their relationships with each other be approached in the same manner as between *individuals* within any state? And should all individuals across the world be given the same rights by everybody else as are usually embodied in the principles of justice that govern the allocation of rights and obligations within any state? There are reasons to believe that there is no clear answer to either of these questions.

There are two main reasons for this. First, insofar as the chief function of principles of justice is to enable people to settle their conflicts without resort to violence and hence to help promote everybody's self-interest, the need for such principles depends on the probability that refusal to abide by them will, in fact, lead to violence or gross failure to promote one's interests. But this probability is not an all-or-nothing matter. It is not a bipolar situation in which probability is either zero or unity. It will vary internationally from one common global problem to another. It is unlikely, for example, that failure to adhere to some internationally agreed conventions governing fishing rights, or respect for some international trade agreements, will lead to war.

Second, individuals are dealing with each other in thousands of different ways all the time. So the scope for disagreements as to what is 'fair' in their dealings – ranging from when one's neighbour can make a noise with his lawn mower to when one can make a big profit by misleading one's clients about the safety of the bonds one is selling to them – is unlimited. The need for very detailed rules governing what is fair and what is not fair is correspondingly almost unlimited. And since it is virtually impossible for the appropriate rules and obligations to be drawn up in such a way as to cover every conceivable contingency, it is inevitable that there should be some authority to which one can appeal for judgement and, if necessary, for retribution. By contrast, the relations between sovereign states are far less common and varied.

Of course, they are becoming more common and more varied, so one can hope that sovereign states will respect Hume's ' . . . three fundamental rules of justice, the stability of possession, its transference by consent, and the performance of promises'.[14] But, for the two reasons given earlier, one should not expect the rules governing relations between sovereign states to be as detailed and varied as the rules pertaining to individuals within any particular state. According to Hume '... *there is a system of morals calculated for princes, much more free that that which ought to govern private persons.*'[15] And he went on to add that '... though the intercourse of different states be advantageous, and even sometimes necessary, yet it is not so necessary nor advantageous as that among individuals, without which it is utterly impossible for human nature ever to subsist'.[16]

The situation is a little like the rules governing any particular sport. It is true that the rules governing some sports are so complicated that one should never play them except accompanied by one's lawyer. But as long as they are basically 'fair' there is no need to agonise over their rationale too much and there is usually adequate scope for variation in the precise details of the rules without their giving an unfair advantage to any one class of participant. For example, if the rules governing the height of the net in tennis were to be drastically modified – say making the net a foot higher – it would give a big advantage to abnormally tall people. But fine adjustments of a fraction of an inch are not likely to cause offence to anybody. Anyway, nobody is obliged to play the game. One can always take up some other sport where physique and agility do not command a premium, like chess. This kind of option is not generally so easy for somebody who does not like the rules of justice prevailing in the country in which he or she is located, since one cannot easily emigrate to another country.

Thus the answer to the question 'How far do we need a detailed theory of global justice anyway?' seems to be that (i) it is less necessary than between individuals, and (ii) it need not be so detailed, so that it does not require as exhaustive analysis of its principles as is required for the principles of justice between individuals within any political entity. But if one asks a different question, namely 'Should the society in whose welfare we are supposed to promote include the welfare of other countries?' the answer could still be 'Yes'. Even if we believe that the gross inequalities in the world are nothing to do with justice, and are simply bad luck, they still call out for remedial action. For – as pointed out earlier – in our individual behaviour we are as much influenced by instinctive sentiments of sympathy and benevolence as by reference to anybody's 'rights' as specified in any theory of justice. To take a trivial example, one may allow one's neighbour to use one's telephone or toilet if his own is out of order without believing that he has any 'right' to do so. One would do so out of a mixture of simple benevolence and neighbourly helpfulness and fraternity. In the same way people who make charitable donations to various causes in poorer countries do not do so out of a conscious respect for some theory of justice.

Of course one cannot be confident that such sentiments and instincts suffice to ensure that certain criteria of minimum conditions of life for all human beings are satisfied. A casual glance at the state of the world suggests that this is not the case. For example, free trade has often failed to help many poor countries because the rules of international trade are biased in favour of rich countries in a way that is 'unjust'.[17] And rich countries often protect, or subsidise, their own economic activities.

Thus none of the earlier reservations concerning the need for a detailed theory of international justice implies that debate over the principles of global justice is pointless. As has been emphasised at various points in this book, ethics does not provide precise answers to conflicts of moral intuitions; it clarifies the conflicts and, where appropriate, indicates what facts are relevant. The same applies to that part of ethics that is about international justice. 'Cosmopolitanism' has raised awareness of the notion of the equality of all human beings in any conception of justice. Against this, the political conception of justice highlights the reliance of most theories of justice on the existence of some sort of authority that can adjudicate between different interpretations of the rules and, where appropriate, punish those who have violated them.

And one need not adopt extreme versions of these two contrasting views. Over the course of time, international agreements and authorities to deal with various international problems gradually and slowly extend across international boundaries countries. The principles that they embody are gradually absorbed into an international system that seems to share certain very basic principles of fairness. This is certainly far from satisfying full-bloodied cosmopolitanism and its ambitious requirement that individuals all over the world have to be treated with equal respect and consideration. But it does, at least, integrate them to varying degrees into the international community by applying some criteria of justice between states that probably go beyond what would be satisfied by simple reliance on Smithian 'sympathy' and that resemble some of the most basic criteria of different theories of justice within any community.

And since the rules of 'fair play' between states need not be so detailed and sophisticated as those between individuals it is likely that adequate and effective rules will be developed over time to deal with specific global problems as they arise. As indicated in the Annex to this chapter, an equitable solution to practical problems, such as a fair allocation of the burden of combating climate change, can be identified with recourse only to certain very general and basic principles of justice that are virtuously unanimously accepted. Full agreement on the details of some totally general theory of global justice is no more likely to be reached than has been the case with theories of justice within any community, about which there has been much debate for millennia. But it can wait for a few more millennia.

7   Annex: How to Share Out Equitably the Burden of Combating Climate Change[18]

Meanwhile, do the various theories briefly outlined earlier throw much light on the problem of how to share out the burden of measures to combat man-made climate change? The answer is 'yes' and 'no'. On the one hand, unsurprisingly, none of the main theories provides an instant blueprint of the way that the burden ought to be shared out. But, on the other hand, this does not mean that we have to feel lost in some moral desert. For some of the underlying principles which are shared by virtually all theories do help arrive at what would seem to be a criterion that would meet with almost universal approval.

7.1   Equity and Efficiency

The Framework Convention on Climate Change agreed at the 1992 Rio de Janeiro World Environmental Conference stated that '...the parties should protect the climate for the benefit of present and future generations of humankind, *on the basis of equity* (my italics) and in accordance with their common but differentiated responsibilities and respective capabilities'.[19] But how difficult would it be to design a method of sharing out the burden of combating man-made climate change that was equitable without unduly sacrificing economic efficiency? The answer is 'not very'.

For example, a uniform carbon tax would lead to an efficient distribution of any reduction in emissions since every (carbon) emitter would seek to equate the tax with his marginal costs of further reductions in emissions. Hence, the marginal costs of emissions reductions would be equalised around the world. And this means that no further reduction in costs could be achieved by switching reductions from any one particular emitter to another. It would be a least-cost method. At the same time, distributional considerations could be dealt with by a suitable distribution of the revenue from the tax. Of course, there would be numerous political and administrative problems with such a solution, but that it not the point here. The point is that the efficiency can be separated from the equity.

The same applies to the method for mitigating climate change that is becoming most widely promoted. This is the method of tradable carbon emissions permits. The basic idea of this method is that, first, some agreement is reached as to the total *global* amount of greenhouse gas emissions that is to be tolerated. Then permits to emit this total amount will be allocated amongst countries, or other agencies, according to some formula that will be agreed in the course of the negotiations. Nobody will be allowed to emit more carbon than allowed by their permits.

But the permits will be tradable, and carbon emitters will presumably buy or sell permits in the light of their own costs of reducing carbon emissions. Some countries may well find it cheaper to reduce their emissions so that they can sell some of their permits. Other countries will find it cheaper to buy permits than to reduce emissions to the amount covered by their initial allocation of permits. This trade in permits will lead to the emergence of a world price for emission permits, which will lead to equal marginal costs of emission reductions across the world in the same way as would a uniform carbon tax.[20]

As with a uniform carbon tax this method is economically 'efficient' in the sense that costs are minimised. The equity problem then is clearly how to allocate the permits in the first place – that is, how to take away valuable and tradable assets from some countries and give them to others. Whatever the relative merits of tradable permits or a carbon tax, international discussion of policy to reduce carbon emissions has been in terms of the former method. This means that the main ethical issue is how the carbon emission permits should be distributed among countries. It is to this problem that I shall now turn.

7.2   The Per capita Allocation of Tradable Permits

One of the most popular criteria for sharing out carbon emission permits is that they be allocated on an equal *per capita* basis. This proposal has a long pedigree going back to an early draft of the (International) Framework Convention leading up to the 1992 Rio

'Earth Summit', and has since been endorsed by other authoritative bodies. For example, the 22nd Report of the (British) Royal Commission on Environmental Pollution, stated that 'an effective, enduring and equitable climate protocol will eventually require emission quotas to be allocated to nations on a simple and equal *per capita* basis'.[21] It is easy to see why this principle has received widespread approval. In terms of ethical principles it is a universal application of the cosmopolitan principle of moral equivalence.

The rule has sometimes been criticised on the grounds that it would encourage some countries to increase their birth rates.[22] It is difficult to take this criticism seriously, since the objective of most – and probably all – poor countries, is not to raise their *total* incomes but to raise their incomes *per head*. Their governments appear to be 'average utilitarians', not 'total utilitarians', though this may come as a big surprise to some of their rulers. But this criticism of the *per capita* rule does seem to have been taken seriously in some circles, as witnessed, for example, by proposals to restrict the population count to the adult population, or some other related benchmark.[23]

The justification of the *per capita* rule is not, of course, that everybody is born with an equal natural right to pollute the atmosphere. The real case for the *per capita* rule would be ' . . . that each human being should have an equal right to an *as-yet unallocated*, scarce, global commons . . . '.[24] In other words, we have only recently understood that if we want to avoid climate catastrophe there is some fixed amount available of atmosphere that is not seriously contaminated by carbon molecules, or what has been called 'carbon space'. It is in that sense that the 'fixed' resource, 'clean air', has been only recently 'discovered'. The argument then is that everybody has an equal right to use it.

The 'cosmopolitan' view would be that a hitherto unappropriated natural resource belongs equally to everybody. It is true that such a cosmopolitan view of property rights does not seem to have prevailed so far in the course of human history, during which time resources – such as coal, oil, bauxite, and so on – are accepted as being the rightful property of whoever first discovers them. On the other hand, if a libertarian/Lockean view of property rights – that is, 'first come first serve' – were to be generally accepted it would absolve past generations from any blame for having already used up more than 'their share' of the scarce resource 'carbon-free atmosphere', for since it was not 'scarce' when they did so they would have had a right to use it up to their heart's content. This has implications for the next widely promoted criterion for sharing out carbon emission permits.

7.3   The 'Historical Debt' Argument

Another widely discussed criterion for an equitable allocation of the burden of climate change mitigation is the so-called 'historical debt' or 'natural debt' criterion. It is difficult to see any merit in this rule. It is usually proposed quite independently of the precise mechanism – such as tradable permits – used to reduce carbon emissions, but could well be incorporated as one of the criteria for the allocation of the permits, and it is convenient to discuss it here as if it were. The basic principle behind this rule is usually stated to be simply that one ought to 'clean up one's own mess'. This principle is usually presented as if it were axiomatic. And it is true that if it were to be applied only to contemporary pollution it would not be difficult to justify it by an appeal to almost any ethical theory. For example, one could appeal to a libertarian principle that, unless suitable compensation is paid, one must not deprive other people of their property, which, in this case, would be their right to a clean atmosphere. Or it could be justified in terms of a game-theoretic penalty for defectors from some social convention.

But, for several reasons, it is difficult to see what ethical justification can be found for penalising people alive today for the 'sins' of their ancestors. First, it is doubtful how far their ancestors had actually sinned. For until the last quarter of the twentieth century polluters could not have known about the consequences of their emissions of carbon dioxide into the atmosphere.

Second, it is not always certain that the long dead polluters were, in fact, the 'ancestors' of many of the people alive today who are expected to pay to 'clean up the mess'. For example, it would be tough on Mexican immigrants to the USA to pay for the carbon emitted many decades ago by American companies who may have been exploiting their *real* ancestors back in Mexico.

Third, even if most of the ancestors of the inhabitants of rich countries could be made morally responsible for their actions, the current generation played no part in the choices their ancestors made, which seems to absolve them of moral responsibility. Collective guilt is generally believed to be ethically unacceptable.

Fourth, as Caney and others point out, the practical obstacles to any identification of the link between people alive today and those responsible for the past emissions by the people who lived decades ago in what are now advanced countries are insuperable.[25]

And finally, if the real objective is to make rich countries bear a greater share of the costs of combating climate change there are easier ways of doing so than embarking on dubious counterfactual investigations and making citizens of rich countries feel guilty about the sins of their grandfathers, let alone other people's grandfathers.

7.4   The 'Ability to Pay' Rule

One of these ways of making the rich bear the burden of combating climate change is simply to adopt an 'ability to pay' rule. There is a perfectly respectable and long-lived tradition in nearly all developed countries of taxing the rich more than the poor in order to pay for communal activities. This rule is widely accepted since it can be justified in terms of a wide range of egalitarian or prioritarian principles discussed in Chapter 16. For example, it might be thought that *unequal* contributions to something, such as total tax revenues, is necessary in order to promote a more *equal* share of something else – such as basic needs or minimum subsistence – to which everybody is often deemed to have a 'right'. Similarly, utilitarians might defend the ability to pay criterion on the grounds that the resulting re-distribution of wealth goes some way towards increasing total utility. 'Post-Rawlsians' like Beitz, Barry, or Pogge might defend some international 'difference principle' on the grounds mentioned previously, namely that the gross inequalities *between* nations now dwarf the differences *within* most nations. Kant would say that no one who applied the categorical imperative would wish to adopt a universal law that denied help to those who 'struggle with great hardships'.[26]

Or, as we have suggested earlier, it may be nothing to do with any *theory* but be a simple application of some instinctive human 'sympathy' or 'beneficence' or 'fraternity'. Thus, because an 'ability to pay' rule can be justified by a wide range of egalitarian theories, it is a rule that enjoys widespread support. It is a criterion that has been behind taxation systems for decades in most countries; it would no doubt be welcome to poorer countries; and is far easier to apply than, say, estimates that purport to allocate 'historical responsibility'.

However, whatever criterion is used to allocate emission permits, it still leaves open the question of whether the permits ought to be given to the governments of the countries concerned or whether, instead, it might be preferable to give some, or all, to some international body that could auction the permits and use the proceeds to assist poor countries reduce the growth of their carbon emissions, or to help the poorest people directly, or to facilitate the monitoring of emissions. The governments of some countries could well use the proceeds from the sale of the permits to bolster their security forces or their overseas bank accounts. This raises the problem which, in this chapter, has been put at the heart of theories of international justice, namely how far one accepts the inviolability of national sovereignty.

Notes

1. Swift, 2001:133.
2. Rawls, 2001:13–14.
3. The World Bank, 2008:Table 1, p. 334. The estimates are at 'purchasing power parities' and so purport to take account of intercountry differences in price levels.
4. Beitz, 1999:516.
5. However, in *Utilitariansim,* ch. 5, John Stuart Mill appears to approve of such special obligations, if only on instrumental grounds as generally conducive to greater utility.
6. Singer, 2002:229–231.
7. Singer, *ibid.:222.*
8. Blackburn, 2001:42. Of course, Kant did make it clear in *The Metaphysics of Morals* that he did not think his categorical imperative would cover every conceivable situation.
9. From Camus, 1956/1974 [my rough translation of 'La Chute' in 1974 Gallimard edition].
10. Joshi, and Skidelsky, 2004:19–21.
11. Joshi and Skidelsky, *ibid.*
12. Barry, 1973:130–131.
13. Hoffman, 1981:156.
14. Hume, 1739:3.2.11.2.
15. Hume, *ibid*:3.2.11.3.
16. Hume, *ibid*:3.2.11.4.
17. This literature relating to the consequences of unequal starting positions in international trade goes back to Balogh, 1963, and possibly much earlier, and the assertion is examined with particular reference to the problem of global justice in Kapstein, 2006:ch. 2.
18. This Annex is based on Ally and Beckerman, 2014. This article contains the statistical estimates of what the different possible distribution criteria entail for groups of countries and for some major individual countries.
19. Intergovernmental Negotiating Committe, 1991:article 3.1.

20. The equilibrium world price of permits will not, however, be the same as a uniform world carbon tax since it will depend on the way the permits are distributed and the corresponding income effects.
21. Royal Commission on Environmental Pollution, 2000:56.
22. See, for example, Jamieson, 2001:301.
23. See references to this and similar proposals in Grubb, 1995:486.
24. Grubb and Sebenius, 1992:205.
25. Caney, 2005.
26. Kant, 1964 edn:90/91. This contains Kant's fourth example of the application of the 'categorical imperative'.

CHAPTER 18

The Boundary in Time: Intergenerational Justice

1 JUSTICE BETWEEN GENERATIONS: A NEW PROBLEM

In the last chapter I asked how we should draw the boundary in space around the society whose economic welfare we are trying to maximise. In this chapter I shall ask how we should draw the boundary in time. Until relatively recently this was, perhaps, a question that could be safely ignored. But during the last few decades we have come to realise that we may be seriously depleting the Earth's resources and damaging the environment that future generations will inherit from us. Hence, whereas the problem of distributive justice within any given society at any point in time has occupied philosophers for over 2,000 years, it now includes distributive justice across generations.[1] Only recently has it been important to ask questions such as 'What is a just distribution of the Earth's resources between us and future generations?' or 'Do we have obligations to future generations?' or 'Do future generations have rights to inherit the same environment as exists now?' These are not factual questions to which there may be definite answers. They are questions about values. How serious are the threats to the welfare of future generations is a factual issue. But the scale and nature of our response is a matter of values. Some philosophers have attempted to ground these values within the framework of general theories of justice. In this chapter we shall briefly examine some of the difficulties that such an attempt must encounter.

© The Author(s) 2017
W. Beckerman, *Economics as Applied Ethics*,
DOI 10.1007/978-3-319-50319-6_18

2   AUTHORITY AND A CONTRACTARIAN THEORY OF JUSTICE

Theories of international justice and theories of intergenerational justice share one major problem – or perhaps one major problem and one slightly less important problem. The *major* shared problem is the problem of 'authority'. In the previous chapter I discussed the importance attached by many philosophers to the existence of some 'authority' in any useful theory of justice between sovereign states. I mentioned that some steps have been taken over the years to establish specific international authorities in certain areas, such as the World Trade Organisation. But sovereign states have continued to guard their sovereignty jealously and have remained free to leave such organisations if, and when, they find it is in their interests to do so. Nevertheless, the question 'How far can there ever be an *international* authority?' is at least debatable. But the question 'How far can there ever be an *intergenerational* authority?' does not make sense. For, in the absence of time travel – and perhaps even then (it is hard to know) – there simply cannot be one.

The less important shared problem is the problem of a contract, which is related to the major problem. For the main function of the authority was to adjudicate between conflicting views of the relevant principles of justice and their application and, where necessary, to ensure that members of society could be punished, in one way or the other, if they broke the terms of the contract. And this also seems to rule out intergenerational justice, since there could not be any contract between different non-overlapping generations. And, clearly, since there cannot be any contract – written or otherwise – between different non-overlapping generations, it no longer matters whether there can be any intergenerational authority to implement it.

Given these difficulties it was perhaps inevitable that Rawls, the pre-eminent exponent of a contractarian theory of justice in recent times, should have concluded, in his *A Theory of Justice*, that '... the question of justice between generations.... subjects any ethical theory to severe if not impossible tests'.[2] Indeed, in this book he devoted only nine pages, out of 587 pages, to the problem of intergenerational justice.

This is not surprising, for two reasons. First, as explained in the last chapter, Rawls was setting out a *'political'* theory of justice, which meant that the principles of justice applied only within some political community that had the authority to enforce its principles. Clearly this cannot apply between generations. Second, Rawls accepted the Humean 'circumstances of justice'. These are described by Rawls as the '...normal conditions under which human cooperation is both possible and necessary...Thus many individuals *coexist together at the same time* on a definite geographical territory'[3] (my italics). The objective circumstances of the Humean concept of justice also include rough equality of power between the parties to the cooperation.

Under these Humean 'circumstances' people can reach some agreement or contract or convention that specifies the rights and obligations of the contracting parties, which, as explained in the previous chapter, is taken by Rawls and others to be a characteristic feature of any theory of justice. Thus, on this conception of justice, if, for example, conditions of inequality of power prevail but, nevertheless, the weaker are treated with decency and respect by the stronger, without any consideration of the advantages that they will derive from their benevolent behaviour, this does not mean that the situation is more 'just'. It merely means that the stronger people are virtuous and behave with decency and compassion according to some highly commendable instincts or sense of moral duty. And in the present context what matters is that, on Hume's 'circumstances' of justice, if people's behaviour towards future generations is motivated by considerations such as love for their children, this may be admirable but is nothing to do with justice. For example, when we bequeath assets to our children (or future generations in general) we do so because we are motivated by ties of affection or benevolence or sympathy, not doing on account of respect for some principles of justice.

A strict application of the Humean 'circumstances of justice' clearly appears to rule out justice between non-overlapping generations. It is obvious that one cannot talk sensibly about the relative degrees of power that different non-overlapping generations have over each other. Nor do we need to make any sort of concession or sacrifice in order to ensure the cooperation of future generations in any common endeavour. Rawls puts it quite bluntly when he says that 'we can do something for posterity but it can do nothing for us. This situation is unalterable, and so the question of justice does not arise'.[4] In short, if it is accepted that the function of principles of justice is to enable people with conflicting interests to live together in peace so that they can benefit from their mutual cooperation, there is no need for a theory of intergenerational justice.

3   JUSTICE AND RIGHTS

Another obstacle to a coherent theory of justice between non-overlapping generations that is not shared with justice between contemporary countries at any point in time arises from the relationship between 'justice' and 'rights'. The attribution of rights' is believed to play a major role in most – and possibly all – serious theories of justice. For example, Rawls's classic exposition of what a theory of justice consists of begins with several references to this relationship between justice and rights. In the space of a few pages (pages 4–7) he repeats several times, if in slightly different words each time, that the principles of justice are those that '...provide a way of assigning rights and duties in the basic institutions of society', or that '...the primary subject of justice is the basic structure of society, or more exactly, the way in which the major social institutions distribute fundamental rights and duties and determine the division of advantages from social cooperation'.[5] Even Barry defines the rules of justice as 'the kind of rules that every society needs if it is to avoid conflict – on any scale from mutual frustration up to civil war. Ideally, rules of justice assign rights and duties to people in their personal and official capacities in such a way that, in any situation, it is clear what each person is entitled or required to do'.[6]

And even if the attribution of rights is not made explicit, theories of justice *implicitly* attribute them according to some criterion or other. For example, in an important article Gregory Vlastos gave a list of 'well-known maxims of distributive justice' such as 'To each according to his *need*' or 'To each according to his *worth*' and so on (Vlastos, 1984, p. 44). Clearly all such principles of justice imply certain rights.

Consider, for example, a contractarian theory of justice. There are various forms of such theories – 'actual', 'hypothetical', 'ideal' contracts and so on – but, with minor adjustments that are irrelevant to the argument here, they can all be represented in one of the maxims on Vlastos's, list, namely 'To everybody according to the *agreement* he has made' (Vlastos, *op.cit.* p. 44). This can then be converted into a proposition about rights, namely 'everybody has a right to what is specified in the contract'. In short, a defining feature of a wide variety of different conceptions of justice is that – explicitly or implicitly – they attribute rights (and hence counterpart duties). This creates special problems when we come to justice between non-overlapping generations. For, as De George pointed out long ago, non-existent people cannot 'have' anything, so they cannot 'have' rights.[7] This seemingly uncontroversial proposition would seem hardly worth discussing, were it not for the fact that it is frequently claimed – particularly in the context of environmental issues – that future non-overlapping generations do have rights.

The problem is that future non-overlapping generations cannot 'have' – in the present tense – rights to anything, simply because properties, such as being green or wealthy or having rights, can be predicated only of some subject that exists. Outside the realm of mythical or fictional creatures or hypothetical discourse, if there is no subject, then there is nothing to which any property can be ascribed.[8] Propositions such as 'X is Y' or 'X has Z' or 'X prefers A to B' make sense only if there is an X. If there is no X then all such propositions are meaningless.[9] Thus the general proposition that future generations cannot have anything, including rights, follows from the meaning of the present tense of the verb 'to have'.[10] Unborn people simply cannot *have* anything. They cannot have two legs or long hair or a taste for Mozart.[11]

In connection with the more specific proposition, namely that future generations have rights to specific assets, such as the existing environment and all its creatures, a second condition has to be satisfied. This is that even people who do exist cannot have rights to anything unless, in principle, the rights *could* be fulfilled (Parfit 1984, p. 365). In the case of rights to particular physical objects, for example, like a right to see a live dinosaur, it is essential that the dinosaurs exist. In the same way that it does not seem to make sense to say 'X has Y' or 'X is Z' if X does not exist, it does not make sense *even when X does exist* to say 'X has a right to Y' if Y is not available or beyond the power of anybody to provide. Thus for the proposition 'X has a right to Y' to be valid, where Y refers to some tangible object, two essential conditions have to be satisfied. First, X must exist, and second, it must be possible, in principle, to provide Y.

In the case of our right to see live dinosaurs, for example, one of these two conditions is not satisfied. We exist, but dinosaurs do not exist. And before the dinosaurs became extinct, the dinosaurs existed but we did not exist, so we could not have any rights to their preservation. If, then, the inseparability of justice and rights set out earlier is accepted, it does seem to confirm the conclusion reached earlier on other grounds, namely that there is no place for a theory of justice between generations.

The argument is really very simple and can be summarised in the following syllogism:

(i) Any coherent theory of justice implies conferring rights on people.
(ii) Future generations of unborn people cannot be said to have any rights.

Therefore, (iii) the interests of future generations cannot be protected or promoted within the framework of any coherent theory of justice.

Of course, both of the first two propositions can be challenged. The first of them reflects a particular conception of justice and rights – which, following Rawls or Barry or others – is essentially that justice is a virtue of institutions and consists of defining the rights and duties of the members of the institutions in question. But other conceptions of justice and rights are certainly plausible. In particular, some philosophers subscribe to conceptions of 'natural justice' – and 'natural fairness' – according to which an injustice exists insofar as somebody is worse off than somebody else through no fault of her own, even if this state of affairs has not been imposed by anybody else and does not reflect a failure of any institution to act according to principles of justice.

The second proposition may be thought by many people to be non-controversial, or even obvious, and to correspond to what is generally understood by the present tense of the verb 'to have'. The claim that future generations do have rights has been supported by some reputable philosophers, and there is even, in Berlin, a 'Foundation for the Rights of Future Generations', that holds international conferences at which various professors solemnly discuss topics such as how to incorporate the rights of unborn people into national political constitutions.

For example, one widely quoted authority on intergenerational equity, Edith Brown Weiss, refers to the Preamble to the Universal Declaration of Human Rights, which states that 'Whereas recognition of the inherent dignity and of the equal and inalienable rights of all members of the human family is the foundation of freedom, justice and peace in the world'. She then goes on to argue that the 'reference to all members of the human family has a temporal dimension, which brings all generations within its scope'. But future generations – of unborn people – are not 'members of the human family'. They are not members of any family, or of any tennis club, or of any national legislature, or of anything at all. They do not exist. The same objection applies to Annette Baier's conclusion that 'So far I have found no conceptual reason for disallowing talk of the rights of future persons. Neither their nonpresence, nor our ignorance of *who* exactly they are, nor our uncertainty concerning how many of them there are, rules out the appropriateness of recognizing rights on their part'.[12] In fact Baier is mistaken. There is no uncertainty at all as to how many future persons there *are*. There aren't any.

Some philosophers have argued that since future people will have interests they have rights, now. For example, the distinguished philosopher, Joel Feinberg, who is also the author of authoritative articles on the concept of 'rights', writes of the interests of future generations that, 'The identity of the owners of these interests is now necessarily obscure, but the fact of their interest-ownership is crystal clear, and that is all that is necessary to certify the coherence of present talk about their rights'. He concludes by saying that 'philosophers have not helped matters by arguing that animals and future generations are not the kinds of beings who can have rights now, that they don't presently qualify for membership, even "auxiliary membership," in our moral community'.[13]

But there seem to be two objections to the argument that because future generations *will* have interests they must *have* rights now.[14] First, having interests is, at best, merely a necessary condition for having rights contemporaneously, not a sufficient condition. Many people have an interest in seeing the horse they have backed to win a race winning it. But they cannot all have a right to such an outcome and, indeed, it would be absurd to maintain that they did. It is not necessary to scrutinise the borderlines between 'interests', 'needs', 'desires', and so on in order to see that we cannot have rights to all that is necessary for the good life. Second, the fact that future generations will have interests in the future, and may well have rights in the future, does not mean that they can have interests today, that is, before they are born. It is sometimes argued that having certain interests – such as 'vital' interests implies having certain rights. But future generations do not at this point in time *have* any interests.

However, for those of us who are concerned about the well-being of future generations, all is not lost. In the same way that justice does not exhaust the whole of morality neither do 'rights'. Consider an example that is often used in discussions of intergenerational justice, namely the case where somebody had made preparations to set off a bomb in, say, 200 years time, or buried some radioactive nuclear waste in an unsafe location. This would harm a lot of people who do not yet exist. According to the previous argument, it would be wrong to say that their rights not to be harmed had been violated. For since they did not exist when the delayed-action bomb was planted, they could not be said to have any rights to be violated. *But, it would still be a very wicked thing to do.* Any system of moral behaviour includes an obligation not to gratuitously inflict grievous harm on people, however removed from us they may be in time or space. One can violate this moral obligation by taking action that would harm people who are not yet born without violating their 'rights' if we were to take advantage of the accidental temporal advantage that we have over them by storing up harm for them that cannot be justified by any need to avoid greater harm to ourselves.

In the same sense that we can harm posterity we can also help posterity. There is, therefore, a moral obligation to take this into account in any policy that affects future generations. In everyday life we do not act as if we have a free hand to do what we like as long as we do not infringe some principle of justice. We would not regard a person who fails to help other people when he can do so at no great cost to himself as being equally virtuous as somebody who does so. It is for this reason, therefore, and not out of respect for some probably unattainable and unnecessary theory of intergenerational justice, that society should take account of the interests of future generations.

4   RAWLS AND 'JUST SAVINGS'

The most obvious way to take account of the interests of future genera-tions is to save for them. As Clark Wolf says, ' . . . one crucial part of any theory of intergenerational justice is an account of whether and how much the present generations ought to save resources for the future rather than destroying or consuming them'.[15] Indeed, it is not clear what else a theory of intergenerational justice has to deal with. Hence, in his 1971 work Rawls attempted to construct a theory of 'just' savings within the frame-work of his contractarian model in order to maintain impartiality between generations. For example, he wrote that 'the parties (in the original position) do not know to which generation they belong . . . ' and that 'since no one knows to which generation he belongs, the question (of finding a just saving principle) is viewed from the standpoint of each'.[16]

However there is a fatal technical difficulty in using the original position in order to arrive at contract between different generations that covers savings. This is that, according to some commentators, the more that the earlier generations are allowed to use up all the Earth's resources the shorter the time span of the human race – that is, the fewer later generations there will be. Since the rules drawn up, therefore, would reduce the number of generations that are represented in the original position it cannot constitute a situation in which all potential generations are represented.

Rawls originally based his 'just savings' rule on the idea that the participants in the original position would have a sentimental interest in the welfare of their descendants. But this rule, too, was fraught with other difficulties.[17] It is basically an *ad hoc* 'motivational assumption'. It no longer represents a negotiated contract between rational, self-interested participants. In other words it implies that Rawls has abandoned the ambition to produce a theory of justice that rescues justice from intuitionism.

But later he accepted that his original proposal was defective and, in 1993, he referred to a better solution that, he said, had been suggested to him in 1972 by Tom Nagel and Derek Parfit and which he set out later in the same work.[18] His version of it was that ' . . . the correct principle is that which members of any generation (and so of all generations) would adopt as the one their generation is to follow and as the principles they would want preceding generations to have followed (and later generations to follow), no matter how far back (or forward) in time' (*op.cit.*, p. 274).[19]

This somewhat Kantian rule has some obvious appeal. For one would not want a rule that allowed every generation to be very stingy in their bequests to future generations since that would have exonerated previous generations from saving much. However, it is still not very convincing since (i) it provides little guidance as to what the just savings principles actually ought to be, or even what they are likely to be; and (ii) it totally fails – like virtually any other coherent theory of intergenerational 'just savings' – to allow for generations to have any view as to what would be the optimal rate of growth of population. And, as Dasgupta points out, ' . . . public policies bearing on fertility and savings decisions can't be kept independent of each other: desirable investment policies are a function of demographic profiles, and defendable population policies depend upon investment rates. The two need to be discussed simultaneously'.[20]

Also, Rawls recognised (contrary to what is sometimes alleged) that a major feature of his theory of justice, namely his famous 'difference principle', was inapplicable between generations. He accepted that his 'difference principle' – that is, that at any point in time, the only inequalities that are allowed to exist in society are those that will improve the position of the worst off members of society – could not apply between generations. But, as he said, 'There is no way for later generations to help the situation of the least fortunate earlier generations. Thus the difference principle does not hold for the question of justice between generations'. He also pointed out that the difference principle between generations would lead to quite unacceptable results.[21] For the first generation would presumably be the poorest generation – not being endowed with any starting capital – and if it cut its own consumption in order to invest for the future it would become even poorer. And it is a basic feature of Rawls's theory of justice that it sets out rules for cooperation between agents for their mutual benefit that are acceptable to all provided it is not at the expense of the worst off. For the more the current generation saves in order to invest for the future, the less it can consume itself, and hence its own standard of living would be reduced even further. This meant that application of the 'difference principle' between generations would rule out economic growth resulting from the accumulation of capital.[22] Rawls's exclusion of the difference principle between generations was subsequently endorsed by various eminent economists, though their conclusions have been challenged by Clark Wolf, who demonstrates that if one does drop the assumption that generations do not overlap, the application of a 'difference principle' between generations need not be rejected.[23]

5   FAIRNESS AND THE ROLE OF INITIAL ENDOWMENTS

Suppose, then, that we abandon a contractarian approach to theory of intergenerational justice and concentrate on some less demanding approach based on a wider notion of 'fairness'. After all, I have repeatedly pointed out in earlier chapters, the 'fairness' of any situation depends partly on value judgements concerning the 'fairness' of the distribution of initial endowments. If we take the view that the concept of 'just' or 'fair' can apply to, say, relations between parties of very unequal strength or unequal initial endowments, it might be easier to construct some principles of what would be 'fair' behaviour towards future generations and 'fair' provision for their welfare. A stress on the possible unfairness of initial endowments corresponds closely to the criticism of the 'mutual advantage' contractarian conception of justice made by the late Brian Barry.

Barry accepts that the Humean 'circumstances of justice' would leave no room for justice between generations.[24] But this is one of the reasons why he rejected them. As I indicated in the previous chapter, Barry would prefer to broaden the scope of a theory of justice so that it would not exclude the notion of injustice in relationships between parties of unequal power. He believes that '... justice as mutual advantage fails egregiously to do one thing that we normally expect a conception of justice to do, and that is provide some moral basis for the claims of the relatively powerless'.[25] He gives the example of the treaties signed between Western settlers and indigenous peoples in the early days of the USA (and many other parts of the world). Such treaties, or agreements, may well have been the best that the weaker parties could accept under the circumstances and to which, therefore, they may have been obliged to enter, but they should still be regarded as 'unjust'.

In the same way that in 1999 Barry broadened the scope of the theory of justice to encompass justice between different countries he broadened it to encompass different generations. He begins with some fundamental principles of justice between contemporaries and then considers how far they can be applied intergenerationally. One of these is the principle of the 'fundamental equality of human beings', which, as indicated in Chapter 17, is a normal axiomatic starting point in *cosmopolitan* theories of justice. Barry says that 'it is precisely because this premise does not make moral standing depend on the time at which people live that principles of justice valid for contemporaries are prima facie valid for intergenerational justice too'.[26]

Barry goes on to select two fundamental principles of justice that he believed can apply intergenerationally. One of these is the principle of responsibility, which is that the current generation would be acting unjustly if it followed policies that made future generations worse off than they would otherwise be. But, unless it is heavily qualified, this would be a very debatable requirement. It is not, in fact, universally accepted without qualification among coexisting people. For example, Utilitarianism would accept harming some people in the interests of the many. Why should it always be unjust to follow policies that *might* conceivably make future generations worse off than they would otherwise be even if this means certainly imposing burdens – and possibly even greater burdens – on some of the people alive today who might be much poorer than future people?

Barry seems to be applying a much more rigorous condition on relationships between different generations than is generally accepted among contemporaries. For he rules out doing harm to future generation even if, in doing so, the present generations suffer a much greater harm. It is not clear that, from the standpoint of, say, a neutral 'Time Lord', this would look like an equitable distribution of wealth between different generations. It certainly would not be sanctioned in a utilitarian approach, such as that followed by Lord Stern in his recent report on the economics of climate change, since total utility over the whole of time would be smaller.[27]

Furthermore, even when redistributing from richer to poorer within any contemporary society one can usually – though not always – know who is going to be affected, and in what way. One has a fairly good idea who are the richer members of society and who are the poorer. But the predictions that Barry makes about the inevitable harmful effects of current environmental practices and population policies on the relative welfare of future generations are very speculative. It is true that climate change could make future generations' welfare much lower than it would otherwise have been. But, if widely accepted projections – including even those used by the International Panel on Climate Change – are to be believed, future generations are likely to be much wealthier than are people today even if climate change means that they would be less wealthy than they would otherwise have been. Of course, in the event of climatic catastrophe, this would no longer be the case.

6   LOCKE'S 'PROVISO'

Attempts to rescue the notion of intergenerational justice are often buttressed by an appeal to the so-called 'Locke's proviso' as justifying the case for not depriving future generations of any resources. This proviso is the phrase '... where there is enough, and as good left in common for others'.[28] But this seems to be an unjustified use of Locke's proviso. What Locke was seeking to do in the chapter 'Of property', in which the aforementioned phrases appear, was to set out his theory of the original justification for the emergence of the rule of property rights.

This started from the assumption that Man had inalienable property rights in himself, and hence in his labour. Hence, if people used their labour to obtain other goods (such as edible game or fruits, etc.) they created a property right in the product in which they had mixed their labour.[29] At an early stage on earth, when there was an abundance of natural resources (he is referring chiefly to land and animals and fruits) – that is, there was no scarcity of such goods – this was sufficient to justify the acquisition of property in land and so on. In other words, this condition was sufficient to justify the acquisition of land and so on when '... there was still enough and as good left'. Locke's repetition of this clause was used by him as part of a literary device to emphasise that he is presenting a theory of the origin and justification of property rights in the state of nature *when there was no scarcity* (my italics).

He hardly ever mentions – let alone discusses – the rules that ought to apply in conditions of scarcity. And when he does so it is just to make casual – and almost parenthetical – remarks to the effect that, under such conditions, the appropriate division of the scarce resource would have to result from the laws upon which interested parties had agreed. He does not discuss what principles should govern such laws and agreements. His emphasis, in the same chapter, on the criterion of mixing one's own labour with the resource that one had appropriated and enclosed, and not using the resource wastefully or not at all, was in the context of widespread unrest at the enclosure of hitherto common land that had been taking place in England from the fourteenth and fifteenth centuries and that led to a landless proletariat in many parts of the country. It was in this that Locke was interested. At no point at all does he show any interest in our obligations to future generations. Of course, this does not preclude speculation as to how Lockean principles concerning property could be applied to the conservation of resources for future generations, though, at first sight, this does not look a very promising line of enquiry, since his suggestion that scarce resources would have to be allocated by laws to which people had agreed rather rules out any intergenerational guidance since non-overlapping generations are unable to agree to anything (a characteristic that they share, of course, with many people alive today).

7   The 'Non-Identity Problem' and Conflicting Intuitions

I have remarked at various points in this book that the main role of ethical theory is to help us sort out our ethical intuitions, particularly when they conflict. A particularly striking case that happens to have a bearing on the question of intergenerational justice is the conundrum known as the 'non-identity problem', which was made famous by J. Narveson and Derek Parfit.[30] This is derived from what is usually known as 'the person-affecting claim' discussed in Chapter 15 above in connection with egalitarianism. One definition of the claim is that 'one situation cannot be worse or better than another if there is no one who is worse or better' (Temkin, (1993:248). The 'person-affecting claim' appears to be intuitively very compelling.

But – adapting one of Parfit's examples – suppose society is faced with two possible policies, one of which is generally referred to as 'sustainable development' policy, and the other is the 'depletion' policy. Whichever policy is adopted will affect which particular people are born in the future. For example, suppose that depletion of the atmosphere's 'carbon space' led to significant climate change. Everybody's lives would be changed. People would engage in different occupations, would live in different places, would meet different people and would get married at different stages of their lives, or produce children at different precise points in time. Hence, the people who will exist under the depletion policy will not be the same people as would have existed under the sustainable development policy. But can the people who will exist under the depletion policy complain they are worse off as a result of that policy?

After all, if that policy had not been pursued they would not have been born. So, if we stick to the person-affecting claim, they cannot say that *they* are worse off. Indeed, it can be argued that as long as they are living lives that are worth living they are better off than they would have been had they not been born at all. So they would have been better off than if the sustainable development policy had been followed since, in that case, they would not have been born at all. Other people would have been born instead. But I have argued in Chapter 14 that such a comparison is meaningless!

So we seem to have a clear case of a conflict of intuitions. On the one hand there is the appeal of the 'person-affecting claim', namely that one situation cannot be worse than another unless it is worse for actual people. This intuition suggests that a depletion policy would not make future people worse off since they would not be the same people as the people who would be alive under a sustainable development policy. On the other hand, it seems that it would be wicked to follow a policy that made the welfare of the people who happen to be alive in the future lower than would have been the welfare of the *different* future people who would have been alive under a different policy. So how can one escape from this dilemma of two apparently compelling but conflicting moral intuitions? Naturally, the 'non-identity problem' has been the subject of enormous debate in the philosophical literature.[31] It is a bit like the 'Liar Paradox' that stimulated many philosophers through the centuries to ask difficult questions about the concept of 'truth'.[32] The non-identity problem provides enormous scope for analysing the concept of 'worse off'.

One possible way out is to accept that different people would be born under different scenarios, so that, under the 'person-affecting claim', it does not make sense to say that they are worse off. This is the simple utilitarian cost-benefit approach, such as is adopted in the *Stern Review* of the climate change problem.[33] A utilitarian could simply say that the welfare of the people who will exist as a result of, say, a 'depletion' policy, will be worse off than would have been the welfare of the *different* people who would exist under the 'conservation' policy.

But what this view amounts to is a rejection of the 'person-affecting claim'. What it implies is that in the place of the person-affecting claim of the form 'one situation cannot be worse or better than another if there is no one who is worse or better' one accepts, instead, the claim that 'one situation *can* be better or worse off than another if it is better or worse for the people in that situation than it would have been for whatever other people might have been in it'. These are two rival definitions of 'worse off' (or 'better off'), and the choice between them is a value judgement to which there can be no objective answer. It is just one more example of the way that ethical theory cannot provide simple answers to conflicts between our ethical intuitions.

It should not be assumed from the previous section, however, that if we accept the second concept of 'worse off' and follow the utilitarian approach, we do not have other problems. Many of the limitations on utilitarianism are discussed in Chapter 10. For a utility maximising Pareto-optimising move requires that the losers can – if only potentially – be compensated while still leaving the gainers better off. Otherwise one has not satisfied the Paretian condition for an improvement, namely that nobody is worse off. But in the intergenerational context, if the losers from any policy happen to be the present generation – for example, people alive today make sacrifices in the interests of posterity – it may not even be a *potential* Pareto-optimising move, let alone an *actual* Pareto-optimising move. For there is no way of ensuring that future generations will compensate the losers in the present generation.

8   CONCLUSION

The conclusion of Chapter 17 was that theories of international justice did not help much to resolve the question of how widely across *space* one ought to draw the boundary of the society in whose economic welfare we are interested. This was for two main reasons, namely (i) mainstream theories of justice relied on the existence of some overall 'authority' that could ensure respect for the principles of justice adopted in whatever units – individuals or states – are concerned; and (ii) mainstream theories of justice – from Hobbes to Rawls – have been 'contractarian'. And respect for sovereignty of independent states made it difficult to arrive at meaningful and enforceable contracts between them except in a limited number of special cases.

These two ingredients of most theories of justice seem to completely rule out the feasibility of constructing a coherent theory of intergenerational justice. And there is a third difficulty. This is that all theories of justice appear to imply some specification of the rights and duties of the people, or entities, covered by them. In particular, it corresponded to the Rawlsian 'political' conception of justice, which referred to the rights and obligations of members of some political community. But it does not seem possible to allocate rights to unborn people, notwithstanding many opinions to the contrary. Future unborn generations cannot 'have' – *in the present tense* – any 'rights' or anything else for that matter.

Thus, for these three reasons, it seems that Rawls was right in doubting whether a coherent theory of justice between generations was attainable.

But should one worry about this? Probably not. From Hume to Rawls it has been widely – though not universally – believed that the function of principles of justice is that it enables members of any society to live more or less in peace and mutual cooperation for the general benefit of them all. It is a way of avoiding conflict of interests finishing up as war or chaos. But as between generations there is no danger of violent conflict anyway. So we may not really need a theory of intergenerational justice.

However, this does not give one a free hand to ignore the interests either of other countries or of distant future generations. It has been argued earlier – particularly at the end of the previous chapter – that there is always a case for old-fashioned beneficence and 'sympathy' for the interests of future generations. As with giving aid to poor countries, so saving resources to ensure a decent future for future generations is a form of the giving aid to the 'right people' that Aristotle included in his conception of virtue.[34]

Thus even without a theory of justice to guide us we still have as a moral obligation not to impose undue harm on future generations and to take account of their interests. To some extent the market mechanism provides for the needs of future generations through the investment that is carried out for purely selfish economic motivations. And over the last thousand years or so it has worked and led to significant economic growth. Also, to some extent one can expect some help from the way that the interests of future generations will be solved by reliance on personal relations between coexisting generations – such as those between parents and their children. For example, the notion of reciprocity that plays a major role in any 'contractarian' theory of justice may play only a negligible part in the relationships between parents and children compared to a spontaneous feelings of affection, and of moral obligation to children for whose existence one is responsible. Such sentiments will usually suffice to ensure that each generation will provide adequately for the next generation. In other words, either (i) natural affection or respect for some conventions of 'duty' between parents and children will suffice to ensure adequate concern for the interests of future unborn generations, or (ii) these interests will be protected by what the philosopher John Passmore called the 'chain of love' (Passmore, 1974). Unfortunately, there are plausible reasons why this might not be enough. In particular, there are good reasons – such as Sen's famous 'isolation paradox' why free markets may not adequately protect the presumed interests of future generations.

Also, on account of limitations on the uncoordinated action of individuals, it is unlikely that the private sentiments of 'sympathy' are adequate to protect and prevent future generations fully from being harmed in ways that most people – in their capacity as citizens of a continuing society rather than in their capacity of private individuals concerned only with their self-interest – will deplore. It is true that, as Wolf has pointed out, it would be useful to have a theory of intergenerational justice as a standard against which one could compare what *actually* happens with what one thinks *ought* to happen.[35] But it is not the absence of such a theory that prevents the interests of future generations from being adequately represented in policy decisions. As with the practical problem of incorporating sympathy and concern with the welfare of other countries into our policies, so the real practical problem on incorporating concern with the interests that future generations into our policies is a problem of the extent to which collective action reflects the sympathies and benevolence of individuals rather than a problem of reaching an agreed theory of intergenerational justice.

NOTES

1. According to Laslett and Fishkin, 'The revival of political theory over the past three decades has taken place within the grossly simplifying assumptions of a largely timeless world...(it) is limited, at most, to the horizons of a single generation who make binding choices, for all time, for all successor generations' (Laslett and Fishkin, (eds.), 1992:1). They go on to describe

recent attempts to bring time into the picture as little more than 'gestures' in that direction. This is, perhaps, rather unfair on Rawls, who discussed intergenerational distributive justice – if rather dismissively – back in 1971, and others, such as Dasgupta (1974), or the contributors to the volumes on the subject edited by Sikora and Barry (1978) or by Partridge (1981). However, Laslett has to be credited with one of the earliest insightful analyses of the relationship between justice between non-contemporaneous generations and contemporaneous cohorts – such as between different age groups (in Laslett and Fishkin, eds., *op.cit.*:24–47).

2. Rawls, 1971:284.
3. Rawls, *ibid.*:126
4. Rawls, *ibid.*:291
5. In similar vein, Vlastos writes that 'Whenever the question of regard, or disregard, for substantially affected rights does not arise, the question of justice or injustice does not arise', or 'Again, whenever one is in no position to govern one's action by regard for rights, the question of justice or injustice does not arise', or 'A major feature of my definition of "just" is that it makes the answer to "is x just?" (where x is any action, decision, etc.) strictly dependent on the answer to another question: "what are the rights of those who are substantially affected by x?"' (Vlastos, 1984:60–61).
6. Barry, 1995:72.
7. De George, 1981.
8. When rights are attributed to mythical or fictional creatures, for example, they are not believed to be rights that exist in the real world and that hence impose any obligations on real-world people, such as us.
9. I am using the term 'meaningless' here to describe propositions such as 'X is Y' when there is no X, although such propositions could be transposed into longer and clumsy propositions that are meaningful, such as 'X exits and if there is an X it has Y', but are false if, in fact, there is no X.
10. This fundamental and apparently decisive point was made by De George (1981). But with some exceptions, notably de-Shalit (1995, and 2000:137), it does not seem to have been given due weight in the literature on this subject.
11. As Dasgupta puts it, 'It would be an error to regard potential persons as a special sort of people' (1993:382/3). The 'unborn' aren't a class of people. It makes no sense to attribute a degree of well-being, low or high or nil, to the states of not being born… 'Possible people aren't actual (or future) people, any more than clay by the river bank is a mud hut. It is actual persons who have feelings, aspirations, needs, claims, projects, and a sense of justice. In short, it is actual persons who are moral agents' (*ibid*:384).
12. Baier, 1981.

13. Feinberg, 1981:148–149. The same argument is advanced at length by Sterba, 1980 and 1998.

14. See, in particular, Feinberg, 1981.

15. Wolf, C., 2010:270.

16. Rawls, 1971:287–288.

17. See critique of this rule in Beckerman and Pasek, 2001:36–40.

18. Rawls, 1993:20, fn.22.

19. A valuable survey of Rawls's views on intergenerational justice is given by Dierksmeier, 2006:ch. 4.

20. Dasgupta, 1993:377.

21. Rawls, 1971:291.

22. See also Brian Barry, 1989:189–202.

23. Wolf, C., 2010:282–287

24. For example, Barry, 1989:189.

25. Barry, 1995:46.

26. Barry, 1999:46.

27. Stern, 2006.

28. Locke, II, ch. V, para. 26.

29. As is well known, Nozick questioned this notion by postulating the example of Mr X pouring some tomato juice (which he owned) into the ocean. According to Nozick, Lockean theory would require us to interpret this as giving Mr X a property right in the ocean, whereas, as Nozick points out, it would be more reasonable to say that the person in question had lost some property (the tomato juice) rather than have gained any (the ocean). This is true, but in all fairness to Locke his theory of property rights has to be seen (i) in the context of the times, when there was much resentment at the enclosure movement, and his claim that property rights could be justified in terms of the effort that the owners had made in order to convert the hitherto unowned resource into their property. This was why he also repeated his insistence on this property right being dependent on the acquired asset not being wasted, as was often the case with much of the hitherto common land that had been enclosed by the landowners without their putting it to any good use; and (ii) in the context of Locke's attempt to establish property rights as one of the basic natural rights that people had in some state of nature.

30. Narveson, 1967, and Parfit, 1984.

31. A very comprehensive study of the 'person-affecting claim' in the context of intergenerational justice is Mulgan, 2008.

32. This is a reference to conundrums such as the one familiar to many school children that goes: 'Socrates said that all Greeks are liars. Socrates was a Greek. So Socrates was a liar. So one should not believe what he said about

all Greeks being liars. So he may have been telling the truth about all Greeks being liars...and so on'. Or, more briefly, 'What I say is untrue', with obvious implications.

33. Stern, 2006.
34. See esp., *Ethics*, 1120a9-b1.
35. Wolf, 1996, 2010.

CHAPTER 19

The Role of Welfare Economics

The numerous value judgements in welfare economics identified in previous chapters mean that the welfare economics input into policy decisions has to be seriously qualified. But they do not mean that it is irrelevant. It merely implies that CBA, which is welfare economics in action, has also to be treated as being a 'decision tool, not a decision rule'.

It is true that some of the technical difficulties of a CBA can never be completely overcome. For example, since we do not have detailed and accurate models of the way that economies work it is impossible to make full allowance for the extent to which market prices and wages differ from the values they would have had if the distribution of initial endowments had corresponded to what one might regard as an 'equitable' distribution, or other market failures.

Also some CBAs in the public sector are badly done. This is not merely on account of a failure to allow for the sort of theoretical issues discussed earlier. It is much more likely to be on account of administrative and managerial defects, such as 'cognitive biases' – that is, 'errors in the way the mind processes information'.[1] This, and related human weaknesses and political pressures, sometimes leads to wildly overoptimistic predictions of likely costs and benefits of public projects by the officials who have an interest in promoting them.

But it is at least possible, in many countries, to do something to correct this sort of weakness in the CBA of major public projects. When this is done a properly conducted CBA will at least indicate which, of a choice of

© The Author(s) 2017
W. Beckerman, *Economics as Applied Ethics*,
DOI 10.1007/978-3-319-50319-6_19

projects, is likely to satisfy both the Paretian conditions for a more efficient resource allocation and the decision-makers' value judgements regarding the distribution of incomes. So there are several reasons why the practical value of welfare economics should not be written off.

First, innumerable decisions have to be taken about very small changes in the economic and social environment. An extreme example would be a project to provide extra street-lighting in some part of town, which is most unlikely to have effects on the whole pattern of relative prices and incomes.

Second, in many micro-decisions it is not feasible, in practice, to compensate somebody who, say, has to lose out in a wait for kidney transplants by refraining from siting some polluting factory in his neighbourhood. It is impossible to ensure that those who gain consumer's surplus from specific public projects compensate those who lose from them. But, although attention has been drawn to the distributional limitations of CBA, in developed societies hundreds or thousands of small projects are being carried out all the time. If they are reasonably accurate CBAs so that the gains from the projects more than offset the losses, on the whole the people who lose on the swings from some projects can hope to gain more on the roundabouts of others. And when this does not suffice the authorities are usually under pressure to promote whatever income distribution society prefers. Democratic governments are under constant pressure to carry out what Peyton Young calls 'macro-equity' in a way that corrects for unwanted changes in income distribution.[2]

Third, although a properly conducted economic CBA can never be more than a part of a broader assessment of any project, along the lines of the 'Franklin's Algebra' mentioned in Chapter 7, it is an essential part.

(i) It prevents an incorrect analysis of the economic costs and benefits of a particular project such as those exposed by Michael Sandel in the Annex to Chapter 14 and helps decision makers to know roughly what is the cost of promoting their particular values.

(ii) It prevents some bad decisions being taken by politicians or officials, who sometimes have their own agendas that may not be those of the public they serve.

The following experience of the author may be relevant. When I was a member of the Royal Commission on Environmental Pollution in the early 1970s I was involved in preparing a report on pollution in British estuaries and coastlines. This involved a visit to a certain County Council that proudly described to the Commission its latest major sewage project designed to clean up some of the rivers running into a large stretch of local coastline in which many people went swimming. The project would cost £x million. On enquiry of the local health authorities it transpired that (i) no lives had been lost from bathing in the 'polluted' coastal waters in question for at least a century; (ii) although some people may have had a stomach upset as a result of doing so, this could not be established in medical statistics for obvious reasons and (iii) if the same £x million were to allocated to other projects designed to improve the health of the local inhabitants, such as better Accident and Emergency services, better maternity care, better cancer treatment, and so on, the drainage project would come nowhere near the top of the list of priorities.

If a CBA had been carried out it is highly unlikely that it would have justified the project in question. Of course, even a less-demanding 'cost-efficiency' test would probably have given it low priority, so this experience does not demonstrate the absolute indispensability of a CBA. But a CBA would have led to the identification and quantification of much relevant information. Given that the project in question would probably not then have passed *any* test, the question arises 'why was it carried out?' The answer probably lies in the realm of local politics, notably in the factors that determine from which group of people the decision makers were mainly drawn.

Thus while a CBA should never be decisive it does, at least, require decision makers to reveal the criteria by which their decisions are made. It introduces a crucial element of transparency into the decision-making process. True, there are important values at stake that cannot be incorporated quantitatively in a CBA. But citizens have a right to know how much, on balance, the decision makers are prepared to pay in the interests of these other values. Thus, for all its numerous weaknesses, there is still a strong case for using in any public policy decision the tools of CBA – tools that are grounded in the basic principles of welfare economics, warts and all. In some cases decision makers will pay excessive respect to CBA so that it will have an undue influence on policy and perhaps lead to unfortunate consequences. But in a democratic community the incidence of such cases is likely to be less than in societies in which decisions are reached by cabals, pressure groups, vested interests and ill-informed participants, free of the discipline of open and public accountability.

And, lastly, the theory of welfare economics provides the theoretical justification for innumerable policies, such as the correction of 'externalities', the restraints on monopolistic power, and the provision of goods and services.

NOTES

1. Flyvbjerg, 2009:349.
2. Peyton Young, 1994.

BIBLIOGRAPHY

Adler, M.D., and Posner, E.A., 2000, *Cost-benefit Analysis: Legal, Economic, and Philosophical Perspectives*, University of Chicago Press.

Aldred, J., 2009, *The Skeptical Economist*, Earthscan, London.

Ally, M., and Beckerman, W., 2014, 'How to Reduce Carbon Emissions Equitably', *World Economics*, 15.

Anand, S., and Hansen, K., 1997, 'Disability-adjusted Life Years: A Critical Review', *Journal of Health Economics*, 16.

Anderson, E., 1999, 'What Is the Point of Equality?', *Ethics*, 109.

Annual Report of the National Institute of Economic and Social Research, 2009, p.13.

Appiah, M., 2001, 'Equality of What?', *The New York Review of Books*, 26 April.

Arneson, R., 2000, 'Luck Egalitarianism', *Ethics*, 110/2.

Arrow, K., 1951/1963 (2nd edn.), *Social Choice and Individual Values*, Cowles Commission, Yale University Press, New Haven and London.

Arrow, K., 1974, *The Limits of Organization*, Norton, New York.

Arrow, K., Cline, W.R., Maler, K-G, Munasinghe, M., 1996, (Intertemporal equity, discounting, and economic efficiency) im Bruce, J.P., Lee, H. and Haites, E.F., *Climate Change, Economic and Social Dimension of Climate Change., Contribution of Working Group III to The Second Assessment Report of the Intergovernmental Panel on Climate Change, Cambridge University Press*.

Atkinson, A., 1972/1980, 'On Measurement of Inequality', reprinted in, *Wealth, Income & Inequality*, Oxford University Press.

Atkinson, A., 1975, *The Economics of Inequality*, Oxford University Press.

Atkinson, A, Piketty, T and Saez, E, 2011, 'Top Incomes in the Long Run of History', *Journal of Economic Literature*, 49.

Atkinson, A., 2015, *Inequality: What Can Be Done*, Harvard University Press.

© The Author(s) 2017
W. Beckerman, *Economics as Applied Ethics*,
DOI 10.1007/978-3-319-50319-6

Australian Government Treasury, 1973, *Economic Growth: Is it Worth Having?* Treasury Economic Paper, No.2, Australian Government Publishing Service, Canberra.

Ayer, A.J., 1973, *The Central Questions of Philosophy*, Weidenfeld and Nicolson, London, and Penguin, Harmondsworth, 1976.

Ayer, A.J., 1990, 'Happiness as Satisfaction of Desires', in Glover, J. (ed.), *Utilitarianism and its Critics*, Macmillan, New York.

Balogh, T., 1963, *Unequal Partners*, Basil Blackwell, Oxford.

Barrett, S., 1992, 'Acceptable Allocations of Tradable Carbon Emission Entitlements in a Global Warming Treaty', in UNCTAD, *Combating Global Warming*, UNO, New York.

Barry, B., 1973, *The Liberal Theory of Justice*, Clarendon Press, Oxford.

Barry, B., 1989, *Theories of Justice*, Harvester-Wheatsheaf, London.

Barry, B., 1995, *Justice as Impartiality*, Clarendon Press, Oxford.

Barry, B., 1999, 'Sustainability and Intergenerational Justice', in Dobson, A.,(ed.) *Fairness and Futurity*, Oxford University Press.

Baier, A., 1981, 'The Rights of Past and Future Persons', in Partridge, *op.cit.*

Beckerman, W., 1978, *Measures of Leisure, Equality and Welfare*, OECD, Paris.

Beckerman, W., 1980, *An Introduction to National Income Analysis*, (3rd edn.), Weidenfeld and Nicolson, London.

Beckerman, W., and Hepburn, C., 2007, 'Ethics of the Discount Rate in the Stern Review on the Economics of Climate Change', *World Economics*, 8/1.

Beckerman, W., and Pasek, J., 2001, *Justice, Posterity and the Environment*, Oxford University Press.

Beitz, C., 1999, 'Social and Cosmopolitan Liberalism', *International Affairs*, 75/3.

Bentham, J., 1789, *An Introduction to the Principles of Morals and Legislation*, Ch. 2, para, 4.

Bernheim, B.D., Berstein, S., Gokhole, J., and Kotlikoff, L.J., 2006, *National Institute Economic Review*, 198, October.

Binmore, K., 1974, *Playing Fair: Game Theory and the Social Contract*, MIT Press, Cambridge, MA.

Binmore, K., 2005, *Natural Justice*, Oxford University Press.

Blackburn, S., 2001, *Ethics: A Very Short Introduction*, Oxford University Press.

Blackburn, S., 2009, 'In Defence of Moral Philosophy', in *Cam* [Cambridge Alumni Magazine], Issue 58, Michaelmas Term.

Blanchflower, D., and Oswald, A., 2004a, 'Well-Being Over Time in Britain and the USA', *Journal of Public Economics*, 84.

Blanchflower, D., and Oswald, A., 2004b, 'Money, Sex, and Happiness: An Empirical Study', in The Behavioral Economics special issue of *the Scandinavian Journal of Economics.*

Brandt, R.B., 1959, *Ethical Theory*, Prentice-Hall Inc., Englewood Cliffs, NJ.

Brighouse, H., and Swift, A., 2006, 'Equality, Priority, and Positional Goods', *Ethics*, 116.

Brocas, Isabelle, and Carrillo, Juan D. (eds.), 2003, *The Psychology of Economic Decisions, Rationality and Well-Being*, Oxford University Press.

Brock, Gillian, 2009, *Global Justice: A Cosmopolitan Account*, Oxford University Press.

Broome, J., 1978, 'Trying to Value a Life', *Journal of Public Economics*, 9.

Broome, J., 1985, 'The Economic Value of Life', *Economica*, 52.

Broome, J., 1991, *Weighing Goods*, Blackwell, Oxford.

Broome, J., 1992, *Counting the Cost of Global Warming*, The White Horse Press, Knapwell, Cambridge.

Broome, J., 1999, *Ethics Out of Economics*, Cambridge University Press.

Broome, J., 2009, 'Why Economics Needs Ethical Theory', in Basu, K., and Kanbur, R. (eds.), *Arguments for a Better World: Essays in Honour of Amartya Sen*, Vol. 1, Oxford University Press.

Brown, C., 2005, 'Priority or Sufficiency...or Both?', *Economics and Philosophy*, 21.

Bruni, L., and Porta, L., 2005, *Economics and Happiness: Framing the Analysis*, Oxford University Press.

Buchanan, J. M., 1954, 'Social Choice, Democracy, and Free Markets', Journal of Political Economy, 62/2.

Buiter, W., 2007, Contribution to a *Financial Times Blog*, [6th June].

Camus, A., 1956/1974., 'La Chute', in 1974 Gallimard edition in volume of Camus's selected works.

Caney, S., 2005, 'Cosmopolitan Justice, Responsibility, and Global Climate Change', *Leiden Journal of International Law*, 18.

Cantril, H., 1985, *The Pattern of Human Concern*, Rutgers University Press, New Brunswick, NJ.

Cavanagh, M., 2002, *Against Equality of Opportunity*, Oxford University Press.

Chang, R. (ed.), 1997, *Incommensurability, Incomparability, and Practical Reason*, Harvard University Press, Cambridge, MA.

Chatterjee, D.K., 2003, 'Moral Distance: An Introduction', *The Monist*, 86/3.

Clark, A., and Oswald, A., 1996, 'Satisfaction and Comparison Income', *Journal of Public Economics*, 70/1.

Clark, D., 2003, 'Concepts and Perceptions of Human Well-Being: Some Evidence from South Africa', *Oxford Development Studies*, 31/2.

Cohen, G.A., 1993, 'Equality of What? On Welfare, Goods, and Capabilities', in Nussbaum, M., and Sen, A. (eds.), *The Quality of Life*, Clarendon Press, Oxford.

Cohen, G.A., 2008, *Rescuing Justice and Equality*, Harvard University Press.

Conly, S., 2013, *Against Autonomy: Justifying Coercive Paternalism*, Cambridge University Press.

Crafts, N., 2003, 'Is Economic Growth Good for Us', *World Economics*, 4/3, July–September.

Crisp, R., 1994: 'Values, Reasons, and the Environment', in A. Belsey and R. Attfield (eds.), *Philosophy and the Natural Environment* (Supplement to Philosophy, 36).

Crisp, R., 2003, 'Equality, Priority and Compassion', *Ethics*, 113.

Crisp, R., 2004, 'How to allocate health care resources: QALYs or the virtues'; http://www.I.u-tokyo.ac.jp/dls/cleth/MedSys/conf/41015CrispR.pdf

Cummins, R.A., 2010, 'Subjective Wellbeing: Homeostatically Protected Mood and Depression: A Synthesis', *Journal of Happiness Studies*, 11.

Dasgupta. P., 1974, 'On Optimum Population Size', in Mitra, A. (ed.) *Economic Theory ad Planning: Essays in Honour Of A.K. Dasgupta*, New Delhi: Oxford University Press.

Dasgupta, P., 1993, *An inquiry into Well-Being and Destitution*, Clarendon Press, Oxford.

Dasgupta, P., 1994, 'Resource Depletion, Research and Development and the Social Rate of Discount', in Layard, R., and Glaister, S. (eds.), *Cost-Benefit Analysis*, Cambridge University Press.

Dasgupta, P., 2001, *Human Well-Being and the Natural Environment*, Oxford University Press.

Dasgupta, P., 2007a, *Economics: A Very Short Introduction*, Oxford.

Dasgupta, P., 2007b, 'A Challenge to Tokyo', *Nature*, 449, September.

Dasgupta, P., 2007c, *National Institute Economic Review*, January.

Dasgupta, P., 2008a, 'Discounting Climate Change', *Journal of Risk and Uncertainty*.

Dasgupta, P., 2008b, *The Welfare Economic Theory of Green National Accounts*, Institute for Advanced Studies, The Hebrew University of Jerusalem University Press.

Dasgupta, P., and D. Ray, 1987, 'Inequality as a Determinant of Malnutrition and Unemployment, 2: Policy', *The Economic Journal*, 97/1.

De George, R., 1981, 'The environment, rights, and future generations', in Patridge, E. (ed.), *Responsibilities to Future Generations*, Prometheus Books, New York.

de Jasay, A, 2010a, 'Inspecting the Foundations of Liberalism',*Economics Affairs*, Institute of Economic Affairs, London.

de Jasay, A., 2010b, Freedom, "'rights' and rights": in *The Collected Papers of Anthony de Jasay*, Indianapolis: The Liberty Fund.

Dierksmeier, C., 2006, 'John Rawls on the Rights of Future Generations', in Tremmel, J.C. (eds.), *Handbook of Intergenerational Justice*, Edward Elgar, Cheltenham, UK.

Dworkin, R., 2000, *Sovereign Virtue*, Harvard University Press, Cambridge, MA.

Easterlin, R.A., 1974, 'Does Economic Growth Improve the Human Lot? Some Empirical Evidence', in David, P.A., and Reder, M.W. (eds.), *Nations and Households in Economic Growth: Essays in Honour of Moses Abramowitz*, Academic Press, New York and London.

Feinberg, J., 1981, 'The Rights of Animals and Unborn Generations', in Partridge, 1981, op.cit.

Finer, S.E., 1966, *Vilfredo Pareto: Sociological Writings*, Blackwell, Oxford.

Fleurbaey, M., 2006, 'Social Welfare, Priority to the Worst Off, and the Dimensions of Individual Well-Being', in Farina, F., and Savagli, E. (eds.), *Inequality and Economic Integration*, Routledge, London.

Flyvbjerg, B., 2009, 'Survival of the Unfittest; Why the Worst Infrastructure Gets Build – and what can we do about it?', *Oxford Review of Economic Policy*, 25/3.

Frank, R.H., 1999, *Microeconomics and Behaviour*, (4th edn.), Irwin McGrawHill, Boston.

Frankfurt, H., 1997, 'Equality and Respect', *Social Research*, 64/1.

Frankfurt, H., 2015, *On Inequality*, Princeton University Press.

Frederick, S., 2003, 'Measuring Intergenerational Time Preference: Are Future Lives Valued Less?', *the Journal of Risk and Uncertainty*, 26/1.

Frey, B.S., and Stutzer, A., 2002, *Happiness & Economics*, Princeton University Press.

Frey, B.S., and Stutzer, A. *et al*, 2008, *Happiness: A Revolution in Economics*, MIT.

Gardiner, S., 2004, 'Ethics and Global Climate Change', *Ethics*, 114(August).

Gardiner, S., 2006, 'Protecting Future Generations: Intergenerational Buck-Passing, Theoretical Ineptitude and a Brief for a Global Core Precautionary Principle', in Tremmel, J.G. (ed.), *Handbook of Intergenerational Justice*, Edward Elgar, Cheltenham, UK, and Northampton, MA.

Gauthier, D., 1986, *Morals by Agreement*, Clarendon Press, Oxford.

Glover, J., (ed.) 1990, *Utilitarianism and its Critics*, London, Collier MacMillan.

———, 1992, 'Future People, Disability, and Screening', in Laslett, P., and Fishkin, J. (eds.), *Justice between Age Groups and Generations*, Yale University Press.

Graaff, J. De V., 1967, *Theoretical Welfare Economics*, Cambridge University Press.

Grubb, M., 1989, *The Greenhouse Effect: Negotiating Targets*, Royal Institute of International Affairs, London.

Grubb, M., 1995, 'Seeking Fair Weather: Ethics and the International Debate on Climate Change', *International Affairs*, 71/3.

Grubb, M., and Sebenius, J.K., 1992, 'Participation, Allocation and Adaptability in International Tradable Permit Systems for Greenhouse Gas Control', OECD *Climate Change Designing a Tradable Permit System*, Paris.

Hahn, F., 1982, 'On Some Difficulties of the Utilitarian Economist', in Sen, A., and Williams, B. (eds.), *Utilitarianism and Beyond*, 1982, Cambridge University Press.

Hands, D.W., 2009 'The Positive – Normative Dichotomy in Economics', in Thagard, P., and Woods, J. (eds.), *Handbook of the Philosophy of Science*, Amsterdam.

Hanley, N., and Spash, C., 1993, *Cost-Benefit Analysis and the Environment*, Edward Elgar, Aldershot, UK.

Hardin, R., 2007, *David Hume: Moral & Political Theorist*, Oxford University Press.

Hargreaves Heap, S., *et al.*, 1992, *The Theory of Choice*, Blackwell, Oxford.

Harsanyi, J.C., 1977/1982, 'Morality and the Theory of Rational Behaviour', repr. in, Sen, A. and Williams, B. (eds.), 1982, *Utilitarianism and Beyond*, Cambridge University Press.

Harkness, S, 2010, 'The contribution of women's employment and earnings to household income inequality: A cross-country analysis', Luxembourg Income Study Working Paper Series, No. 531.

Hart, H.L.A., 1975, 'Rawls on Liberty and its Priority', in Daniels, N. (ed.), *Reading Rawls: Critical Studies of A Theory of Justice*, Blackwell, Oxford.

Hausman, D.M., and McPherson, M.S., 1994, 'Economics, Rationality, and Ethics', in Hausman, D.M. (ed.), *The Philosophy of Economics: An Anthology* (2nd edn.), Cambridge University Press.

Hausman, D.M., and McPherson, M.S., 2006, *Economic Analysis, Moral Philosophy, and Public Policy*, (2nd edn.), Cambridge University Press, Cambridge, U.K. and New York.

Hausman, D.M., and McPherson, M.S., 2009, 'Preference Satisfaction and Welfare Economics', *Economics and Philosophy*, 25/1.

Hayek, F.A., 1960, *The Constitution of Liberty*, Routledge and Kegan Paul, London and Henley.

Hirsch, F., 1977, *The Social Limits to Growth*, Routledge and Kegan Paul, London and Henley.

Hoffman, S., 1981, *Duties Beyond Borders: On Limits and Possibilies of Ethical International Politics*, Syracuse University Press.

Holmes, S., and Sunstein, C., *The Costs of Rights: Why Liberty Depends on Taxes*, W.W. Norton, New York.

Hooker, B., 2000, *Ideal Code, Real World: A Rule-Consequentialist Theory of Morality*, Oxford University Press.

Horkheimer, M., 1933, 'Materialism and Metaphysics', translation published in O'Connell, M. (ed.), 1999, *Critical Theory: Selected Essays*, Continuum Press, New York.

House of Lords Select Committee on Economic Affairs, 2008, *The Economic Impact of Immigration*, www.publications.parliament.uk/pa/ld/ldeconocaff.htm.

Hudson, W.D. (ed.), 1969. *The Is-Ought Question: A Collection of Papers on the Central l Problems in Moral Philosophy*, London: Macmillan.

Hume, D., 1739, *A Treatise of Human Nature*, all references here are to the on-line version prepared by Peter Millican, at, www.davidhume.org.

Hume, D., 1751, *An Enquiry Concerning the Principles of Morals*, 1998 edition, Beauchamp, T. (ed.), Oxford University Press.

Intergovernmental Negotiating Committee (INC), 1991, Annex I to the *Report of the Intergovernmental Negotiating Committee for a Framework Convention on Climate Change: United Nations Framework Convention on Climate Change*, Document A/Ac. 237/18 (Part II)/Add.1, United Nations, New York, May 1991.

Jamieson, D., 2001, *Climate Change and Global Environmental Justice*, Blackwell, Oxford.

Jarowsky, P., 2015, 'Architecture of Segregation: Civil Unrest, the Concentration of Poverty, and Public Policy', *Financial Times*.

Jevons, W.S., [1871]/1970, *The Theory of Politcial Economy*, Harmondsworth. UK; Penguin Books.

Jones, C., 2005, *Applied Welfare Economics*, Oxford University Press.

Jones-Lee, M.W., 1989, 'Safety and the Saving of Life', in Jones-Lee (eds.), *The Economics of Safety and Physical Risk*, Blackwell, Oxford, repr. in, Layard, R., and Glaister, S. (eds.), 1994

Jones-Lee, M.W., Hammerton, M., and Philips, P.R., 1985, 'The Value of Safety: Results of a National Sample Survey', *The Economic Journal*, 95.

Joshi, V., and Skidelsky, R., 2004, 'One World', in *The New York Review of Books*, 25th March.

Kahneman, D., 2011, *Thinking, Fast and Slow*, Farrar, Straus and Giroux.

Kahneman, D., and Deaton, A., 2010, *A High Income Improves Evaluation of Life but Not Emotional Well-being*, Center for Health and Well-being, Proceedings of the National Academy of Sciences, 106/38.

Kant, I., 1785/1964, *Groundwork of the Metaphysics of Moral*, trans. Paton, H.J., Harper and Row, New York.

Kapstein, E.B., 2006, *Economic Justice in an Unfair World*, Princeton University Press.

Kay, J., 2007, 'The Failure of Market Failure', *Prospect*, August, 2007:p. 36.

Kenny, A., and Kenny, C., 2006, *Life, Liberty and the Pursuit of Utility*, Imprint Academic, UK.

Klemperer, P., 2007, 'Why Economists don't Know All the Answers about Climate Change', http://voxen.org/index.php?q=node/440.

Korsgaard, C., 1993, 'Commentary on Contributions by Sen and Cohen', in Nussbaum, M., and Sen, A. (eds.), *op.cit.*

Kymlicka, W., 2002, *Contemporary Political Philosophy: An Introduction*, (2nd edn.), Oxford University Press.

Laslett, P., and Fishkin, J. (eds.), 1992, *Justice between Age Groups and Generations*, Yale University Press.

Layard, R., 2003, '*Happiness: Has Social Science a Clue?*', Lionel Robbins Memorial Lectures 2002/3, March.

Layard, R., and Glaister, S., 1994, *Cost-Benefit Analysis*, (2nd edn.), Cambridge University Press.

Lerner, A., 1971, 'Priorities and Efficiency, *American Economic Review*, 61, September.

Little, I.M.D., 1952, 'Social Choice and Individual Values', *Journal of Political Economy*, 60, October. reprinted in various collections including Little, 1999, *Collections and Recollections*, Clarendon Press, Oxford.

Little, I.M.D., 1957, *A Critique of Welfare Economics*, (2nd edn.), Oxford University Press.

Little, I.M.D., 2002, *Ethics, Economics, & Politics*, Oxford University Press.

Little, I.M.D., and Mirrlees, J.A., 1974, *Project Appraisal and Planning for Developing Countries*', Heinemann Educational Books, London.

Lukes, S., 1997, 'Comparing the Incomparable', in Chang, R. (ed.), *op.cit.*

Marmot, M., 2004, *The Status Syndrome: How Social Standing Affects our Health and Longevity*, Times Books/Henry Holt, New York.

Marmot, M., 2015, *The Health Gap: The Challenge of the Unequal World*, Bloomsbury, London.

McKerlie, D., 2013, *Justice between the Young and the Old*, Oxford University Press.

Meade, J., 1976, *The Just Economy*, George Allen and Unwin, London.

Mill, J.S., 1861/2003, '*Utilitarianism*', in Mary Warnock, (ed.), *Utilitarianism and On Liberty*, Blackwell, Oxford, 2003.

Miller, D., 2009, 'Global Justice and Climate Change', in Peterson, G. (ed.), *The Tanner Lectures in Human Values*, University of Utah Press, Salt Lake City.

Mishan, E.J. 1971a, 'Evaluation of Life and Limb: A Theoretical Approach', *Journal of Political Economy*, 79.

Mishan, E.J., 1971b, *Cost-Benefit Analysis*, George Allen and Unwin, London.

Mishan, E.J., 1981, *Introduction to Normative Economics*, Oxford University Press.

Mishan, E.J., 1982, 'Recent Contributions to the Literature on Life Valuation: A Critical Assessment', in Jones-Lee, M.W. (ed.), *The Value of Life and Safety*, North Holland Publishing Company.

Mishan, E.J., and Quah, E., 2007, 'The Value of Life', in Mishan, E.J., and Quah, Euston (eds.), *Cost-Benefit Analysis (5th edition)*, Routledge and Kegan Paul, London and New York.

Mishel, L, Gould, E, and Bivens, J, 2015, 'Wage Stagnation In Nine Charts', *Economic Policy Institute*, January 6, 2015.

Morris, N., and Vines, D., 2014, *Capital Failure: Rebuilding Trust in Financial Services*, Oxford University Press.

Mulgan, T., 2008, *Future People: A Moderate Consequentialist Account of Our Obligations to Future Generations*, Cambridge University Press.

Mulhall, S., and Swift, A., 2003, 'Rawls and Communitarians', in Freeman, S. (ed.), *The Cambridge Companion to Rawls*, Cambridge University Press.

Mulhall, S., and Swift, A., 1996, *Liberals and Communitarians*, Blackwell, Oxford.

Nagel, T., 1979, *Mortal Questions*, Cambridge University Press.

Nagel, T., 2005, 'The Problem of Global Justice', *Philosophy & Public Affairs*, 33/2.

Narveson, J., 1967, 'Utilitarianism and new generations', *Mind*:76.

New Economics Foundation, 2016, *Looking through the Wellbeing Kaleidoscope: Results from the European Social Survey*.

Ng, Y.-K., 1983, *Welfare Economics: Introduction and Development of Basic Concepts*, (2nd edn.), Macmillan, London.

Nickell, S., 2009, 'Putting children to work', *Prospect*, September, London.

Nordhaus, W., and Tobin, J., 1972, *Is Growth Obsolete?*, National Bureau of Economic Research, New York.

Norman, R., 1983, *The Moral Philosophers: An Introduction to Ethics*, Oxford University Press.

Nozick, R., 1974, *Anarchy, State, and Utopia*, Basic Books, New York, and Blackwell, Oxford.

Nozick, R., 1989, *The Examined Life*, Simon and Schuster, New York.

Nussbaum, M., 2000, *Women and Human Development: The Capabilities Approach*, Cambridge University Press.

Nussbaum, M., 2001, 'The Costs of Tragedy: Some Moral Limits on Cost-Benefit Analysis', in Adler, M.D., and Posner, E.A. (eds.), *Cost-benefit analysis, Legal, Economic, and Philosophical Perspectives*, University of Chicago Press.

Nussbaum, M., 2005, 'Building a Better Theory of Well-Being', in Bruni, L., and Porta, L. (eds.), *Economics and Happiness: Framing the Analysis*, Oxford University Press.

Nussbaum, M., and Sen, A. (eds.), 1993, *The Quality of Life*, Oxford University Press for the United Nations University.

O'Donnell, G., Deaton, A., Durand, M., Halpern, D., and Layard, R., 2014, *Wellbeing and Policy Report*, Legatum Institute.

O'Neill, O., 1991, 'Transnational Justice', in Held, David (ed.), *Political Theory Today*, Polity Press, Oxford.

OECD, 2012, 'Income Inequality and Growth: The Role of Taxes and Transfers', OECD Economics Department Policy Notes, No 9.

OECD, 2013, *Guidelines on Measuring Subjective Well-being*, Paris.

OECD, 2014, *Trends in Income Inequality and its Impact on Economic Growth*, Social, Employment and Migration Working Paper, No.163.

Offer, A., 2006, *The Challenge of Affluence*, Oxford University Press.

Office of National Statistics (U.K.), 2008, *The Blue Book: 2007 edition*, Table 1.1, London.

Okun, A., 1971, 'Social Welfare has no Price Tag', in *Survey of Current Business*, July, U.S. Department of Commerce, Washington, DC.

Okun, A., 1975, *Equality and Efficiency: The Big Tradeoff*, The Brookings Institution, Washington, DC.

Ostry, D., and Berg, A., *et al.*, 2014, *Redistribution, Inequality, and Growth*, IMF Staff Discussion Note, SDN/14/02.

Oswald, A., 2014, *Happiness Around the World*, Lecture delivered at St Gallen, Switzerland.

Parfit, D., 1984, *Reasons and Persons*, Oxford University Press.

Parfit, D., 1991, 'Equality or Priority', *[The Lindley Lecture]*, University of Kansas.

Partridge, E. (ed.), 1981, *Responsibilities to Future Generations*, Prometheus Books, New York.

Passmore, J., 1974, *Man's Responsibility for Nature*, Duckworth, London.

Peyton Young, H., 1994, *Equity: In Theory and Practice*, Princeton University Press, Princeton, NJ.

Phelps, E. (ed.), 1973, *Economic Justice*, Penguin, Harmondsworth, UK.

Pigou, A.C., 1932, *The Economics of Welfare*, (4th edn.), London, Macmillan.

Piketty, T., 2014, *Capital in the Twenty First Century*, 2014, English translation published by Harvard University Press.

Pogge, T., 1992, 'Cosmopolitanism and Sovereignty', *Ethics*, 101: 48–49

Popper, K., 1966, *The Open Society and Its Enemies*, Routledge & Kegan Paul, London.

Proto, E., and Oswald, A. 2015, National Happiness and Genetic Distance: A Cautious Exploration'. Warwick Economics Research Papers.

Rawls, J., 1971, *A Theory of Justice*, Harvard University Press, Cambridge, MA.

Rawls, J., 1993, *Political Liberalism*, Columbia University Press, New York.

Rawls, J., 1998, *The Law of Peoples*, Harvard University Press, Cambridge, MA.

Rawls, J., 2001, *Justice as Fairness: A Restatement*, [ed. E. Kelly], Harvard University Press, MA.

Raz, J., 1986, *The Morality of Freedom*, The Clarendon Press, Oxford.

Reich, R.B., 2015, *Saving Capitalism: For the Many, Not the Few*, Knopf.

Robbins, L., 1945, *The Nature and Significance of Economic Science*, (2nd edn.), Macmillan, London.

Rothenberg, J., 1961, *The Measurement of Social Welfare*, Prentice-Hall, Inc, New Jersey.

Royal Commission on Environmental Pollution. 2000, *Energy-The Changing Environment*, The Stationary Office, London.

Royal Commission on the Distribution of Income and Wealth, Report No 7: Fourth Report on the Standing Reference, July 1979, Cmnd 7595, p. 17.

Sandel, M., 1998, *Liberalism and the Limits of Justice*, (2nd edn.), Cambridge University Press, Cambridge, UK.

Scanlon, T., 1998, *What We Owe to Each Other*, Cambridge, MA, Bellnap Press of Harvard University Press.

Satyamurti, C., 1987, *Broken Moon*, Oxford University Press, p.12.

Scheffler, S. (ed.), 1988, *Consequentialism and Its Critics*, Oxford University Press.

Schelling, T.C., 1968, 'The Life That You Save May Be Your Own', in Chase, S.B. (eds.), *Problems in Public Expenditure Analysis*, Brookings Institution, Washington, DC.

Schelling, T.C., 1987, 'Value of Life', in Eatwell, J., Milgate, M., and Newman, P. (eds.), *The New Palgrave Dictionary of Economics*, Macmillan, London and New York, 793–796.

Schelling, T.C., 1995, "Intergenerational Discounting", *Energy Policy*, 23(4–5): 395–401

Scitovsky, T., 1941, 'A Note on Welfare Propositions in Economics', *The Review of Economic Studies*, 77.

Scott, M.F.G., MacArthur, J.D., and Newberry, D.M.G., 1976, *Project Appraisal in Practice*, Heinemann Educational Books, London.

Sen, A., 1970, *Collective Choice and Social Welfare*, Holden-Day, San Francisco, and Oliver & Boyd, London.

Sen, A., 1982, 'Equality of What?', repr. in Sen, A. (ed.), *Choice, Welfare and Measurement*, Blackwell, Oxford.

Sen, A., 1982a, *Rational Fools: A Critique of the Behavioural Foundations of Economic Theory*, reprinted in Sen, 1982b.

Sen, A., 1982b, *Choice, Welfare and Measurement*, Blackwell, Oxford.

Sen, A., 1984, *Resources, Values and Development*, Blackwell, Oxford.

Sen, A., 1986, 'Adam Smith's Prudence', in Lall, S., and Stewart, F. (eds.), *Theory and Reality in Development*, Macmillan, Basingstoke and London.

Sen, A., 1987, *On Ethics and Economics*, Blackwell, Oxford.

Sen, A., 1992, *Inequality Reexamined*, Russel Sage Foundation, New York, and Clarendon Press, Oxford.

Sen, A., 1993, 'Capability and Well-Being', Nussbaum, M., and Sen, A (eds.), *op.cit.*

Sen, A., 1999, *Development as Freedom*, Oxford University Press.

Sen, A., 2000, 'The Discipline of Cost-Benefit Analysis', in Adler, M.D. and Posner, E.A. (eds.), *Cost-Benefit Analysis, Legal, Economic, and Philosophical Perspectives*, University of Chicago Press.

Sen, A., 2009, *The Idea of Justice*, Alan Lane, London.

Shue, H., 2010, 'Deadly Delays, Saving Opportunities', in Gardiner, S., Caney, S., Jamieson, D., and Shue, H. (eds.), *Climate Ethics: Essential Readings*, Oxford University Press, New York:, 2010.

Singer, P., 1993, *Practical Ethics* (2nd edn.), Cambridge University Press.

Singer, P., 2002, *One World, the Ethics of Globalization*, 2nd edn., Yale University Press.

Sikora, R., and Barry, B. (eds.), 1978, *Obligations to Future Generations*, Temple University Press, Philadelphia.

Smart, J.J.C., 1973, 'Negative Utilitarianism', in *Smart and Williams*, 1973.

Smart, J.J.C., and Williams, B., 1973, *Utilitarianism: For and Against*, Cambridge University Press.

Sobhee, S K., 2011, 'Greater Female Employment Participation as a Catalyst to Reducing Income Inequality in Developing Countries'. Paper presented at the International Conference on Applied Economics (ICOAE), Perugia, Italy, 26–28 Aug 2011.

Sterba, J., 1980, 'Abortions and the Rights of Distant Peoples and Future Generations', *Journal of Philosophy*, 77.

Sterba, J., 1998, *Justice for Here and Now*, Cambrridge University Press.

Stern, N., 2006, *The Economics of Climate Change: The Stern Review*, Cambridge University Press.

Stern, N., 2008, The Economics of Climate Change', the Richard T Ely lecture, *American Economic Review, Papers and Proceedings*, May.

Stern, N., 2009, *A Blueprint for a Safer Planet*, The Bodley Head, London.

Stevenson, B., and Wolfers, J., 2008, 'Economic Growth and Subjective Well-Being: Re-assessing the Easterlin Paradox', *Brookings Papers on Economic Activity*, Spring.

Stiglitz, J., 2012, *The Price of Inequality*, Penguin Books, Harmondsworth, UK.

Stiglitz, J., 2015, *The Great Divide: Unequal Societies and what we can do about them*. W. W. Norton.

Stiglitz, J., Sen, A., and Fitoussi, J.-P., 2009, *Report by the Commission on the Measurement of Economic Performance and Social Progress*, Paris.

Streeten, P., 1984, 'Basic Needs: Some Unsettled Questions', *World Development*, 973–978.

Streeten, P., 1994, 'Human Development: Means and Ends', *American Economic Review*, 84/2.

Streeten, P., 1998, 'Human Rights and Their Indicators', *Human Development and Human Rights Report of the Oslo Symposium*, 2–3 October.

Streeten, P., and Burki, S.J., Ul Haq, M., Hicks, N., and Stewart, F., 1981, *First Things First, Meeting Basic Human Needs in Developing Countries*, Oxford University Press, New York.

Sugden, R., 2008, 'Why Incoherent Preferences do not Justify Paternalism', *Constitutional Political Economy*, 19.

Sugden, R., and Williams, A., 1978, *The Principles of Practical Cost-benefit Analysis*, Oxford University Press.

Sunstein, C., 2004, 'Lives, Life Years, and Willingness to Pay', *Columbia Law Review*, 104.

Sunstein, C., 2005, *Laws of Fear*, Cambridge University Press.

Sunstein, C., 2014, *Valuing Lives: Humanizing the Regulatory State*, University of Chicago.

Swift, A., 2001, *Political Philosophy: A Beginners' Guide for Students and Politicians*, Polity Press, Cambridge U.K.

Tan, K.-C., 2005, 'International Toleration: Rawlsian versus Cosmopolitan', *Leiden Journal of International Law*, 18.

Temkin, L., 1993, *Inequality*, Oxford University Press.

Thaler, R.H., and Sunstein, C., 2008, *Nudge: Improving Decisions about Health, Wealth and Happiness*, Yale University Press.

Tobin, J., 1970/1973, 'On Limiting the Domain of Inequality', *Economic Journal*, 97/1.

Tobin, J., *The Intellectual Revolution in United States Policy Making*, The Noel Burton Lecture, University of Essex.

United Nations Development Programme, 2006/7, United Nations High Commissioner for Human Rights, Royal Ministry of Foreign Affairs, Norway, pp. 88–96.

Usher, D., 1973, 'An Imputation to the Measure of Economic Growth for Changes in Life Expectancy', in Moss, M (ed.), 1973, *The Measurement of Economic and Social Performance*, National Bureau of Economic Research, New York.

Viscussi, K., 1993, 'The Value of Risks to Life and Health', *Journal of Economic Literature*, XXX1(December).

Viscussi, K., and Kip, W., and Aldy, J.E., 2003, 'The Value of a Statistical Life: A Critical Review of Market Estimates throughout the World', *The Journal of Risk and Uncertainty*, 27/1.

Vlastos, G., 1984, Justice and Equality, in Waldron, J. (ed.), *Theories of Rights*, Oxford University Press.

Walzer, M., 1983, *Spheres of Justice*, Blackwell, Oxford.

Warnock, M. (ed.), 2003, *Utilitarianism and On Liberty*, (2nd edn.), Blackwell, Oxford.

Weale, M., 2009, 'Commentary: The Burden of the National Debt', *National Institute Economic Review*, January.

Weisbrod, B.A., 1971, 'Costs and Benefits of Medical Research: A Case Study of Poliomyelitis', *Journal of Political Economy*, 79/3.

Weitzman, M., 2007, 'The Stern Review of the Economics of Climate Change', *Journal of Economic Literature*, 45/3.

Wight, J.B., 2015, *Ethics in Economics*, Stanford University Press.

Wildaum, G., and Mitchell, T., 2016, 'China Income Inequality Among World's Worst', *Financial Times*, 14 January.

Wilkinson, R., and Pickett, K., 2011, *The Spirit Level: Why Equality is Better for Everyone*, Penguin Books, Harmondsworth, U.K.

Wilkinson, T.M., 2004, 'The Ethics and Economics of the Minimum Wage'', *Economics and Philosophy*, 20.

Willetts, D., 2010, *The Pinch*, Atlantic Books, London.

Williams, B., 1969, 'The Idea of Equality', in Warnock, G. (ed.), *Moral Concepts*, Oxford University Press.

Wolf, C., 1996, 'Markets, Justice, and the Interests of Future Generations', *Ethics and the Environment*.

Wolf, C., 2005, 'Intergenerational Justice', in Frey, R.G., and Helman, C.H. (eds.), *Blackwell Companion to Applied Ethics*, Blackwell, Oxford.

Wolf, C., 2010, 'International Justice and Saving', in Gauss, G., Favor, K., and LaMont, J. (eds.), *Essays on Ethics and Economics*, Stanford University Press.

Wolf, S., 1982/1998, 'Moral Saints', reprinted in Cahn S., and Mackie, P. (eds.), 1998, *Ethics, History, Theory, and Contemporary Issues*, Oxford University Press.

Wolff, J., 1998, 'Fairness, Respects and the Egalitarian Ethos', *Philosophy and Public Affairs*, 27 (2).

World Bank, 2008, *World Development Report*, World Bank, Washington, DC.

World Happiness Reports, since 2012, Helliwell, J.F., Layard, R., Sachs, J. (eds.), *For the Sustainable Development Solutions*, Newark, USA.

Author Index

© The Author(s) 2017
W. Beckerman, *Economics as Applied Ethics*,
DOI 10.1007/978-3-319-50319-6

Subject Index

© The Author(s) 2017
W. Beckerman, *Economics as Applied Ethics*,
DOI 10.1007/978-3-319-50319-6

Printed in Great Britain
by Amazon

55712060R00180